Harbrace
College
Handbook

BRIEF THIRTEENTH EDITION

Harbrace
College
Handbook

BRIEF THIRTEENTH EDITION

John C. Hodges

Winifred Bryan Horner
Texas Christian University

Suzanne Strobeck Webb
Texas Woman's University

Robert Keith Miller
University of St. Thomas

HARCOURT
BRACE

HARCOURT BRACE COLLEGE PUBLISHERS
Fort Worth   Philadelphia   San Diego   New York   Orlando   Austin
San Antonio   Toronto   Montreal   London   Sydney   Tokyo

Publisher: **Christopher P. Klein**
Executive Editor: **Michael Rosenberg**
Acquisitions Editor: **John Meyers**
Product Manager: **Ilse Wolfe West**
Developmental Editor: **Michell Phifer**
Project Editor: **Matt Ball**
Senior Art Director: **Brian Salisbury**
Senior Production Manager: **Kathleen Ferguson**

Mary Stoughton and EEI Communications for copyediting and
editorial services

ISBN: 0-15-508133-0
Library of Congress Catalog Card Number: 97-72208

Copyright © 1998 by Harcourt Brace & Company

All rights reserved. No part of this publication may be reproduced or
transmitted in any form or by any means, electronic or mechanical,
including photocopy, recording, or any information storage and
retrieval system, without permission in writing from the publisher.

Requests for permission to make copies of any part of the work should
be mailed to: Permissions Department, Harcourt Brace & Company,
6277 Sea Harbor Drive, Orlando, Florida 32887-6777.

This work is derived from HARBRACE COLLEGE HANDBOOK,
Thirteenth Edition, copyright © 1998, 1994, 1990, 1986, 1984, 1982,
1977, 1972, 1967, 1962, 1956 by Harcourt Brace & Company.
Copyright 1951, 1946, 1941 by Harcourt Brace & Company.
Copyright renewed 1990 by Cornelia Hodges and Audrey Welch.
Copyright renewed 1984 by Cornelia Hodges and J.N. Hodges.
Copyright renewed 1979, 1974, 1969 by Cornelia Hodges.

HARBRACE is a registered trademark of Harcourt Brace & Company.

Copyrights and Acknowledgments appear on page C-1 and constitute a
continuation of the copyright page.

Address for orders:
Harcourt Brace College
Publishers
6277 Sea Harbor Drive
Orlando, FL 32887-6777
1-800-782-4479

Address for editorial
correspondence:
Harcourt Brace College Publishers
301 Commerce Street, Suite 3700
Fort Worth, TX 76102

Website address:
http://www.hbcollege.com

Harcourt Brace & Company will provide complimentary supplements
or supplement packages to those adopters qualified under our adoption
policy. Please contact your sales representative to learn how you
qualify. If as an adopter or potential user you receive supplements you
do not need, please return them to your sales representative or send
them to: Attn: Returns Department, Troy Warehouse, 465 South
Lincoln Drive, Troy, MO 63379.

Printed in the United States of America

7 8 9 0 1 2 3 4 5 6   039   9 8 7 6 5 4 3 2 1

Preface

The *Harbrace College Handbook, Brief Thirteenth Edition* is a compact version of the *Harbrace College Handbook*. Yet the Brief Thirteenth Edition contains the same number of chapters and more complete coverage in each chapter than any other brief handbook available. The Brief Thirteenth Edition offers practical, well-organized, and easily accessible advice for writers. Specific examples demonstrate the principles of writing that are applicable to both course work and professional tasks, and frequent cross-references establish how these principles inform each other.

The Brief Thirteenth Edition is a complete revision of the Twelfth Edition. While recognizably the same book that generations of writers have come to trust, the handbook is now easier to use and understand. To revise it, we followed several principles:

1. Whenever possible, we have explained the reasons for specific elements of grammar, style, punctuation, and mechanics. Students learn faster and write better when they understand the reasons behind the rules.

2. We have updated the examples, drawing principally on contemporary American writers and including examples of student work.

3. In sample sentences that are revised to illustrate the principles being taught, we have introduced handwritten corrections so that the revision is more readily apparent.

4. We have deleted all exercises from the handbook and offer them to students in a separate supplement with new paragraph-length exercises and heavily revised sentence exercises. For instructors, we provide a separate answer key to the exercises.

5. We have significantly expanded our discussion of writing with computers; further, we have integrated this discussion throughout the book and identified the sections with an icon instead of isolating this material in a separate chapter.

6. Similarly, we have expanded our discussion of writing difficulties common to dialect and ESL, doing so *in context* rather than placing these concerns in a separate chapter. This decision is in response to changing national demographics and our determination not to make international students feel as if their needs were being addressed only as an afterthought. Because American students face many of these problems as well, some concepts are not separated out as relating only to ESL students.

7. We have eliminated the "Notes" and reduced the number of "Cautions" to make the text more straightforward and to give more emphasis to the "Cautions" that remain.

Those familiar with past editions will also note some major structural changes. To emphasize our commitment to writing as a process, we have divided what used to be a single chapter, "The Whole Composition," into two: "Planning and Drafting Essays" and "Revising and Editing

Essays." Three versions of a new student essay illustrate these chapters, and we have expanded our discussion of invention and revision. Similarly, we divided what had been a one-hundred-page chapter on the research paper into two: "Research: Finding and Evaluating Sources" and "Research: Using and Citing Sources." This division makes it easier for students to locate information. "Finding and Evaluating Sources" now contains a significantly expanded discussion of how to use electronic resources; "Using and Citing Sources" discusses the most recent MLA and APA guidelines and illustrates writing from sources with two new student essays.

In response to requests from users, we have created two other chapters new to this edition. "Writing under Pressure" builds on material previously located in "Writing for Special Purposes" to give it more emphasis and make it more useful. Chapter 32, "Writing Arguments," expands on the discussion of critical thinking introduced in Chapter 31 and helps students understand an important type of academic writing previously unaddressed in the book.

At the same time, we have consolidated two short chapters: We have located the discussion of superfluous commas in the chapter on the comma and combined what used to be separate chapters on sentence unity and sentence consistency.

Although many instructors are familiar with the traditional sequence of the *Harbrace's* chapters, we recognized that a significant number of faculty would prefer an alternate edition with a different chapter order. With this in mind, we have unified our discussion of the sentence by moving chapters devoted to "Effective Sentences" next to those devoted to sentence grammar. In doing so, we were able to reposition "Misplaced Parts and Dangling Modifiers" in the context of sentence grammar and to unify our discussion of pronoun use.

Other changes followed these decisions. We moved the chapter on manuscript format to immediately precede the "Larger Elements" section. This heavily revised chapter, now titled "Document Design," appears just before the section on the writing process. Reflecting the fact that editing concerns are usually addressed late in the writing process, all chapters on mechanics have moved toward the back of the book (from Part II to Part V). Chapters devoted to punctuation, however, have moved forward so that student writers can see the relationship between understanding the conventions that govern punctuation and writing effective sentences.

We have also improved the internal order of other chapters. Material on writing in a straightforward style has moved from "Good Usage" to "Conciseness," and tone is now treated as a revision issue rather than a planning issue.

Although it has been reorganized according to the chapter order of the new full-length *Harbrace,* the *Brief* is a handbook first and a rhetoric second. Within each division, most chapters are still located next to chapters that previously neighbored them. Also, we have tried to change existing chapter titles and subtitles as little as possible. And while we have made the book easier to teach and easier to consult, we have not compromised its well-established integrity. On the contrary, we have worked hard to improve it. The new chapter arrangement is based on research of instructor preferences and on our own extensive classroom experience. As a result, the new edition will respond to the changing needs of writers well into the next century.

The following supplements accompany the *Harbrace College Handbook, Thirteenth Edition.*

Instructor Supplements

Instructor's Manual

Harcourt Brace Guide to Teaching First-Year Composition

Harcourt Brace Sourcebook for Teachers of Writing

Harcourt Brace Guide to Teaching Writing with Computers

Harcourt Brace Guide to Writing across the Curriculum

Diagnostic Test Package to accompany the Harbrace Handbook, 13e

Transparency Acetates to accompany the Harbrace Handbook, 13e

Instructor's Correction Chart

Test Bank to accompany the Harbrace Handbook, 13e

Student Supplements

Exercises to accompany the Harbrace College Handbook, Brief 13e

Harbrace College Workbook, 13e

Harbrace Basic Writer's Workbook

Harbrace ESL Workbook

Working Together: A Collaborative Writing Guide

Harcourt Brace Guide to Peer Tutoring

Harcourt Brace Guide to Citing Electronic Sources

Resourceful Reader, 4e

Writing in the Disciplines, 3e

Merriam Webster's Dictionary (softcover)

Merriam Webster's Collegiate Dictionary, 10e

Software

Writing Tutor V

Harbrace Online 3.1

Harbrace CD-ROM

ExaMaster Test Bank to accompany the Harbrace Handbook, 13e

For additional information on the supplemental materials available for *Harbrace*, please visit the *Harbrace* Web site at http://www.harbrace.com/english

Acknowledgments

For the material on English as a Second Language, a feature new to the Thirteenth Edition, we are indebted to **Judith B. Strother** at the Florida Institute of Technology and **Irene Juzkiw** at the University of Missouri. Their special expertise added a much needed feature to *Harbrace*.

The following individuals gave us their advice and experience, which shaped the Thirteenth Edition.

Focus Group Participants

Donald Andrews, *Chattanooga State Technical Community College;* Mary Jo Arn, *Bloomsburg University;* Susan Becker, *Illinois Central College;* Honora Berninger, *Hillsborough Community College;* Tim Biehl, *Tarrant County Junior College;* Tracy Bird, *Hillsborough Community College (student);* Cathy Bridges, *Hillsborough Community College (student);* Teresa Chasteen, *Hiwassee College;* Carol Cinclair, *Brookhaven College;* Sean Claflin, *Hillsborough Community College (student);* Linda Clark, *Maryville College;* Mark Dawson, *Faulkner University;* Cody Dolnick, *University of San Diego;* Josh Edmonson, *Hillsborough Community College (student);* Dave Esselstrom, *Azusa Pacific University;* Bernie Felder, *St. Joseph's University (student);* Sally Fitzgerald, *Chabot College;* Angela Forsman, *University of South Florida (student);* Jim Frank, *Cleveland State Community College;* Jean Marie Fuhrman, *University of Central Florida;* Judith Gallagher, *Tarrant County Junior College;* Danny Glover, *University of South Florida (student);* Barbara Goldstein, *Hillsborough Community College;* Adrienne Goslin, *Cleveland*

State University; Michele Grantle, *St. Joseph's University (student);* Angie Green, *Lee College;* Rusty Green, *University of South Florida (student);* Mary Beth Gugler-Matthews, *Pasco-Hernando Community College;* Patsy Hammontree, *University of Tennessee-Knoxville;* George Hanson, *University of California at San Diego;* Beth Hedengren, *Brigham Young University;* Kathryn Henkins, *Mt. San Antonio College;* Susan Hines, *Middle Georgia College;* Mary Hostenner, *St. Joseph's University (student);* Maggie Jenkins, *Pellissippi State Technical Community College;* Myra Jones, *Manatee Community College;* Jim Knox, *Roane State Community College;* Robert Lamm, *Arkansas State University;* Ernest Lee, *Carson-Newman College;* Susan Lowdermilk, *Texas Wesleyan University;* John Martino, *California Polytechnic State University-Pomona;* Melissa Mazzei, *University of South Florida (student);* Jeanne McDonald, *Waubonsee Community College;* Alan Merickel, *Tallahassee Community College;* Judy Michna, *DeKalb College-Dunwoody;* Robert Miller, *Tennessee Temple University;* Jody Millward, *Santa Barbara City College;* Jason Murray, *Pasco-Hernando Community College (student);* Marlene Musinca, *Villanova University (student);* Jennifer Olsone, *St. Joseph's University (student);* Mary Padget, *Tennessee Technical University;* Karen Peterson, *Hillsborough Community College (student);* Ron Puckett, *Polk Community College;* Bob Renk, *Trinity Valley Community College;* Ashley Richmond, *Delaware County Community College (student);* Stephanie Sanchez, *University of South Florida (student);* Jack Scanlon, *Triton College;* Marie Schein, *Tarrant County Junior College;* Karen Sidwell, *St. Petersburg Junior College;* Laurel Smith, *Vincennes University;* Marcia Songer, *East Tennessee State University;* Barbara Stewart, *Long Beach City College;* Megan Striker, *St. Joseph's University (student);* Bill Summer, *Delaware County Community College (student);*

Brian Talbert, *Villanova University (student);* Michelle
Tarlene, *Delaware County Community College (student);*
Tom Tuggle, *Gainesville College;* Donte Williams, *Pasco-
Hernando Community College (student);* Michael Wood-
ard, *St. Joseph's University (student);* and Driek Zirinsky,
Boise State University

Phone Interviews

Paul Clee, *Tacoma Community College;* Joseph Colavito,
Northwestern State University; Cynthia Denham, *Snead
State Community College;* Gabrielle Gautreaux, *University
of New Orleans;* Eloise Grathwohl, *Meredith College;* An-
gie Green, *Lee College;* Diana Kilpatrick, *Palm Beach
Community College;* Bruce Kirle, *Trident Community Col-
lege;* John Launt, *Central Piedmont Community College;*
Dara Llewellyn, *Florida Atlantic University;* Mike Mat-
thew, *Tarrant County Junior College;* and Lisa Williams,
Jacksonville State University

Manuscript Reviewers

Dorothy Ashe, *West Hills Community College;* Myrtle B.
Beavers, *Okaloosa Walton Community College;* Jon G.
Bentley, *Albuquerque Technical-Vocational Institute;* Tim
Biehl, *Tarrant County Junior College;* Steven Brahlek,
Palm Beach Community College; Ann Camy, *Red Rocks
Community College;* Thomas E. Fish, *Cumberland Col-
lege;* Gabrielle Gautreaux, *University of New Orleans;*
Lynn M. Grow, *Broward Community College;* Ruby John-
son, *Wallace State Community College;* George M. Kelly,
Hinds Community College; Wanda Martin, *University of
New Mexico;* Barbara McMichael, *Gwinnett Technical In-
stitute;* Kathryn Raign, *University of North Texas;* Eula
Thompson, *Jefferson State Community College;* Heide-
marie Z. Weidner, *Tennessee Technical University;* and
Lisa Williams, *Jacksonville State University*

Marketing Phone Interviews

Donald Andrews, *Chattanooga State Technical Community College;* Linda Bensel-Meyers, *University of Tennessee-Knoxville;* Lorraine Cadet, *Grambling State University;* George Cox, *Johnston Community College;* Margaret DeHart, *Trinity Valley Community College;* MaryBeth DeMeo, *Alvernia College;* Wendy Jones, *County College of Morris;* Paul Kleinpoppen, *Florida Community College at Jacksonville;* Carol Lowe, *McLennan Community College;* Judy Michna, *DeKalb College-Dunwoody;* Bill Newman, *DeKalb College;* Mary Padget, *Tennessee Technical University;* Ken Rosen, *University of Southern Maine;* Marcia Songer, *East Tennessee State University;* Bill Spencer, *Delta State University;* and Ken Wolfskill, *Chowan College*

Marketing Survey Participants

Elizabeth Addison, *Western Carolina University;* David Anderson, *Butler County Community College;* Gordon Anderson, *Delgato Community College;* Vic Aquino, *Green River Community College;* Rozel Arant, *Northeast Louisiana University;* Ellen Arl, *University of Southern California at Sumter;* Dorothy Ashe, *West Hill Community College;* Charles Avinger, *Washtenau Community College;* Jan Balakiam, *Kean College;* Juanita Barnes, *Grambling State University;* Carol Bays, *Northern Michigan University;* Sue Bennett, *New Mexico Junior College;* Dianne Bladel, *Florida Community College at Jacksonville;* Valerie Blue, *Nashville State Technical College;* William Bode, *Southern College;* Jesse Bogan, *Morris Brown College;* Odon Bologan, *Delaware State University;* Gene Booth, *Albuquerque Technical-Vocational Institute;* Steven Brahlek, *Palm Beach Community College;* Floyd Brigdon, *Trinity Valley College;* Jessica Bryan, *Troy State University;*

Patricia Burnes, *University of Maine-Orono;* Russell Burrows, *Weber State University;* Lorraine Cadet, *Grambling State University;* Susan Calovini, *Austin Peay State University;* Mike Campbell, *Yakima College;* Ayne Cantrell, *Middle Tennessee State University;* Linda Carmichael, *East Tennessee State University;* Allison Carpenter, *University of Delaware;* Jerry Carr, *Hinds Community College;* Julie Cary, *Georgia State University;* Harriet Castratsaro, *Indiana University at Bloomington;* Judy Cheatham, *Greensboro College;* Merlin Cheney, *Weber State University;* Elizabeth Chesla, *Polytechnic University;* Dennis Ciesielski, *Peru State College;* Dennis Clark, *Eastern Illinois University;* Sarah Cogne, *West Liberty State College;* Rocky Colavito, *North Western State University;* Anna Coles, *Baldwin-Wallace College;* Elaine Coneq, *Southwest Mississippi Community College;* Mark Connelly, *Milwaukee Area Technical College;* Judith Corbin, *Eastern Illinois University;* Moira Cordel, *University of Detroit Mercy;* Richard Cornelius, *Bryan College;* George Cox, *Johnston Community College;* Anne Crane, *St. Edwards University;* Patricia Crane, *Nazarene Bible College;* Carol Creekmore, *DeKalb College at Rockdale Center;* Leslie Cronin, *Widener University;* Marilyn Curall, *Valencia Community College;* Martha Davenport, *Olympia College;* MaryBeth DeMeo, *Alvernia College;* Cynthia Denham, *Snead State Community College;* C. J. Denne, *College of New Rochelle;* Dennis Dooley, *Wofford College;* Paul Drake, *Spartenburg Technical College;* Sean Dugan, *Mercy College;* Sallie Duhling, *Gainesville College;* Mike Eason, *Tarrant County Junior College;* Donna Edsel, *Muskingum College;* Mark Edmonds, *St. Leo College;* Jolly Faught, *Cumberland College;* Steve Feldman, *George Mason University;* Donald Fritz, *University of Texas Pan American;* Hank Galmish, *Green River Community College;* James Gamble, *University of Arkansas at Monticello;*

Maryanne Garbowsky, *County College of Morris*; Bill
Gary, *Henderson Community College*; Gabrielle Gau-
treaux, *University of New Orleans*; Louise Gearhart, *Hog-
erstown Junior College*; Julia Gergits, *Youngstown State
University*; Jim Gilchrist, *Iowa State University*; Karen
Gillenwaters, *Brazo Sport College*; Margaret Gillio,
Northern Michigan University; Owen Gilman, *St. Joseph
University*; Lewis Graham, *Olympia College*; Eileen Greg-
ory, *University of Dallas*; Kevin Griffith, *Capital Univer-
sity*; Huey Guagliardio, *Louisiana State University-Eunice*;
Rachel Guppta, *Charles Mott Community College*; Janet
Haddock, *Northeast Louisiana University*; Joanne Haen,
Kansas City Community College; Carol Hall, *Victoria Col-
lege*; Jeff Hammond, *St. Mary College of Maryland*; Elree
Harris, *Westminster College*; Judy Hart, *Frank Phillips
College*; Susan Hartman, *Reading Community College*;
Jane Haywood, *University of Mary Hardin Baylor*; Betty
Lou Heimbold, *University of Cincinnati-Clermont Col-
lege*; Doris Helbig, *Florida Atlantic University*; Cindy
Hess, *Elizabethtown College*; Alice Hines, *Hendrix Col-
lege*; Michael Hood, *Belmont Abbey College*; Sue How-
ard, *Duquesne University*; Tom Hruska, *Northern Michi-
gan University*; Marsha Huntineton, *Everett Community
College*; John Hyman, *The American University*; Deborah
Jacobs, *Prestonburg Community College*; Melanie John-
son, *Wallace State Community College*; Wendy Jones,
County College of Morris; Nancy Kennedy, *Edmonds
Community College*; Janice Kidd, *Lake Land College*;
Lola King, *Trinity Valley College*; Paul Kleinpoppen, *Flor-
ida Community College at Jacksonville*; Jim Knox, *Rowan
State Community College*; Dan Landau, *Santa Monica
College*; Susan Lang, *Southern Illinois University at Car-
bondale*; Rosemary Lanshe, *Broward Community College*;
Russ Larson, *Eastern Michigan University*; Gail Laurson,
Southeast Community College; Ernest Lee, *Carson New-*

man College; William Lenz, Chatham College; Diane Lestourgeon, Widener University; Sarah Liggett, Louisiana State University; Salvatore Lisanti, Westchester Community College; Frank Littler, Palm Beach Community College; Alice Loftin, Tusculum College; Kim Long, Shippensburg University; Richard Louth, Southeast Louisiana University; Carol Lowe, McLennan Community College; Laura Maas, Olivet College; Cheryl Martin, Roanoke-Chowan Community College; Linda Martin, Florida Community College; Linda McGinley, West Liberty State College; Tom McKay, Truman College; Victoria McLure, South Plains College; Barbara McMillan, Union University; John Moore, East Illinois University; Nelda Moore, Jones County Community College; Janet Morczek, Daly College; David Moreland, Louisiana State University; John Morris, Cameron University; Tina Murdock, Clear Creek Baptist Bible College; Christopher Nielson, Widener University; Connie Nunley, Truett McConnell Junior College; Susan Oldrive, Baldwin-Wallace College; Penny Olson, Bay Mills Community College; Peter Olson, Hillside College; Mary O'Reilly, Rider University; Joyce O'Shay, Stark Technical College; Sam Overstreet, Maryville College; Pat Palmer, Olympia College; Nancy Parker, Embry Riddle Aeronautical University; Jane Parks, Dalton College; Mildred Pate, Georgia Southern University; Mary Peddicord, Pearl River Community College; Rita Perkins, Camden County College; Donna Prescott, Green Mountain College; Janice Quass, Grand View College; Carole Raybourn, Morehouse College; Mary Jo Reiff, University of Kansas; David Rosen, University of Maine at Machias; Ken Rosen, University of Southern Maine; Kenny Rowlette, Liberty University; Rebecca Rowley, Clovis Community College; Mark Schmidt, University of Arkansas at Monticello; Geoffrey Schramm, University of Maryland at College Park; Kathleen Sherfick, Albion College; George

Shields, *Kentucky State University;* Erlene Smith, *Pearl River Community College;* William Smith, *Piedmont College;* Marcia Songer, *East Tennessee State University;* Jacqueline Stark, *Los Angeles Valley College;* Philip Stirling, *Ferris State University;* Jim Stuart, *Kellogg Community College;* Marilyn Styne, *Wilbur Wright College;* Joan Sweitzer, *Lake City Community College;* George Teffner, *University of Pittsburgh at Bradford;* Sandra Thompkins, *Hiwassee College;* Nancy Tuten, *Columbia College;* Linda Underhill, *Alfred University;* Louis Van Keuren, *Green Mountain College;* Ben Varner, *University of Northern Colorado;* Frank Vaughan, *Campbell University;* Donna Walker-Nixon, *University of Mary Hardin Baylor;* James Wallace, *University of Akron;* Jonathan Walters, *Norwich University;* W. G. Walton, *Meredith College;* Jay Ward, *Thiel College;* Bill Waterson, *Lees McRae College;* Michael Webster, *Grand Valley State University;* Bob Welsh, *Webster University;* Mike Westerfield, *Michigan Christian College;* Katherine Wheatcroft, *Bucknell University;* Ron Wheeler, *Johnson Bible College;* Judy Whitis, *Olivet Nazarene University;* Jeanne Williams, *Southwest Mississippi Community College;* Ken Wolfskill, *Chowan College;* Jim Wood, *Green River Community College;* Randall Woodland, *University of Michigan-Dearborn;* Laura Writer, *Ottawa University;* and Norma ZanRheenes, *Western Michigan University*

For the daunting task of copyediting and proofreading the manuscript, we thank Mary Stoughton, Senior Editor, and the staff at EEI Communications.

For help with details from research to manuscript preparation, we are indebted to Camille Langston, Susan Perry, Denise Stodola, and Paul Teske.

Finally we wish to give special thanks to the editorial and marketing staff at Harcourt Brace for their two and a half years of preparation for the Thirteenth Edition: Michael Rosenberg, Executive Editor for English; John Meyers, Acquisitions Editor; Michell Phifer, Developmental Editor; Ilse Wolfe West, Senior Product Manager; Kimberly Allison, Special Projects; and Katie Frushour and Laura Newhouse, Editorial Assistants. From the production staff, for their amazing efforts to bring all phases of this edition together, we thank Matt Ball, Project Editor; Kathy Ferguson, Senior Production Manager; and Brian Salisbury, Senior Art Director.

Contents

EFFECTIVE SENTENCES

DICTION

MECHANICS

LARGER ELEMENTS

Grammar

Grammar

Chapter 1

Sentence Sense

Writing a clear, precise sentence is an art you can master by knowing the different kinds of sentences and the ways they function. You can also revise more effectively if you recognize the different parts of speech and the ways they work together. (For explanations of unfamiliar terms, see the **Glossary of Terms.**)

The parts of a sentence   An English sentence divides into two parts.

SUBJECT + PREDICATE

Gabriel + hung the picture on the wall.

The **towel + is wet.**

The **subject** is what the sentence is about and answers the question "Who?" or "What?" The **predicate** says something about the subject and contains a word that expresses action or state of being.

1a   Verbs form the predicate of sentences.

A verb functions as the predicate of a sentence or as an essential part of the predicate.

Marco **walks.** [verb by itself]

Marco **walks** very fast. [verb plus modifier]

Verbs can be compound, that is, composed of more than one verb.

Marco **walks** and **arrives** on time.

A verb can consist of more than one word. The **auxiliary** is often called a *helping verb*. (See chapter 7 for a complete discussion of verbs.)

The fight **had started** by then.

Mara **should go** now.

Other words sometimes intervene between the auxiliary and the verb.

Television **will** never completely **replace** radio.

Verbs with prepositions Verbs followed by a preposition are called **phrasal verbs**. A preposition combines with a verb to mean something different from the verb standing alone. Some examples of verbs with prepositions are *look up, phase out, watch out, put off*. If a phrasal verb has a direct object, the preposition can come before or after the object.

She **looked** the word **up** in the dictionary.

She **looked up** the word in the dictionary.

If the object is a pronoun, the preposition must follow.

She **looked** it **up** in the dictionary.

ESL The meanings of such verbs can be found in a good ESL dictionary, together with an explanation of whether or not they are separable.

1b   Subjects, objects, and complements can be nouns, pronouns, or word groups serving as nouns.

(1) Subjects of verbs

Except for imperatives, all grammatically complete sentences contain stated subjects.

> Louisiana *produces* delicious yams.

In commands or requests, the subject is often understood.

> [You] *Take,* for example, Louisiana.

Subjects of verbs may be compound.

> **Louisiana** and **North Carolina** grow yams.

Subjects usually precede verbs. Common exceptions occur in questions and after the words *there* and *it*.

> *Was* the *book* interesting? [verb + subject]
>
> There *were* no *refusals.* [there + verb + subject]

(2) Objects of verbs

Verbs denoting action often require a **direct object** to receive or show the result of the action. Such verbs are called **transitive** verbs. (See chapter 7.) Sometimes a word that shows to whom or for whom the action occurred (**indirect object**) comes between the verb and the direct object.

> The clerk sold **her** the expensive **briefcase.** [indirect object: *her*; direct object: *briefcase*]

To identify a direct object, use the subject and the verb in a question ending with *whom* or *what*.

Juana silently took his hand.

Subject and verb: **Juana took**

Juana took WHAT? **hand**

Direct object: **hand**

Direct and indirect objects of verbs can be compound.

She likes **peas** and **spinach**.

We offered **Elena** and **Octavio** a year's membership.

(3) Subject and object complements

A **subject complement** refers to, identifies, or qualifies the subject and helps complete the meaning of forms of *be,* linking verbs (such as *seem, become*), and sensory verbs (such as *feel, smell, taste*). These verbs are often called **intransitive verbs**. (See chapter 7.)

Leilani is my **sister**. [*Sister* identifies *Leilani*.]

The rose smelled **sweet**. [*Sweet* describes *rose*.]

An **object complement** refers to, identifies, or qualifies the direct object.

We elected Jesse **president**.

The flaw made it **worthless**.

(4) Word order

Careful study of the five most common sentence patterns will reveal the importance of word order.

Pattern 1

SUBJECT + VERB.

The **lights** on the patrol car **flashed** ominously.

Pattern 2

> ## SUBJECT + VERB + OBJECT.

Kenya's **athletes** often **win** the **marathon**.

Pattern 3

> ## SUBJECT + VERB + INDIRECT OBJECT
> ## + DIRECT OBJECT.

The **company will** probably **send me** a small **refund**.

Pattern 4

> ## SUBJECT + LINKING VERB
> ## + SUBJECT COMPLEMENT.

My son's **name is** Aaron.

Pattern 5

> ## SUBJECT + VERB + DIRECT OBJECT
> ## + OBJECT COMPLEMENT.

I **named** my **son** Aaron.

1c   There are eight parts of speech.

Words are traditionally grouped into eight parts of speech: **verbs, nouns, pronouns, adjectives, adverbs, prepositions,** conjunctions, and **interjections**. A dictionary labels words according to their parts of speech. Some words have only one classification—for example, *notify* (verb), *sleepy* (adjective). Others can function as two or more parts of speech. The label of a word therefore depends on its use in a given sentence.

They dragged the sled **up** the hill. [preposition]

She follows the **ups** and downs of the market. [noun]

"They have **upped** the rent again," he complained. [verb]

The **up** escalator is broken again. [adjective]

Hopkins says to look **up** at the skies! [adverb]

(1) Verbs

A verb is an essential part of the predicate. (See **1a.**)

He **is** no longer **writing** those dull stories.

Suffixes frequently used to make verbs are *-ize* and *-ify:*

terror (noun)—*terrorize, terrify* (verbs)

real (adjective)—*realize* (verb)

! **CAUTION** Verbals (infinitives, participles, and gerunds) cannot function as the predicate. (See **1d.**)

(2) Nouns

Nouns function as subjects, objects, complements, appositives, and modifiers, as well as in direct address and in absolute constructions. Nouns name persons, places, things, ideas, animals, and so on. The articles *a, an,* and *the* signal that a noun is to follow.

McKinney drives a **truck** for the **Salvation Army**.

Suffixes frequently used to make nouns are *-ance, -ation, -ence, -ism, -ity, -ment, -ness,* and *-ship*.

> *relax, depend* (verbs)—*relaxation, dependence* (nouns)
>
> *kind, rigid* (adjectives)—*kindness, rigidity* (nouns)

Words such as *father-in-law, Labor Day,* and *swimming pool* are generally classified as *compound nouns*.

E S L   *Count/noncount nouns*   (See **16a(1)** for use of articles.)

Count nouns represent individual items that can be counted and not viewed as a mass, such as *child*.

Count nouns can be either singular or plural and are preceded by words such as *many, a few,* and *several* with the plural. Use either indefinite (*a, an*) or definite articles (*the*) with count nouns.

Noncount nouns, such as *humor* or *furniture,* represent an abstract concept, a mass, or a collection and do not have an individual existence. Modifiers such as *much* or *a little* can be used with noncount nouns but never *a* or *an*. They usually have only a singular form.

---

(3) Pronouns

A pronoun can substitute for a noun. Pronouns change form according to their function. (See chapter **6**.)

> **They** bought **it** for **her**.   **Everyone** knows **that**.

(4) Adjectives

Adjectives modify or qualify nouns and pronouns—and sometimes gerunds. (See page 12.)

These difficult decisions, whether **right** or **wrong**, affect all of us.

Suffixes such as *-able, -ant, -ic, -ish, -less,* and *-y* can be added to certain verbs or nouns to form adjectives:

accept, repent (verbs)—*acceptable, repentant* (adjectives)

angel, effort (nouns)—*angelic, effortless* (adjectives)

The articles *a, an,* and *the* are often classified as adjectives. Noun modifiers are also often classified as adjectives.

(5) Adverbs

Adverbs modify verbs, adjectives, and other adverbs: *rarely* saw, *very* short, *practically never* loses. In addition, an adverb can modify a verbal, a phrase, or a clause.

Adverbs that modify the sentence as a whole are called *sentence modifiers.* They are separated from the rest of the sentence by a comma.

Honestly, Jo wasn't speeding.

(6) Prepositions

A preposition establishes a relationship such as space, time, or manner between its object and another part of the sentence. The preposition with its object (and any modifiers) is called a *prepositional phrase.*

With great feeling, Martin Luther King, Jr., expressed his dream **of freedom**.

The preposition may follow its object, and it can be placed at the end of the sentence:

What was he complaining **about**? [*What* is the object.]

Phrasal prepositions can contain more than one word.

According to Georgeanne, it was a bad experience.

Phrasal Prepositions (two or more words):

according to	due to	in spite of
along with	except for	instead of
as for	in addition to	out of
because of	in case of	up to
by means of	in front of	with the exception of

ESL Some prepositions, such as *by/until,* pose special problems. *Until* means a continuing situation that will come to an end at a definite time in the future. *By* means an action that will happen at or before a particular time in the future.

I will finish my work **by** six o'clock.

I will be away **until** next Tuesday.

(For other preposition problems, consult the **Glossary of Usage** or one of the ESL resources listed in chapter **13**.)

---

(7) Conjunctions

Conjunctions are connectors. The **coordinating conjunctions** (*and, but, or, for, nor, so, yet*), as well as the correlatives (*both–and, either–or, neither–nor, not only–but also, whether–or*), join sentence elements of equal grammatical rank. (See also chapter **10**.) The **subordinating conjunctions** (such as *because, if, since, when, where*) join subordinate clauses to independent clauses. (See **1e(2)**.)

Words like *consequently, however,* and *therefore* (see the list on page 22) serve as conjunctive adverbs.

Don seemed bored in class; **however,** he did listen and learn.

(8) Interjections

Interjections are exclamations. They can be followed by an exclamation point or by a comma.

Wow! Oh, that's a surprise.

 A phrase is a group of words that functions as a single part of speech.

A **phrase** is a word group that lacks a subject and/or a predicate and functions as a single part of speech (noun, verb, adjective, adverb).

(1) Kinds of phrases

Phrases are generally classified as follows:

Verb Phrases   The flowers **have wilted.**

Noun Phrases   **The heavy freeze** killed **fruit trees.**

Prepositional Phrases   Parking **on campus** is prohibited.

Participial Phrases   **Exploring the beach,** we found many treasures. The picnic ground, **covered with trash,** looked pretty bad.

Gerund Phrases   **Swimming across the lake** is fun.

Infinitive Phrases   He wanted **to go to the movie.**

Absolute Phrases   The star left the gym, **reporters following him eagerly.**

Appositive Phrases   John, **my brother,** is here today.

Give special attention to verb forms in word groups used as nouns, adjectives, or adverbs. Although such verb forms (called *verbals*) are much like verbs, they cannot function as the predicate of a sentence. Verbal phrases can serve only as adjectives, adverbs, or nouns.

(2) Phrases used as nouns

Verbal phrases

Verbal phrases function as adjectives, nouns, or adverbs. **Gerund phrases** are always used as nouns. **Infinitive phrases** are often used as nouns.

Nouns	Phrases Used as Nouns
The **decision** is important.	**Choosing a major** is important. [gerund phrase]
She likes the **job**.	She likes **to do the work.** [infinitive phrase]
He uses my garage for **storage.**	He uses my garage for **storing his auto parts.** [gerund phrase]

Appositive phrases

An **appositive phrase** identifies, explains, or supplements the meaning of the word it adjoins.

Johnnycake, **a kind of cornbread,** is native to New England.

(3) Phrases used as modifiers

Prepositional phrases nearly always function as adjectives or adverbs. **Infinitive phrases** can also be used as adjectives or adverbs. **Participial phrases** are used as adjectives. **Absolute phrases** are used as adverbs. (See also **sentence modifier** in the **Glossary of Terms.**)

Adjectives	Phrases Used as Adjectives
It was a **sad** day.	It was a day **for sadness.** [prepositional phrase]
A **destructive** tornado roared through the city.	**Destroying everything in its path,** a tornado roared through the city. [participial phrase]

My **wet** clothes felt cold.	**Soaked with water,** my clothes felt cold. [participial phrase]
Adverbs	**Phrases Used as Adverbs**
Drive **carefully.**	Drive **with care on wet streets.** [prepositional phrases]
She sang **joyfully.**	She sang **to express her joy.** [infinitive phrase]
Today I could feel the warm sun on my face.	**My eyes shaded against the glare,** I felt the warm sun on my face. [absolute phrase]

 ## 1e Recognizing clauses helps in analyzing sentences.

A clause is a group of related words that contains a subject and a predicate.

(1) Independent clauses

An **independent clause** has the same grammatical structure as a sentence and contains a subject and a predicate.

The boy chased the dog, although he couldn't catch him.

(2) Subordinate clauses

A **subordinate clause** is a group of words that contains a subject and a predicate but cannot stand alone. Such clauses often begin with words like *because* and *since*.

Maria received the gold medal **because her performance was flawless.**

Subordinate clauses provide additional information about the independent clause. A subordinate clause is grammatically dependent and functions within a sentence as an adverb, an adjective, or a noun.

> I had to leave early **because I became ill.** [adverb clause]

> Geologists know **why earthquakes occur.** [noun clause]

The following conjunctions are commonly used to introduce subordinate clauses.

Words Commonly Used as Subordinating Conjunctions:

after	how	though
although	if	unless
as (far/soon) as	in case	until
as though	no matter how	when, whenever
because	once	where, wherever
before	since	whether
even if	so that	while
even though	than	why

Relative pronouns also serve as markers of those subordinate clauses called **relative clauses.** (See chapter **6.**)

that	what	which	who, whoever
whom, whomever		whose	

Subordinate clauses used as nouns

Nouns	Noun Clauses
The **news** may be false.	**What the newspapers say** may be false. [subject]
I do not know his **address**.	I do not know **where he lives.** [direct object]
Give the tools to **Rita**.	Give the tools to **whoever can use them best.** [object of a preposition]

That before a noun clause can often be omitted.

> I know she will come.

Subordinate clauses used as modifiers

Adjective clauses and adverb clauses serve as modifiers.

Adjective clauses Adjective clauses usually begin with relative pronouns but may sometimes begin with words such as *where* or *why*.

Adjectives	Adjective Clauses
The **golden** window reflects the sun.	The window, **which shines like gold,** reflects the sun.
My sister lives in a **peaceful** town.	The town **where my sister lives** is peaceful.

Adverb clauses Adverb clauses are ordinarily introduced by subordinating conjunctions.

Adverbs	Adverb Clauses
Next, the disk controller failed.	**After I backed up my files,** the disk controller failed.
His popularity dropped **locally.**	His popularity dropped **where people knew him.**

1f Sentences may be analyzed by form and function.

The form of a sentence is identified by the number and kinds of clauses it contains. The function of a sentence refers to its purpose.

(1) Examining sentence forms

a. A **simple sentence** consists of a single independent clause:

I **had lost** my passport.

b. A **compound sentence** consists of at least two independent clauses and no subordinate clauses:

I had lost my passport, but **I did not worry about it.**

c. A **complex sentence** has one independent clause and at least one subordinate clause:

Although I had lost my passport, I did not worry about it.

d. A **compound-complex sentence** consists of at least two independent clauses and at least one subordinate clause:

When I lost my passport, **I ordered** a new one, but **I did not worry** about it.

(2) Examining the purpose or function of sentences

English sentences make statements (**declarative**), ask questions (**interrogative**), give commands or make requests (**imperative**), and make exclamations (**exclamatory**).

Declarative	She refused the offer.
Imperative	Refuse the offer now.
Interrogative	Did she refuse the offer? She refused, didn't she? She refused it?
Exclamatory	What an offer! And she refused it!

In your writing, make sure you use the forms and functions that most effectively express your thoughts.

Chapter 2

Sentence Fragments

A **fragment**, an incomplete sentence starting with a capital and ending with a period, is ordinarily avoided in formal writing.

> He enjoys shrubs. **Which help screen him from the street.**
>
> Raymond began to tap out the rhythm. **First on the table and then on the counter.**

Fragments are often phrases or subordinate clauses. Fragments can be corrected by making them independent sentences or by connecting them to an adjoining sentence.

> He enjoys shrubs. **They help screen him from the street.**
>
> Raymond began to tap out the rhythm, **first on the table and then on the counter.**

Testing for fragments   You can ask three questions to help identify fragments:

1. Is there a verb? If not, supply one or attach the fragment to a related sentence (**2a**). Remember, a verbal is not a verb.
2. Is there a subject? If not, supply one or attach the fragment to a related sentence (**2a**).
3. Is there a subordinating conjunction? If so, remove it or attach the subordinate clause to a related sentence (**2b**).

Occasionally, writers deliberately use fragments. For example, writing that mirrors speech often contains grammatically incomplete sentences. Similarly, exclamations and answers to questions are often single words, phrases, or subordinate clauses.

Unbelievable! No pain, no gain.

Why does Camilla's radio always play classic rock? **Because that is her favorite kind of music.**

⚠ **CAUTION**   Have a good reason for any sentence fragment you allow to stand.

2a   Phrases are sometimes mistakenly punctuated as sentences.

Verbal phrases, prepositional phrases, parts of compound predicates, and appositives are sometimes written as fragments. They can be revised in one of the ways listed below.

1. *Make the phrase into a sentence by supplying the missing subject and/or verb.*

   He reached the top. ^He was^ Panting and puffing all the way.

   I'm getting an ice cream cone. ^I want^ One scoop of chocolate swirl and one of butter pecan.

2. *Attach the fragment to a related sentence.*

   He reached the top,^top,^ Panting and puffing all the way.

   I'm getting an ice cream cone. ^with^ One scoop of chocolate swirl and one of butter pecan.

2b Subordinate clauses are sometimes mistakenly punctuated as sentences.

These fragments can be revised in one of the ways listed below.

1. *Remove the subordinating conjunction and supply the missing elements.*

   They tried to understand Arturo's objections. ~~Which~~ ^{They} were unfounded.

2. *Attach the fragment to a related sentence.*

   They tried to understand Arturo's ~~objections. Which~~ ^{objections, which} were unfounded.

3. *Reduce the fragment to a single-word modifier and include it in the related sentence.*

   They tried to understand Arturo's ^{unfounded} objections. ~~Which were~~ ~~unfounded.~~

Chapter 3

Comma Splices and Fused Sentences

A **comma splice** consists of two independent clauses joined simply by a comma. A **fused sentence** (also called a *run-on*) occurs when neither a conjunction nor appropriate punctuation joins two independent clauses.

Comma Splice   The current was swift, he swam to shore.

Fused Sentence   The current was swift he swam to shore.

Comma splices and fused sentences can be corrected by separating the clauses or by joining them.

To separate:

1. Clauses may be separated by placing a period after each.

   The current was swift. He swam to shore.

2. Clauses may be separated by a semicolon.

   The current was swift; he swam to shore.

To link and relate:

1. A comma can be inserted before the appropriate coordinating conjunction (*and, but, or, nor, for, so, yet*—see **17a**).

   The wind was cold, **so** they decided not to walk.

2. One clause can be subordinated to the other (see **17b**).

   The wind was so cold **that** they decided not to walk.

   Because the wind was cold, they decided not to walk.

3. One of the clauses can become an introductory phrase (see **17b**).

Because of the cold wind, they decided not to walk.

ESL   *For students who learn British English as a second language*   British usage commonly links independent clauses with a comma. When writing for American readers, however, follow the American practice.

3a Commas occur between independent clauses only when they are linked by a coordinating conjunction.

Comma Splice   Women's roles have changed in recent decades, women now make up a larger percentage of the workforce.

Revised   Women's roles have changed in recent decades, **for** women now make up a larger percentage of the workforce. [coordinating conjunction *for* added]

OR   Women's roles have changed in recent decades; women now make up a larger percentage of the workforce. [A semicolon separates the clauses.]

Comma Splice   I ran over some broken glass in the parking lot, it did not puncture my tires.

Revised   I ran over some broken glass in the parking lot, **but** it did not puncture my tires. [coordinating conjunction *but* added]

OR   **Although** I ran over some broken glass in the parking lot, it did not puncture my tires. [Addition of *although* makes the first clause subordinate: see **17b**.]

3b Semicolons occur before conjunctive adverbs or transitional phrases between independent clauses.

Comma Splice   Sexual harassment is not just a women's issue, after all, men can be sexually harassed too.

Revised   Sexual harassment is not just a women's issue; after all, men can be sexually harassed too. [independent clause; *transitional phrase,* independent clause]

Fused Sentence   The nineteenth-century European imperialists left arbitrary boundaries in Africa therefore, each country is composed of a mix of cultures.

Revised   The nineteenth-century European imperialists left arbitrary boundaries in Africa; therefore, each country is composed of a mix of cultures. [independent clause; *conjunctive adverb,* independent clause]

Below is a list of frequently used conjunctive adverbs and transitional phrases.

Conjunctive adverbs: *Beginning of paragraphs.*

also	however	next
anyway	instead	otherwise
besides	likewise	still
consequently	meanwhile	then
finally	moreover	therefore
furthermore	nevertheless	thus

Transitional phrases:

after all	even so	in other words
as a result	for example	in the second place
at any rate	in addition	on the other hand
at the same time	in fact	

Chapter 4

Adjectives and Adverbs

Adjectives and adverbs qualify, restrict, or intensify the meaning of other words. They also describe degrees of comparison. **Adjectives** modify nouns and pronouns; **adverbs** modify verbs, adjectives, and other adverbs.

Adjectives	Adverbs
a **quick** lunch	eat **quickly**
She looked **angry**.	She looked **angrily** at me.

Adverbs can also modify verbals (gerunds, infinitives, participles) and whole clauses as well. (See **1c**.)

Walking rapidly is good for you. [adverb *rapidly* modifying gerund *walking*, which serves as the subject]

The *-ly* ending is associated with adverbs formed from adjectives (*lightly*), but adjectives formed from nouns also have the *-ly* ending (*cost, costly*). A number of words can function as either adjectives or adverbs (*fast, well*), and a few adverbs have two acceptable forms (*quick, quickly; slow, slowly*).

The articles *a, an,* and *the* are often classified as adjectives.

ESL   See **16a(1)** for the use of articles.

4a   Adverbs modify verbs, adjectives, and other adverbs.

Leela played her part ~~perfect~~. *perfectly* [The adverb *perfectly* modifies the verb *played*.]

The plane departs at ~~a reasonable~~ *a reasonably* early hour. [The adverb *reasonably* modifies the adjective *early*.]

Most dictionaries still label the following as informal usage: *sure* for *surely*, *real* for *really*, and *good* for *well*.

Informal   The Broncos played **real good**.
Formal   The Broncos played **very well**.

4b   There is a distinction between adverbs used to modify verbs and adjectives used as subject complements.

A common error is to use an adjective as an adverb or an adverb as an adjective.

The actor looked *angry*. [subject complement]
The actor looked up *angrily*. [adverb]

4c   Many adjectives and adverbs change form to indicate the degree of comparison.

Generally, short adjectives and adverbs form the comparative by adding *-er* and the superlative by adding *-est*.

large, larger, largest

quick, quicker, quickest

Most two-syllable adjectives with stress on the first syllable also add *-er* or *-est*. For words whose base form ends in *-y*, change the *-y* to *-i*.

lucky, luckier, luckiest

Longer adjectives and most adverbs form the comparative by using *more* (or *less*) and the superlative by using *most* (or *least*).

fortunate, more/less fortunate, most/least fortunate

rapidly, more/less rapidly, most/least rapidly

A few common modifiers have irregular forms.

little, less, least

good/well, better, best

bad/badly, worse, worst

(1) The comparative denotes a greater degree or refers to two in a comparison.

Make sure to complete the comparison, and make clear what the subject is being compared with. The conjunction *than* signals the second element.

The area is **bigger** now **than** it was five years ago.

Dried apples are **more** nutritious per pound **than** fresh apples.

Note that the comparison may be implied by the context.

She wrote **two** papers, and the instructor gave her a **better** grade on the second.

The comparative form when used with *other* sometimes refers to more than two.

Bert can run **faster** than the *other* players.

(2) The superlative denotes the greatest degree or refers to three or more in a comparison.

The interests of the family are **best** served by open communication.

Bert is the **fastest** of the three runners.

(3) A double comparative or superlative is incorrect.

Our swimming hole is much ~~more~~ shallower than Crystal Lake.

That was the ~~most~~ funniest movie.

4d   A single rather than a double negative is correct.

The use of two negatives within a clause to express a single negation is considered incorrect.

He did **not** keep ~~no~~ records.

I can~~not~~ do **no**thing about it.

Because **hardly, barely,** and **scarcely** already denote severely limited or negative conditions, use of **not, nothing,** or **without** with these modifiers creates a double negative.

I could~~n't~~ **hardly** quit in the middle of the job.

ESL   Writers often use up to three adjectives to modify a noun. English requires that the adjectives occur in the following order: determiners, subjective opinion (beautiful, happy, angry), physical description (size, shape, age, and color), origin, material, purpose.

  that ugly brick building   their large English watercolor

  Dad's old threshing machine   a round Italian pizza dish

Chapter 5

Coherence: Misplaced Parts and Dangling Modifiers

Keeping related parts of the sentence together and avoiding dangling modifiers makes meaning clearer to your reader.

5a   **Placing modifiers near the words they modify clarifies meaning.**

The meaning of the following sentences changes according to the position of the modifiers.

> Natasha went out with **just** her coat on.
> Natasha **just** went out with her coat on.
> **Just** Natasha went out with her coat on.

(1) Place modifiers such as *almost, only, just, even, hardly, nearly,* and *merely* immediately before the words they modify.

> The truck |only| costs| $2,000.

> He |even| works\ during his vacation.

(2) Place a modifying prepositional phrase to indicate clearly what the phrase modifies.

> Arne says |that he means to leave| in the first paragraph|.

(3) Place adjective clauses near the words they modify.

I put the chair |in the middle of the room |that I purchased|.

(4) Revise "squinting" constructions—modifiers that may refer to either a preceding or a following word.

I agreed|the next day|to help him|.

5b   There are several ways to revise dangling modifiers.

Dangling modifiers   Dangling modifiers are primarily verbal phrases that do not clearly refer to other words or phrases in the sentence. The words in the sentence can be rearranged, or words can be added, to make the meaning clear.

Dangling	*Taking our seats,* the game started.
Revised	*Taking our seats,* **we waited** for the game to start.
Dangling	The evening passed very pleasantly, *watching* a late movie.
Revised	**We** passed the evening very pleasantly, *watching* a late movie.
Dangling	On *entering* the stadium, the size of the crowd surprised Theo.
Revised	On *entering* the stadium, **Theo** was surprised at the size of the crowd.
Dangling	*When only a small boy,* my father took me with him to Chicago.
Revised	*When* **I was** *only a small boy,* my father took me with him to Chicago.

Chapter 6

Pronouns

Pronouns have a number of forms (cases) that show their relation to other parts of the sentence.

> **I** [subject] want **my** [modifier showing possession] cousin to help **me** [direct object].

I, the subject, is in the *subjective* case; *my,* showing possession, is in the *possessive* case; and *me,* the object, is in the *objective* case.

ESL   Although many languages include the subject pronoun in the verb, in English it must be stated except in certain imperatives. (See **1b(1)**.)

Pronouns also have singular and plural forms.

> **We** want **our** cousins to help **us**.

The personal pronouns   Personal pronouns identify the speaker (first person: *I, we*), the person spoken to (second person: *you*), and the person or thing spoken about (third person: *he, she, it, they*). The pronouns *I, we, he, she,* and *they* have distinctive forms for all three cases and for both singular and plural. *You* is the same in both singular and plural, and *you* and *it* change case form only in the possessive.

	Singular	Plural
Subjective	I	we
	you	you
	he, she, it	they
Possessive	my, mine	our, ours
	your, yours	your, yours
	his, her, its	their, theirs
Objective	me	us
	you	you
	him, her, it	them

The pronouns *my, our, your, him, her, it,* and *them* combine with *self* or *selves* to become **intensive/reflexive pronouns**, which are used primarily for emphasis.

Jake, **himself**, brought it here.

Intensive/reflexive pronouns also often refer to a noun or pronoun already mentioned in the sentence.

Jake saw a picture of **himself**.

■ **CAUTION** Do not use *myself* or *me* in place of *I* in a compound subject.

Jake and ~~myself~~ *I* brought it here.

Jake and I
~~Me and~~ Jake brought it here.

Hisself and *theirselves* are not accepted in formal English; instead, use *himself, themselves.*

James and Jerry painted the house by ~~theirselves~~ *themselves*.

Relative pronouns Relative pronouns (*who, whom, which, whose,* and *that*) introduce clauses that refer to a noun in the main clause.

Julieta, who is my sister, lives in Atlanta.

Who, whose, and *whom* ordinarily refer to people; *which* to things; and *that* to either.

	Singular or Plural
Subjective	who, which, that
Possessive	whose
Objective	whom, which, that

6a   Pronouns agree with their antecedents.

Pronouns should agree in number and gender with the noun or phrase (antecedent) to which they refer.

The cousins gave us **their** [plural modifier] help.

George gave us **his** [masculine pronoun] help willingly. Lucinda, on the other hand, gave us **her** [feminine pronoun] help grudgingly.

When referring to a noun that can include both men and women, you can avoid the pronoun *he* by dropping the pronoun.

A student should hand ~~his~~ papers in promptly.

You can also avoid the problem by recasting in the plural, in the passive, or in the imperative.

Students should hand their papers in promptly. [plural]

Papers are to be handed in promptly. [passive]

Hand your papers in promptly. [imperative]

6b Pronouns refer to the nouns immediately preceding them.

The meaning of each pronoun should be immediately obvious. To avoid any confusion, repeat the antecedent, use a synonym for it, or recast your sentence.

(1) Clear antecedents

When a pronoun could refer to either of two antecedents, the reader is confused. Recasting the sentence or replacing the pronoun with a noun makes the antecedent clear.

In talking with   Juan admitted
~~Juan told~~ Peter that he had made a mistake. [Whom does *he*

refer to?]

that
The books were standing on the shelf ~~which~~ needed sorting.

[Did the books or the shelf need sorting?]

(2) Clear references

If a pronoun is too far away from its antecedent, the reader may have to backtrack. A pronoun that refers to a modifier can also obscure meaning. Recasting the sentence to bring pronoun and antecedent closer together or substituting a noun for the obscure pronoun will clarify meaning.

Remote	The *sophomore* found herself president of a group of animal lovers, *who* was not a joiner of organizations. [*Who* is too far removed from the antecedent *sophomore*.]
Better	The **sophomore, who** was not a joiner of organizations, found herself president of a group of animal lovers.

| Obscure | Before Ellen could get to the jewelry store, *it* was all sold. [reference to a modifier] |
| Better | Before Ellen could get to the jewelry store, all the **jewelry** was sold. |

(3) Broad or implied references

Pronouns such as *it, this, that, which,* and *such* may refer to a specific word or phrase or to the sense of a whole clause, sentence, or paragraph.

> Some people think that the fall of man had something to do with sex, but that's a mistake.   —C. S. LEWIS   [*That* refers to the sense of the whole clause.]

When used carelessly, broad references can make writing unclear. Make the antecedent explicit rather than implicit.

> Lois said she would stay in Yuma for a year. This ^remark^ suggests that she is happy. [*This* has no expressed antecedent.]

> My father is a music teacher. ~~It~~ ^Teaching music^ is a profession that requires much patience. [*It* has no expressed antecedent.]

(4) Awkward use of *it*

Awkward	It was no use trying.
Revised	**There was** no use trying.
	OR
	Trying was useless.

6c   Pronoun form in compound constructions varies.

Multiple *subjects or subject complements* are in the subjective case.

She and her father buy groceries on Saturday morning.

I thought **he or Dad** would come to my rescue.

It was **Maria and I** who solved the problem. [See **6g**.]

The pronoun *I* occurs last in a compound construction.

Multiple objects of prepositions are in the objective case.

between Merrill and ~~I~~ *me*   with Amanda and ~~I~~ *me*

You can test the case of a pronoun after a preposition by eliminating the accompanying noun or pronoun.

Gabriel gave it to (Edwyn and) me.

Multiple objects of verbs or verbals and *subjects of infinitives* are in the objective case.

Clara may appoint **you or me**. [direct object]

He gets nowhere by scolding **Bea or him**. [object of gerund]

Dad wanted **Sheila and me** to keep the old car. [subject of the infinitive]

If an appositive follows a pronoun, normal case rules still apply.

~~Us~~ *We* students need this.

Dylan told ~~we~~ *us* girls to go home.

6d   The use of a pronoun in its own clause determines its case.

(1) *Who* or *whoever* as the subject of a clause

The subject of a verb in a subordinate clause takes the subjective case, even when the whole clause is used as an object:

I forgot **who** won the game. [*Who* is the subject of the clause *who won the game.*]

He has consideration for **whoever** needs his help. [*Whoever* is the subject of the clause *whoever needs his help.*]

(2) *Whom* for all pronouns used as objects

Whom, the form used for the object of a verb or a preposition in a subordinate clause, is often misused.

They helped the people ~~who~~ *whom* they liked.

I don't know ~~who~~ *whom* he voted for.

In spoken English, the pronoun *who* is commonly used when it occurs as the first word in the sentence, even when it is the object of a verb or preposition. Dictionaries increasingly accept this usage, although in formal writing it is better to use the traditional *whom.*

Informal   **Who** do you want to speak to?
Formal   **Whom** will they elect president?

(3) Pronouns after *than* or *as*

In sentences with implied (rather than stated) elements, the choice of the pronoun form is important to meaning:

She likes Clarice more than **I**. [subjective case, meaning "more than I like Clarice"]

She likes Dana more than **me**. [objective case, meaning "more than she likes me"]

6e   A pronoun before a gerund uses the possessive form.

The possessive form of the pronoun is used before a gerund (a verb form ending in *-ing* and used as a noun).

I appreciated ~~him~~ *his* helping Denise.

⚠️ **CAUTION** The *-ing* ending marks both gerunds and participles. A participle is used as an adjective; a gerund is used as a noun. The possessive case precedes gerunds, but not participles. The sentences below have different meanings. In the first *sitting* is a participle modifying *the man* who annoys us; in the second his *sitting* is what annoys us.

The man sitting [participle modifying *man*] at the desk annoyed us.

The man's sitting [gerund acting as subject] at the desk annoyed us.

6f Pronouns use the subjective form for a subject complement.

That certainly could be **she** sitting near the front.

It was **I** who first noticed the difference.

Informal English accepts *It's me* (*him, her, us,* and *them*).

Chapter 7

Verbs

Verbs show what someone (or something) does, when an action occurred, and whether it is hypothetical or conditional. They are the heart of a sentence.

Tense Verbs change form to show whether an action happened in the present, the past, or the future. English traditionally recognizes six tenses: three simple tenses and three perfect tenses.

Simple Tenses

Present: We often write letters.
Past: After graduation, we wrote letters.
Future: We will write letters after graduation.

Perfect Tenses

Present: We have written letters since graduation.
Past: We had written letters after graduation.
Future: We will have written letters before graduation.

ESL To express the idea that an action happened at some unspecified time, English uses the simple tenses, either present or past. To specify the complex time relationships of completed actions, English speakers combine the auxiliary verb *have* with one of the principal forms of the verb to form the perfect tense.

Regular and irregular verbs A **regular verb** takes the -*d* or -*ed* ending to denote the past tense.

Regular *laugh (laughs), laughed*

Irregular verbs form their past tense in other ways.

Irregular *eat (eats), ate
run (runs), ran*

Auxiliary verbs **Auxiliary verbs** (or helping verbs) combine with other verbs to indicate tense, voice, or mood. **Modal auxiliary verbs** join the present form of the verb to make requests, give instructions, and express doubt, necessity, or probability.

Checklist of Auxiliary Verbs			✓
Auxiliary Verbs		**Modal Auxiliary Verbs**	
be	have	shall	may
am	has	should	might
is	had		must
are		will	
was	do	would	
were	does		can
been	did		could
being			

Although the auxiliary always precedes the basic verb, other words may intervene.

Television **will** never completely **replace** newspapers.

E S L   In English, when more than one auxiliary precedes a basic verb, the modal comes first.

We should have been basting the turkey more often.

Forms of be   The most irregular verb in the English language is *be*. Following is a list of forms of *be* in the present and past tenses.

	First	Second	Third	
Present	I am	you are	he/she/it is	[singular]
	we are	you are	they are	[plural]
Past	I was	you were	he/she/it was	[singular]
	we were	you were	they were	[plural]

Some dialects use *be* in place of *am, is,* or *are,* the present forms of *be*. Some dialects also use *be* with the present participle to indicate habitual action. In formal written English, use the conventional forms of *be*.

She be a fine hockey player.

He be walking to class.

E S L   English recognizes two kinds of verbs, those that express states of being (**stative** verbs) and those that express action (**dynamic** verbs). Some verbs have two meanings, one stative, the other dynamic: I have [possess] time to waste. [stative] I was having [experiencing] trouble understanding him. [dynamic]

Voice   Voice indicates the relationship between the action of the verb and the subject. **Active voice** emphasizes the subject as the **doer** of the action. **Passive voice** makes the subject the *receiver*. To make a verb passive, use the appropriate form of *be* with the base verb.

Active   The dog **chases** the cat. [The subject *dog* acts on the object *cat*.]

Passive   The cat **is chased** by the dog. [The subject *cat* is acted upon. The prepositional phrase identifying the doer of the action could be omitted.]

The active voice is clearer, more concise, and more vigorous than the passive. Use passive voice only when you have good reason. (See **11d(1)**.)

Transitive and intransitive verbs   The subject and object of an active verb switch places when a verb becomes passive. This transformation is possible only with verbs that accept a direct object—**transitive verbs**. Although an **intransitive verb** can take a subject complement, it does not accept a direct object and cannot be made passive.

Transitive   The hammer **bent** the nail. [*Nail*, the direct object, receives the action of *hammer*.]

Intransitive   The bell **looks** fragile. [The subject complement, *fragile*, identifies *bell*.]

Some verbs can be transitive or intransitive.

Transitive   Claudia **studies** the book.

Intransitive   Claudia **studies** all night.

Mood   Mood indicates writers' attitudes. The **indicative mood** makes statements, the **imperative mood** issues commands or requests, and the **subjunctive mood** expresses situations that are hypothetical or conditional.

The following conjugation of the verb *see* shows tense, person, voice, and mood. It also shows how auxiliary verbs make a verb passive and form the perfect tenses.

THE CONJUGATION OF A VERB

Indicative Mood

Active Voice   *Passive Voice*

Present Tense

Singular	*Plural*	*Singular*	*Plural*
1. I see	we see	I am seen	we are seen
2. you see	you see	you are seen	you are seen
3. one (he/she/it) sees	they see	one (he/she/it) is seen	they are seen

Past Tense

1. I saw	we saw	I was seen	we were seen
2. you saw	you saw	you were seen	you were seen
3. one saw	they saw	one was seen	they were seen

Future Tense

1. I shall (will) see	we shall (will) see	I shall (will) be seen	we shall (will) be seen
2. you will see	you will see	you will be seen	you will be seen
3. one will see	they will see	one will be seen	they will be seen

Present Perfect Tense

1. I have seen	we have seen	I have been seen	we have been seen
2. you have seen	you have seen	you have been seen	you have been seen
3. one has seen	they have seen	one has been seen	they have been seen

Past Perfect Tense

1. I had seen	we had seen	I had been seen	we had been seen
2. you had seen	you had seen	you had been seen	you had been seen
3. one had seen	they had seen	one had been seen	they had been seen

Future Perfect Tense
(seldom used)

1. I shall (will) have seen	we shall (will) have seen	I shall (will) have been seen	we shall (will) have been seen
2. you will have seen	you will have seen	you will have been seen	you will have been seen
3. one will have seen	they will have seen	one will have been seen	they will have been seen

Imperative Mood

Present Tense

See. Be seen.

Subjunctive Mood

Active Voice *Passive Voice*

Present Tense

Singular	if I, you, one see	if I, you, one be seen
Plural	if we, you, they see	if we, you, they are seen

Past Tense

Singular	if I, you, one saw	if I, you, one were seen
Plural	if we, you, they saw	if we, you, they were seen

Present Perfect Tense

Singular	if I, you, one have seen	if I, you, one have been seen
Plural	if we, you, they have seen	if we, you, they have been seen

Past Perfect Tense (same as the Indicative)

7a   Verbs must agree with their subjects.

Agree means that if a subject is plural, the verb must have a plural form, and if the subject is singular, the verb must have a singular form.

Singular   The **rose** in the vase **is** wilted. [*rose is*]

Plural   The **roses** in the vase **are** wilted. [*roses are*]

Only present-tense verbs change form to indicate the number and person of their subjects. It is easy to confuse the endings of *verbs* (where -*s* indicates **singular**) with those of *nouns* (where it indicates **plural**).

subject + *s*	verb + *s*
The students need attention.	The student needs attention.

If the subject is singular but is not *I* or *you,* the verb needs the -*s* ending. Since grammar checkers cannot catch agreement errors, it pays to be alert for situations that cause them.

(1) Other words between the subject and the verb

The **rhythm** of the pounding waves **is** calming. [*Waves* is the object of a prepositional phrase, not the subject.]

Phrases such as *along with, as well as, in addition to, including* generally introduce a prepositional phrase and do not affect the number of the subject.

Her **salary** in addition to tips **is** just enough to live on.

(2) Endings of subjects and verbs not clearly sounded in rapid speech

Economists seem concerned.

(3) Subjects joined by *and*

My two best **friends** and my **fiancé hate** each other.

The **coach** and the **umpire were** at home plate.

A compound subject that refers to a single person or unit takes a singular verb.

The **creator** and **director** of *Schindler's List* **is** Spielberg.

(4) Subjects joined by *either . . . or*

Either Patty or Tom **was** asked to preside.

If one subject is singular and one is plural, the verb agrees with the subject nearer to the verb.

Neither the basket nor the **apples were** expensive.

Neither the apples nor the **basket was** expensive.

(5) Inverted word order or *there* + *verb* constructions

Hardest hit by the snows **were** the large **cities** of the Northeast.

There **are** several **ways** to protect yourself from a tornado.

(6) Relative pronoun (*who, which, that*) subjects

It is the **doctor who** often **suggests** a diet.

It is among the **books that are** out of print.

He is one of **those who agree** with my decision. [*Who* refers to *those*, a plural pronoun.]

(7) Indefinite pronouns

Each, either, one, everybody, and *anyone* are singular.

Either of them **is willing** to shovel the driveway.

Everybody in our apartment building **has** a parking place.

All, any, some, none, half, and *most* can be either singular or plural.

Wendy collects comic books; **some are** very valuable.

The bank would not take the money because **some was** foreign.

Use a singular verb with singular subjects preceded by *every* or *each* and joined by *and*:

Every cat and dog in the county **has** to be vaccinated.

Each fork and spoon **has** to be dried carefully.

Each after a plural subject does not affect the verb form:

The cat and the dog **each have** their good points.

(8) Collective nouns and phrases

Collective nouns and phrases refer to a group of individual things as a unit. Whether they require a singular or a plural verb depends on whether the sentence refers to the group as a whole or to the individual items.

> **ESL** *For students who learn British English as a second language* British usage treats collective nouns as plural. Treat collective nouns as singular when writing for American readers.
>
> **British** The committee **are** meeting tonight.
>
> **American** The committee **is** meeting tonight.

Singular (regarded as a unit):

The **committee is** meeting today.

Ten million gallons is a lot of oil.

Plural (regarded as individuals or parts):

The **majority** of us **are** in favor.

Ten million gallons of oil **were spilled**.

Most writers still use *data* and *media* as plural nouns in formal written English.

Formal The media **have** shaped public opinion.

Formal The data **are** in the appendix.

(9) Nouns plural in form but singular in meaning

Nouns that look plural but are treated as singular include *economics, news,* and *physics.*

Economics **is** important for a business major.

Some nouns (such as *athletics, politics,* and *sheep*) can be singular or plural.

Statistics is an interesting subject. **Statistics are** often misleading.

7b Verbs have at least three principal parts.

The three principal parts of verbs are the simple present form (*see*), the past form (*saw*), and the past participle (*seen*). The present participle (*seeing*) is often considered a fourth principal part. This checklist of principal parts includes regular and irregular verbs that are sometimes misused.

Checklist of Principal Parts of Verbs ✓

Present	Past	Past Participle
arise	arose	arisen
ask	asked	asked
attack	attacked	attacked
awaken	awakened OR awoke	awakened
bear	bore	borne/born
begin	began	begun
blow	blew	blown
break	broke	broken
bring	brought	brought
burst	burst	burst
choose	chose	chosen
cling	clung	clung
come	came	come
dive	dived OR dove	dived
do	did	done
drag	dragged	dragged
draw	drew	drawn
drink	drank	drunk
drive	drove	driven
drown	drowned	drowned
eat	ate	eaten

continued

continued from previous page

		✓
fall	fell	fallen
fly	flew	flown
forgive	forgave	forgiven
freeze	froze	frozen
get	got	got OR gotten
give	gave	given
go	went	gone
grow	grew	grown
hang (things)	hung	hung
hang (people)	hanged	hanged
happen	happened	happened
know	knew	known
ride	rode	ridden
ring	rang	rung
rise	rose	risen
run	ran	run
see	saw	seen
shake	shook	shaken
shrink	shrank OR shrunk	shrunk OR shrunken
sing	sang OR sung	sung
sink	sank OR sunk	sunk
speak	spoke	spoken
spin	spun	spun
spit	spat	spat
spring	sprang OR sprung	sprung
steal	stole	stolen
sting	stung	stung
stink	stank OR stunk	stunk
strive	strove OR strived	striven OR strived
swear	swore	sworn
swim	swam	swum
swing	swung	swung
take	took	taken
tear	tore	torn

continued

continued from previous page

throw	threw	thrown ✓
wake	woke OR waked	woken OR waked
wear	wore	worn
weave	wove	woven
wring	wrung	wrung
write	wrote	written

Some verbs are easy to confuse and tricky to spell:

PRINCIPAL PARTS OF TROUBLESOME VERBS

Present	Past	Past Participle	Present Participle
lay	laid	laid	laying
lead	led	led	leading
lie	lay	lain	lying
loosen	loosened	loosened	loosening
lose	lost	lost	losing
pay	paid	paid	paying
set	set	set	setting
sit	sat	sat	sitting
study	studied	studied	studying

! **CAUTION** It is sometimes hard to remember a needed *-d* or *-ed* in such expressions as *supposed to* or *used to* when the sound is not emphasized in speech.

Yesterday, I ~~ask~~ asked myself, Is the judge prejudice_d?

He ~~use~~ used to smoke.

7c Tense forms express differences in time.

(1) The meaning of tense forms

Tense is not the same as time. For instance, as the following examples show, the present tense form is not restricted to present time. It can refer to past and future occurrences as well. Auxiliaries and other words in the sentence can also indicate time.

Present tense (timeless or habitual present, now)

> I **see** what you meant by that remark.
>
> Dana **uses** common sense. [habitual action]
>
> Blind innocence **sees** no evil. [universal or timeless truth]
>
> Joseph Conrad **writes** about the human heart. [literary present]
>
> The store **opens** next week. [future time]
>
> I **am trying** to form an opinion. [present progressive form indicating action occurring now]

ESL In English, the present progressive expresses action that is occurring now, whereas the simple present expresses activities that occur at an unspecified time (timeless or habitual present):

I am boiling eggs.	The act of boiling eggs is occurring now.
I boil eggs.	The act of boiling eggs is habitual.

Past tense (past time, not extending to the present)

> I **ate** the cake.

We **were continuing** our work. [continuing action in the past]

Adolpho **used to be** happy. [COMPARE "Adolpho was happy then."]

Future tense (at a future time, sometime after now)

We **will see** the movie.

He **will be having** his dinner. [progressive]

Present perfect tense (sometime before now, up to now)

I **have taken** the prize.

Has Michelle **been using** her talents? [progressive]

Past perfect tense (before a specific time in the past)

After Shawn **had left** for work, he realized it was a holiday.

Had they **been sailing** along the coast? [progressive]

Future perfect tense (before a specific time in the future)

Our bumpers **will have rusted** by the time he changes his mind.

The future perfect is almost always replaced by the simple future.

After graduation, I **will have seen** [*or* **will see**] my dreams come true.

(2) Logical sequence of tense forms

Combinations of tense forms can make fine distinctions in relation to time.

When the speaker **finished**, everyone **applauded**. [Both actions took place at the same definite time in the past.]

When I **had been** here for two weeks, I **learned** that my application **had been denied**. [The *had* before *been* indicates a time before the action described by *learned* and *denied*.]

7d Although rare, the subjunctive mood is still used for specific purposes.

The subjunctive mood occurs in fixed expressions such as *as it were* and is also used to express certain other meanings.

Forms for the subjunctive

For the verb *be:*

> PRESENT, singular or plural: **be**
>
> PAST, singular or plural: **were**

For all other verbs with third-person singular subjects, the subjunctive omits the characteristic *-s* ending:

> PRESENT, singular only: **see** [The *-s* ending is dropped.]

Subjunctives are used under the following conditions:

1. **After such verbs as *demand, urge, request, suggest***

   I demand that the parking ticket **be** voided.

   I suggested that she **move** to a new apartment.

2. **To express wishes or a hypothetical, highly improbable, or contrary-to-fact condition**

   I wish I **were** in Ashville.

   If I **were** you, I'd accept the offer.

3. **As *had* rather than *would have* in *if* clauses**

   If he ~~would have~~ *had* arrived earlier, he wouldn't have lost the sale.

Effective
Sentences

Effective Sentences

Chapter 8

Sentence Unity: Consistency

Good writing is unified. It does not contain unrelated ideas, mixed constructions, or faulty predication. It is consistent throughout.

8a Making the relationship of ideas in a sentence clear helps the reader.

Unrelated   Alaska has majestic glaciers, but most Americans must travel great distances. [gap in thought]

Related   Alaska has majestic glaciers, but **to see them** most Americans must travel great distances.

8b Arranging details in a clear sequence makes your point clear.

Although detail makes writing more interesting, too much can be distracting. Do not include details that are not necessary.

Excessive   When I was only sixteen, I left home to attend a college that was nearby and that my uncle had graduated from twenty years earlier. [If the detail about the uncle is important, include it in another sentence.]

8c Mixed metaphors and mixed constructions are illogical.

A **mixed metaphor** combines different images, creating an illogical comparison.

Mixed	Her climb up the ladder of success was nipped in the bud.
Revised	She slipped on her climb up the ladder of success. OR Before her career could blossom, it was nipped in the bud.

A sentence that begins with one kind of construction and shifts to another is a **mixed construction**. Mixed constructions often omit the subject or the predicate.

Mixed	When Win plays the accordion attracts attention. [adverb clause + predicate; no subject]
Revised	When Win plays the accordion, she attracts attention. [adverb clause + main clause] OR Win's playing of the accordion attracts attention. [subject + predicate]

8d Faulty predication can lead to problems.

Faulty predication occurs when the subject and predicate do not fit together logically.

Faulty	An example of discrimination is an apartment owner, after he has refused to rent to people with children. [The refusal, not the owner, is an example of discrimination.]

| Revised | An example of discrimination is an apartment owner's refusal to rent to people with children. |

8e   Unnecessary shifts are disconcerting.

Avoid abrupt, unnecessary shifts—from past to present, from singular to plural, or from one perspective to another.

(1) Faulty *is . . . when, is . . . where,* or *is . . . because* constructions

| Faulty | The reason the package arrived so late is because he didn't mail it soon enough. |
| Revised | The package arrived so late because he didn't mail it soon enough. |

(2) Consistent tense, mood, and person

Arlo **believed** in nuclear power while Mary ~~believes~~ *believed* in solar power. [both verbs in the past tense]

If I **were** not so stupid and he ~~was~~ *were* not so naive, we would have known better. [both verbs in the subjunctive mood]

I had to exercise daily and ~~the rowing **machine** was especially despised.~~ *I especially despised* the rowing **machine.** [persons made consistent]

When using the literary or historical present, avoid slipping from the present into the past tense. (See the **Glossary of Terms.**)

Romeo and Juliet **marry** secretly and ~~died~~ *die* together in the tomb within the same hour. [verbs in present tense]

(3) Consistent person and number (See also 6b.)

If a person is *you are* going to improve, you should work harder. [Both subjects are in the second person.]

The team is counting on winning ~~their~~ *its* game. [Both *team is* and *its* are singular.]

(4) Shifts between direct and indirect discourse (See also 10a.)

Janet wondered how the thief got the computer out and why ~~didn't he~~ *he didn't* steal the TV.

(5) Consistent tone and style

It seemed to Romeo that Juliet's face was as white as ~~the underbelly of a fish.~~ *a lily*

Chapter 9

Subordination and Coordination

Subordination and **coordination** establish relationships between ideas. Subordinate structures make the ideas they express appear less important than ideas expressed in main clauses. In the following sentence, the subordinate clause is italicized; the main clause is boldface.

Since it was pouring rain, **the game was canceled.**

When two ideas in a sentence are equal, they are expressed in coordinate structures. In the following example, ideas of equal importance are expressed in two main clauses.

They did their best, and they ran the course.

Coordination in words and phrases also gives equal structural emphasis to equal ideas.

a **stunning** and **unexpected** conclusion

in the attic or **in the basement**

(See 1e for subordinate and main clauses.)

60

9a Careful subordination can combine a series of related short sentences into longer, more effective units.

Choppy   I was taking eighteen hours of course work. I wanted to graduate in three years. It turned out to be too much. I also had a full-time job at the newspaper. I just couldn't do both.

Revised   I was taking eighteen hours of course work, because I wanted to graduate in three years, but it turned out to be too much. Since I already had a full-time job at the newspaper, I just couldn't do both.

Use some of the following subordinate structures to relate less important ideas to the main one.

(1) Adjectives and adjective phrases

Choppy   The limbs were covered with ice. They sparkled in the sunlight. They made a breathtaking sight.

Better   **Sparkling in the sunlight,** the **ice-covered** limbs made a breathtaking sight. [participial phrase and hyphenated adjective]

(2) Adverbs and adverb phrases

Choppy   Season the chicken livers with garlic. Use a lot of it. Fry them in butter. Use very low heat.

Better   **Heavily** season the chicken livers with garlic, and **slowly** fry them in butter. [coordination]

Choppy	His face was covered with white dust. So were his clothes. The man looked like a ghost.
Better	**His face and clothes white with dust,** the man looked like a ghost. [absolute phrase]

(3) Appositives and contrasting elements

Choppy	Her comments were uncalled for and unnecessary. They were mean. And everyone noticed them.
Better	Everyone noticed her mean, unnecessary, and uncalled-for comments.

(4) Subordinate clauses

Subordinate clauses are linked to main clauses by subordinating conjunctions and relative pronouns that signal **time** (*after, before*), **place** (*where, wherever*), **reason** (*as, because*), **condition** (*although, if*), or **addition** (*that, who*). (See page 14 for a list of these markers.)

Choppy	The blizzard ended. Then helicopters headed for the mountaintop. It looked dark and forbidding.
Better	**As soon as the blizzard ended,** helicopters headed for the mountaintop, **which looked dark and forbidding.**

9b   Faulty or excessive subordination can confuse the reader.

Faulty	Chen was only a substitute pitcher, winning half of his games.
Better	Although Chen was only a substitute pitcher, he won half of his games. [*Although* establishes the relationship between the ideas.]

Excessive   Some people who are not busy and who are in-
            secure when they are involved in personal rela-
            tionships worry all the time about whether their
            friends truly love them.

Better   Some insecure, idle people worry about whether
            their friends truly love them. [two subordinate
            clauses reduced to adjectives]

Chapter 10 | Parallelism

Parallelism contributes to ease in reading by making ideas that are parallel in meaning parallel in structure. Parallel elements appear in lists or series, in compounds, in comparisons, and in contrasting elements.

I like to swim, to dance, and ~~having~~ *to have* fun.

In the following examples, verbals used as subjects and complements are parallel in form.

To define flora is **to define** climate. —NATIONAL GEOGRAPHIC

Seeing is **believing**.

10a Similar grammatical elements need to be balanced.

For parallel structure, balance nouns with nouns, prepositional phrases with prepositional phrases, and clauses with clauses.

(1) Parallel words and phrases

The Africans carried with them a pattern of kinship
that emphasized ‖ collective survival,
                ‖ mutual aid,
                ‖ cooperation,
                ‖ mutual solidarity,
                ‖ interdependence,
       and ‖ responsibility for others.
                                 —JOSEPH L. WHITE

She had ‖ no time to be human,
       ‖ no time to be happy.   —SEAN O'FALLON

(2) Parallel clauses

I remember Iyatiku's sister, Sun Woman,
‖ who held so many things in her bundle,
‖ who went away to the east.   —PAULA GUNN ALLEN

(3) Parallel sentences

‖ When I breathed in, I squeaked.
‖ When I breathed out, I rattled.   —JOHN CARENEN

10b Parallels need to be clear to the reader.

Repeating a preposition, an article, the *to* of the infinitive,
or the introductory word can make parallel structure clear.

The reward rests not ‖ in the task
            but ‖ in the pay.
                          —JOHN KENNETH GALBRAITH

I was happy in the thought
         ‖ **that** our influence was helpful
  and ‖ **that** I was doing the work I loved
  and ‖ **that** I could make a living out of it.   —IDA B. WELLS

10c Correlatives can be used with parallel structures.

With the correlatives (*both . . . and, either . . . or, neither . . . nor, not only . . . but also, whether . . . or*), parallel structures are required.

The team not practices

~~Not~~ only ~~practicing~~ at 6 a.m. during the week, but ~~the team~~

also scrimmages on Sunday afternoons.

OR

does the team practice   *it*

Not only ~~practicing~~ at 6 a.m. during the week, but ~~the team~~

also scrimmages on Sunday afternoons.

Chapter 11

Emphasis

You can emphasize ideas by using subordination and co-ordination (9), parallelism (10), and exact word choice (14) and also by writing concisely (15). This chapter presents additional ways to emphasize material.

11a Words at the beginning or end of a sentence receive emphasis.

~~In today's society, most~~ G good jobs *today* require a college education ~~as part of the background you are supposed to have.~~

~~I could hear the roar of~~ Traffic *roared* outside my hotel room in Chicago ~~when I was there.~~

The colon and the dash often precede an emphatic ending. (See also 21d and 21e.)

> In short, the freedom that the American writer finds in Europe brings him, full circle, back to himself, with the responsibility for his development where it always was: in his own hands.
> —JAMES BALDWIN

> Until fairly recently, the pattern was that the father and sons worked, and, to whatever extent their earnings allowed, the mothers and daughters were supposed to display culture, religion, luxury, and other assorted fine feelings of society—in addition to seeing that the housework got done.
> —JUDITH MARTIN

11b When surrounded by cumulative sentences, a periodic sentence receives emphasis.

In a **cumulative sentence,** the main idea comes first; less important ideas or details follow. In a **periodic sentence,** however, the main idea comes last, just before the period.

Cumulative   History has amply proved that large forces can be defeated by smaller forces superior in arms, organization, morale, and spirit.

Periodic   That large forces can be defeated by smaller forces superior in arms, organization, morale, and spirit has been amply proved by history.

Because cumulative sentences are more common, the infrequently used periodic sentence is often the more emphatic.

11c When ideas are arranged from least to most important, the most important idea receives emphasis.

They could hear the roar of the artillery, the crash of falling timbers, the shrieks of the wounded.

Benefiting from much needed rest, moderate medication, and intensive therapy, he eventually recovered from despair.

11d Forceful verbs can make sentences emphatic.

(1) The active is more emphatic than the passive voice.

Active voice emphasizes the *doer* of the action by making the doer the subject of the sentence. **Passive voice** emphasizes the *receiver* of the action, minimizes the role of the doer, and results in wordier sentences.

Active   All citizens should insist on adequate medical care.

Passive   Adequate medical care should be insisted on by all citizens.

Sentences in the passive voice are often less precise: "The race was won" leaves unanswered the question of who did the winning. The passive voice is appropriate, however, when the doer of an action is unknown or unimportant.

Passive   The television set was stolen. [The thief is unknown.]

When reporting research, scientific writers often choose the passive voice to preserve objectivity and to emphasize the work being done rather than who is doing it.

Passive   The experiment was conducted under carefully controlled conditions over several months.

Unless they have a strong reason to use the passive voice, good writers prefer the active voice.

(2) **Action verbs and forceful linking verbs are more emphatic than forms of *have* or *be*.**

Forms of *have* or *be*, when used without an action verb, rob writing of energy and forcefulness. The real action often lies in a verbal or in the object or complement.

Our college is always ~~the winner of~~ *wins* the conference.

The meat ~~has a~~ *smells* rotten ~~smell~~.

You can ~~be more effective at~~ *solve* a problem ~~by~~ *more effectively if you* understand-ing the problem first.

11e   Repeating important words gives them emphasis.

Although good writers avoid unnecessary repetition (chapter 15), they also understand that deliberate repetition emphasizes key terms.

> We forget all too soon the things we thought we could never forget. We forget the loves and the betrayals alike, forget what we whispered and what we screamed, forget who we are.
>
> —JOAN DIDION

When you decide to repeat a word for emphasis, make sure that it conveys an idea central to your purpose.

11f   Inverting the standard word order of a sentence gives it emphasis.

> At the feet of the tallest and plushiest offices lie the crummiest slums.   —E. B. WHITE   [COMPARE "The crummiest slums lie at the feet of the tallest and plushiest offices."]

11g   A short sentence following one or more long ones is emphasized.

> In the last two decades there has occurred a series of changes in American life, the extent, durability, and significance of which no one has yet measured. No one can.   —IRVING HOWE

Chapter 12 | Variety

Varying the kinds of sentences you use can make your writing lively and distinctive. Compare the two paragraphs below. Both express the same ideas in virtually the same words. Variety in sentence structure and length, however, gives one paragraph a stronger rhythm than the other.

Not Varied

This account is *about* television only in part. I don't mean to cast it as an evil appliance. I will be describing phenomena that appear on television often, but they are also on the radio and in magazines and everywhere else. They are parts of modern life. Television covers an extraordinary amount of territory in twenty-four hours. I could find fifty references to any topic. [six sentences: five simple, one compound; all starting with the subject; three starting with *I*]

Varied

But only in part is this account *about* television, which I don't mean to cast as an evil appliance. Often I will be describing phenomena that appear on television, but they are also on the radio and in magazines and everywhere else, because they are parts of modern life. The amount of territory that television covers in twenty-four hours is extraordinary— I could find fifty references to any topic that interested me. [three sentences: one complex, one compound-complex, and one compound; first sentence subject/verb order reversed; four dependent clauses]   —THE *NEW YORKER*

71

12a A series of short, simple sentences sounds choppy.

You can lengthen sentences by showing how the ideas are subordinate or coordinate. (See chapter **9**.)

Choppy   The Maine coast and the Oregon coast look very much alike. The houses by the water, however, are different. It's a matter of architectural style.

Effective   Although the Maine coast and the Oregon coast look very much alike, the architectural style of the houses by the water is different.

12b Writing sounds monotonous when too many sentences begin the same way.

Most writers begin more than half their sentences with the subject. Although this pattern is normal, relying too heavily on it can make your writing monotonous.

(1) Begin with an adverb or an adverbial clause.

Suddenly a hissing and clattering came from the heights around us. —DOUGLAS LEE [adverb]

Even though baseball is essentially the same, the strategy of play then and now is different.
                              —JAMES T. FARRELL   [adverbial clause]

(2) Begin with a prepositional phrase or a verbal phrase.

Out of necessity they stitched all of their secret fears and lingering childhood nightmares into this existence.
                              —GLORIA NAYLOR   [prepositional phrase]

Looking out of the window high over the state of Kansas, we see a pattern of a single farmhouse surrounded by fields, followed by another single homestead surrounded by fields.

—WILLIAM OUCHI   [participial phrase]

(3) Begin with a conjunctive adverb or a transitional expression.

Difficulty in finding a place to park is one factor keeping people from shopping downtown. **Moreover,** public transportation has become too expensive. [conjunctive adverb]

This legislation will hurt the economy. **In the first place,** it will cost thousands of jobs. [transitional expression]

(4) Begin with an appositive, an absolute phrase, or an introductory series. (See 9a.)

A town of historic interest, Sante Fe also has many art galleries. [appositive]

His fur bristling, the cat attacked. [absolute phrase]

Light, water, temperature, minerals—these affect the health of plants. [introductory series]

12c   Stringing simple sentences together to make compound sentences is less effective than experimenting with sentence structure.

If you normally write short, simple sentences, and then revise by just linking them with *and* or *but,* your writing will still lack variety. To revise, use one of the following methods.

(1) Make a compound sentence complex.

Compound   Seafood is nutritious, and it is low in fat, and it has become available in a greater variety.

Complex   Seafood, which is nutritious and low in fat, has become available in a greater variety.

(2) Use a compound predicate in a simple sentence.

Compound   She caught the bird, and next she held it so its feet were still, and then she slipped a yellow band around its leg.

Simple   She caught the bird, held it so its feet were still, and slipped a yellow band around its leg.

(3) Use an appositive in a simple sentence.

Compound   J. T. Nichols was an old-fashioned naturalist, and he spent his life studying birds and turtles.

Simple   J. T. Nichols, an old-fashioned naturalist, spent his life studying birds and turtles.

(4) Use a prepositional or verbal phrase added to a simple sentence.

Compound   The rain was torrential, and we could not see where we were going.

Simple   Because of the torrential rain, we could not see where we were going.

Compound   The town is near the interstate, and it attracted commuters, and its population grew rapidly.

Simple   The town, located near the interstate, attracted commuters and grew rapidly in population.

12d When surrounded by declarative sentences, a question, an exclamation, or a command adds variety.

What was Shakespeare's state of mind, for instance, when he wrote *Lear* and *Antony and Cleopatra*? It was certainly the state of mind most favourable to poetry that there has ever existed. —VIRGINIA WOOLF

Now I stare and stare at people, shamelessly. Stare. It's the way to educate your eye. —WALKER EVANS

Diction

Diction

Chapter 13

Good Usage

There is a difference between the words used in informal writing and conversation and the more formal language appropriate for college and business writing. A dictionary includes usage labels to distinguish between the two. Words labeled **non-** or **substandard** are usually inappropriate for edited American English.

It helps to have ready access to a good, recent desk dictionary. The date is important because language is constantly changing. Many desk dictionaries are available either in paperback or on CD-ROM, both of which usually include the same information. The pocket version, which is useful for spelling and a quick definition, omits important information on usage and derivation.

ESL The following dictionaries are recommended for nonnative English speakers.

Longman Dictionary of English Language and Culture, 1992.

Longman Language Activator, 1993. (a cross between a dictionary and a thesaurus)

The Newbury House Dictionary of American English, 1996.

Oxford ESL Dictionary, 1994.

13a Dictionaries provide information beyond the definition of a word.

Reading the introductory material and noting the meaning of any special abbreviations will help you understand the information your dictionary provides.

Spelling, syllabication, and pronunciation

You can check spelling and word division as well as pronunciation of unfamiliar words. A key to sound symbols appears at the bottom of the entry pages.

Parts of speech and inflected forms

The dictionary also labels the possible uses of words in sentences—for instance, *tr. v., adj*. It identifies the various ways that nouns, verbs, and modifiers change form to indicate number, tense, and comparison.

Word origin/etymology

The origin of a word—also called its etymology—can be useful in understanding its meaning.

Definitions

Definitions are listed in different order in different dictionaries. Often they are ordered according to how common they are.

Usage

Most dictionaries give guidance on usage, showing how the word has been used in context.

Synonyms

Dictionaries always list synonyms, sometimes with detailed explanations of subtle differences in meaning. When such discussions are used in conjunction with a thesaurus, they are extremely helpful.

13b Most dictionaries label words according to dialectical, regional, or stylistic usage.

Dictionaries provide guidelines for the appropriate use of words, and many words carry labels that act as guides for appropriate use.

(1) Colloquial or informal

Words labeled **colloquial** or **informal** are common to speech and used by writers in dialogue and informal writing. In college writing, unlabeled words are preferred.

Informal	dopey	belly button
Formal	stupid	navel

(2) Slang

Slang covers a wide range of words that are variously considered breezy, excessively informal, or taboo. Slang is usually avoided in college writing.

(3) Regionalisms

Regional or dialectal usages are normally avoided in writing outside the region where they are current.

(4) Nonstandard and substandard

Words and expressions labeled nonstandard or substandard should not be used in formal writing, except possibly in direct quotations.

13c Writers consider their audience when selecting words to convey meaning and appropriate tone.

(1) Technical words

In writing for the general reader, avoid unnecessary technical language. *Jargon,* technical language tailored specifically for a particular occupation, can be an efficient shortcut for specialized concepts, but you should use jargon only when you can be sure that your readers understand it.

(2) Inclusive language

Making language inclusive means treating men and women equally. For example, many feel that women are excluded when *man* is used to refer to both men and women.

Man's twentieth-century achievements are impressive.

Also, avoid stereotyping sex roles—for example, assuming that all nurses are women and all doctors are men.

Inappropriate	Appropriate
the common man	the average person
male nurse	nurse
mankind	humanity, people

policeman	police officer
weatherman	meteorologist
Have your *mother* send a snack.	Have your **parent** send a snack.
The law should prohibit one with a drinking problem from driving *his* car.	The law should prohibit one with a drinking problem from driving **a** car.

(3) Confusion of *sit/set* and *lie/lay* and *rise/raise*

Thinking of these verbs in pairs and learning their principal parts can help you remember which form to use.

Present	Past	Past Participle	Present Participle
sit	sat	sat	sitting
lie	lay	lain	lying
rise	rose	risen	rising
set	set	set	setting
lay	laid	laid	laying
raise	raised	raised	raising

Set, lay, and *raise* mean "to place or put something somewhere." *Sit, lie,* and *rise* mean "be seated," "get into a horizontal position," or "get up."

Sit	Sit down. He sat up.
Set	I set the clock. It had been set there.
Lie	Lie down. He lay there for hours.
Lay	We laid these aside. These had been laid aside.
Rise	I rise before daylight. I rose even earlier yesterday.
Raise	I raise the window each night. I raised the window last night.

Chapter 14

Exactness

When drafting (chapter **28**), choose words that express your ideas and feelings. When revising (chapter **29**), make those words exact, idiomatic, and fresh.

14a   Accurate and precise word choice conveys meaning efficiently.

(1) Accuracy is essential.

Select words that state your point exactly.

The figures ~~inferred~~ *implied* that enrollment had increased. [*Infer* means "to draw a conclusion from evidence." For example: From the figures, I inferred that enrollment had increased. *Imply* means "to suggest," so *implied* is the exact word for the sentence as drafted.]

Jennifer spends too much money on clothes, ~~and~~ *but* she earns it herself. [*And* adds or continues; *but* contrasts. In this case, negative and positive information are contrasted.]

(2) Definitions clarify the precise meaning of words.

A short dictionary definition may be adequate when you need to define a term or a special meaning of a word.

> Here *galvanic* means "produced as if by electric shock."

Giving a synonym or two may clarify the meaning.

> *Magendo,* or black-market corruption, is flourishing.
> —KEN ADELMAN

Writers frequently show what a word means by giving examples.

> Many homophones (*be* and *bee, see* and *sea*) are not spelling problems.

A formal definition first states the term to be defined and puts it into a class, then differentiates the term from other members of its class.

> A phosphene [term] is a luminous visual image [class] that results from applying pressure to the eyeball [differentiation].

(3) Connotations enrich meaning.

The **denotation** of a word indicates what it names. For example, the noun *beach* denotes a sandy shore. The **connotation** is what the word suggests or implies. *Beach,* for instance, may connote surf, water sports, sunburn, or even gritty sandwiches. The challenge for writers is to choose words that are most likely to evoke the appropriate connotations.

> One reason I recommend Mr. Krueger is that he is so ~~relent-less.~~ *persistent* [*Relentless* has negative connotations inappropriate for a recommendation.]

I love the ~~odor~~ *aroma* of freshly baked bread. [Many odors are un-

pleasant; *aroma* sounds more positive.]

ESL   Your ability to understand connotations will
improve as your vocabulary improves. When you learn a
new word that seems to mean exactly what another word
means, ask a native speaker if these words have different
connotations.

---

(4) **Specific and concrete words are usually stronger than
general and abstract ones.**

A **general** word is all-inclusive, indefinite, and sweeping in
scope. A **specific** word is precise, definite, and limited.

General	Specific	More Specific/Concrete
food	fast food	cheeseburger
prose	fiction	short stories

An **abstract** word deals with concepts, with ideas. A **concrete** word signifies particular objects, what can be
touched, heard, or seen.

Abstract	democracy, loyal, evil, hate, charity
Concrete	mosquito, spotted, crunch, grab

As you select words, be specific and concrete. For example, instead of *bad*, consider using a more precise
adjective.

bad planks:	rotten, warped, termite-eaten
bad children:	rowdy, rude, ungrateful, perverse, spoiled

Notice what a difference specific, concrete words can make
in expressing an idea and how specific details can expand
or develop ideas.

Vague   A big bug got stuck in my candle and died.

Specific   A golden female moth, a biggish one with a two-inch wingspread, flapped into the fire, dropped abdomen into the wet wax, stuck, flamed, and frazzled in a second.   —ANNIE DILLARD

The need to be specific does not necessarily conflict with the need to be concise. (See chapter **15**.) Simply substituting one word for another can often make it far easier to see, hear, or smell what you are hoping to convey.

I ~~had an accident~~ *fell out of the canoe* while trying to ~~catch a fish.~~ *land a muskie*

Abstract words are exact when they are used to express abstractions—"immortal," "compassion," "endurance." When you use abstract words, make sure you do so with good reason.

(5) **Figurative language can contribute to exactness.**

Figurative language uses words in an imaginative sense. Simile and metaphor are the chief **figures of speech**. A **simile** is the comparison of dissimilar things using *like* or *as*. A **metaphor** is an implied comparison of dissimilar things not using *like* or *as*.

Similes

He was like a piece of rare and delicate china which was always being saved from breaking and finally fell.

—ALICE WALKER

The thick blood welled out of him like red velvet, but still he did not die.   —GEORGE ORWELL

Metaphors

His money was a sharp pair of scissors that snipped rapidly through tangles of red tape.   —HISAYE YAMAMOTO

We refuse to believe that the bank of justice is bankrupt.

—MARTIN LUTHER KING, JR.

Single words are often used metaphorically:

> We always **sweep** the leaves off the sidewalk. [literal]
>
> He seems likely to **sweep** her right off her feet. [metaphorical]

For faulty metaphors, see **8c**.

Other figures of speech include **personification** (attributing to nonhumans characteristics possessed only by humans), **paradox** (a seemingly contradictory statement), and **irony** (a deliberate incongruity between what is stated and what is meant). Figures such as these can contribute to lively, memorable writing even if they do not always contribute to exactness.

 14b   Exact word choice requires an understanding of idioms.

An **idiom** is an expression whose meaning differs from the individual meanings of its elements. Occasionally the idiomatic use of prepositions proves difficult. For instance, *agree* may be followed by *about, on, to,* or *with*. The choice depends on the context. Writers sometimes have trouble with expressions such as these:

> comply **with** rules
> conform **to/with** standards
> in accordance **with** policy
> inferior **to** ours

Many idioms—such as *to mean well, raining cats and dogs*—cannot be understood from the individual meanings of their elements. As you encounter idioms that are new to you, master their meanings just as you would when learning new words.

ESL   The context in which idioms appear will often help you understand their meaning. For example, if you read, "I never eat broccoli because I can't stand it," you would probably understand that *not to be able to stand something* means *to dislike something*. If you are confused about the meaning of an idiom, check an idiom dictionary.

14c   Fresh expressions are more distinctive than worn-out ones.

Such expressions as *bite the dust* or *smooth as silk* were once striking and effective. Excessive use, however, has drained them of their original force and made them **clichés**. Some **euphemisms** (pleasant-sounding substitutions for more explicit but possibly offensive words) are not only trite but wordy or awkward—for example, *correctional facility* for *jail* or *pre-owned* for *used*. Faddish or trendy expressions like *be into* (as in "I am into dieting") were so overused that they quickly became clichés.

Nearly every writer uses clichés from time to time because they are so much a part of the language. But experienced writers often give a fresh twist to an old saying.

> I seek a narrative, a fiction, to order days like the one I spent several years ago, on a gray June day in Chicago, when I took a roller-coaster ride on the bell curve of my experience.
> —GAYLE PEMBERTON
> [COMPARE frequent references elsewhere to being on "an emotional roller coaster."]

Chapter 15

Conciseness: Avoiding Wordiness and Needless Repetition

Unnecessary words or phrases distract readers and blur meaning. Good writers know how to make their points concisely.

Wordy In the early part of August, a hurricane was moving threateningly toward Houston.

Concise In early August, a hurricane threatened Houston.

15a Words or phrases that add nothing to the meaning should be omitted.

(1) Redundancy

Restating a key point in different words can help readers understand it. But if you use additional words to convey meaning already conveyed by the words you've written, your work will suffer from redundancy.

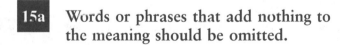

Ballerinas auditioned ~~in the tryouts~~ for *The Nutcracker*.

Each actor has a unique talent ~~and ability that he or she uses in his or her acting.~~

In the phrases below, useless words appear in brackets.

yellow [in color]   circular [in shape]

[basic] essentials   return [back]

bitter[-tasting] salad   small[-size] potatoes

because [of the fact that]   [true] facts

[really and truly] fearless   the oil [that exists] in shale

(2) Unnecessary words

~~In the event that~~ *If* taxes are raised, expect complaints ~~on the part of the~~ *from* voters.

One or two words can replace expressions such as these:

at this point in time   **now**

in an employment situation   **at work**

in spite of the fact that   **although**

on account of the fact that   **because**

One exact word can say as much as many inexact ones. (See also **14a**.)

spoke in a low and hard-to-hear voice   **mumbled**

(3) Expletives

There followed by a form of *to be* is an *expletive*—a word that signals that the subject will follow the verb. Because expletives shift emphasis away from the subject, they can result in the use of unnecessary words.

~~There were t~~*T*hree children playing *ed* in the yard.

It is also an expletive when it lacks an antecedent and is followed by a form of *be*.

Learning to ski ~~It is easy~~ to learn to ski.

The *it* construction is necessary only when there is no logical subject. For example: It is going to snow.

15b Combining sentences or simplifying phrases and clauses can eliminate needless words.

A carpet of blue-green grass
~~The grass was like a carpet. It~~ covered the whole playing field.

~~The color of the grass was blue green.~~

Some ~~phony~~ unscrupulous brokers are ~~taking money and sav-~~ *cheating*

~~ings from elderly~~ old people ~~who need that money because~~

~~they planned to use it as a retirement~~ *out of their* pension~~s~~.

15c Repetition is useful only when it improves emphasis, clarity, or coherence.

~~Your teacher is unlike my teacher.~~ Your teacher likes teaching better than mine ~~does~~.

We will not rest until we have pursued every lead, inspected every piece of evidence, and interviewed every suspect. [In this case, the repetition of *every* is useful because it emphasizes the writer's determination.]

15d Pronouns and elliptical constructions can eliminate needless repetition.

Instead of needlessly repeating a noun or substituting a clumsy synonym, use a pronoun. If the reference is clear (6b), several pronouns can refer to the same antecedent.

The hall outside was empty. ~~The hall~~ *It* had dirty floors, and *its* the walls ~~of this corridor~~ were covered with graffiti.

An **elliptical construction** (the omission of words that will be understood by the reader without being repeated) helps the writer of the following sentence be concise.

> Speed is the goal for some swimmers, endurance [is the goal] for others, and relaxation [is the goal] for still others.

Sometimes commas mark omissions that avoid repetition.

> My family functioned like a baseball team; my mom was the coach; my brother, the pitcher; and my sister, the shortstop.

15e   A clear, straightforward style is preferable to an ornate one.

An ornate or flowery style calls attention to your words rather than your ideas. Although different styles are appropriate for different situations, you should usually keep your writing simple and straightforward.

> Ornate   The majority believes that the approbation of society derives from diligent pursuit of tasks.
>
> Simple   Most people believe that success results from hard work.

ESL   In cultures shaped by different traditions, being direct and straightforward might be considered rude, but this is not the case in the United States. If you feel that you are being rude when you write straightforward English, consider your word choice (chapter **13**) and your tone (**29a**). By making careful choices, it is possible to be both straightforward and polite.

Chapter 16

Clarity and Completeness

In rapid speech we omit words because our listeners do not hear them. For example, instead of "We had better study hard" a listener might hear "We better study hard." *Had* must be included in writing to make the meaning clear.

16a Articles, pronouns, conjunctions, or prepositions are sometimes necessary.

(1) Use of articles

Review material on count and noncount nouns. (See **1c(2)**.)

 E S L Indefinite articles

A and *an* are used with singular countable nouns in the following situations:

with descriptive or general nouns

> **a** house   **an** orange

with something mentioned for the first time

> Our history professor assigned **an** exam.

with the meaning of *one*, not *more*

> I chose **a** piece of fruit from the basket.

Use *a* before a consonant sound: **a** yard, **a** university. Use *an* before a vowel sound: **an** *apple,* **an** *hour.*

Plural count nouns use words such as *some* or *any.*

some magazines   **any** books

Definite articles

The is used with singular or plural noncount nouns in the following situations:

when the noun has been previously introduced or when you and the reader know what you are referring to

We must leave **the** building now.

We will have a quiz. **The** quiz will cover chapter 2.

when the noun is unique

the Vietnam Memorial

when an ordinal number (fourth, sixth) or superlative (least, best) comes before the noun

the eighth day of the month

the least expensive

Omission of the article

The article is omitted entirely in a number of cases.

with another determiner

Sign up for this new course.

before a plural countable noun that does not refer to a specific item

Buy oranges and apples.

before a plural noun that has a general meaning

> Everyone wants benefits.

The article is omitted in certain common expressions: *go to school, go to class, go to college, go to bed*

(2) Omitted prepositions

Two prepositions may be required after different verbs to make the meaning clear.

> I neither believe _in_ nor approve of those attitudes.

16b Auxiliaries omitted in speech are necessary in writing to avoid awkwardness.

Revision eliminates the awkwardness in the following sentence.

> Voter turnout has never _been_ and will never be 100 percent.

16c Complete comparisons are needed in writing to complete the meaning if it is not suggested by the context.

> He is taller *than his brother*.

> People think television is more violent *than it used to be*.

Comparisons can be completed by other words in the sentence or by the context.

> In the next century, people will need more education.

16d The intensifiers *so* and *too* need a completing phrase or clause.

In informal writing, a completing phrase is often omitted after intensifiers used for emphasis.

My hair is **so** long.

It is just **too** much.

In formal writing, intensifiers are followed by a completing phrase or clause.

My hair is **so** long **that I must get it cut today**.

It is just **too** much **for me to try to do**.

Punctuation

Punctuation

Chapter 17

The Comma

If you understand the following four principles, you will see through most of the mystery surrounding commas and find them easier to use consistently.

Commas

- come before coordinating conjunctions when they link independent clauses.
- follow introductory adverb clauses and, usually, introductory phrases.
- separate items in a series (including coordinate adjectives).
- set off nonrestrictive and other parenthetical elements.

17a Commas come before a coordinating conjunction that links independent clauses.

The minutes would pass, and then suddenly Einstein would stop pacing as his face relaxed into a gentle smile.

—BANESH HOFFMANN

Justice stands upon Power, or there is no Justice.

—WILLIAM S. WHITE

There was no voice apart from his, yet he appeared to be chatting in friendly, excited tones with some other person.

—WOLE SOYINKA

When a sentence contains multiple clauses, a comma comes before each coordinating conjunction.

> I chose to follow in the footsteps of my unconventional Aunt Esther, and I have never regretted my choice, but I think my mother never approved of me.

When the clauses are short, the comma can be omitted before *and, but,* or *or,* but not before *for, nor, so,* or *yet.* (See also page 20.)

> I liked the haircut and it made me actually look forward to my future fame. —AMY TAN

17b A comma usually follows introductory words, phrases, and clauses.

(1) Adverb clauses before independent clauses

> When you write, you make a sound in the reader's head.
> —RUSSELL BAKER

> The safest automobile on the road is expensive, but if I consider the protection it offers, I cannot find the cost unreasonable. [adverb clause preceding the second independent clause]

If the omission does not make reading difficult, writers may omit the comma after an introductory adverb clause, especially when the clause is short.

A comma is usually unnecessary when the adverb clause follows the independent clause.

> I should have no difficulties establishing my citizenship in the tribe because my grandmother's name can be found on the Dawes roll. [*Because* introduces an adverbial clause.]

(2) Introductory phrases before independent clauses

Prepositional phrases

From the deck, I could not see my father, but I could see my mother facing the ship, her eyes searching to pick me out.
—JAMAICA KINCAID

If the comma after an introductory prepositional phrase is not necessary to prevent misreading, it can be omitted:

For safety the university installed call boxes linked directly to campus security.

Other types of phrases

Having traveled nowhere, she believed the rest of the world was like her own small town. [participial phrase—see also **1d** and **1e**]

The language difference aside, life in Germany doesn't seem much different from life in America. [absolute phrase—see also **17d(7)**]

Introductory words

Furthermore, the person responsible for breaking or damaging university equipment will be fined. [transitional expression—see the lists on page 22]

Yes, I bought my tickets yesterday. No, I didn't pay cash. [introductory *yes* or *no*]

Commas are not used after phrases that begin inverted sentences. (See also **11f.**)

With the hurricane came the tornadoes.

17c Commas separate items in a series (including coordinate adjectives).

A series contains three or more parallel elements. (See chapter 10.)

(1) Words, phrases, and clauses in a series

A pet should be trusting, obedient, and intelligent. [words]

My job requires me to start work at 7 a.m., to drive to three different towns every day, and to carry heavy repair equipment upstairs. [phrases]

My idea of a great vacation spot is one where no telephone rings, someone else fixes me great food, and I sit on the porch all day and read mystery novels. [clauses]

If items in a series contain internal commas, you can make the meaning clear by separating the items with semicolons. (See 18b.)

(2) Coordinate adjectives

Coordinate adjectives are two or more adjectives that modify the same noun or pronoun. One test for coordinate adjectives is to switch them; another is to put *and* between them. If the meaning does not change, the adjectives are coordinate. Commas separate coordinate adjectives not linked by a coordinating conjunction.

It is a waiting, silent, limp room. —EUDORA WELTY [*Waiting, silent,* and *limp* all modify *room.*]

Walking along the rushing, shallow creek, I slipped on a rock and sank above my boot tops into a small, still pool. [*Rushing* and *shallow* modify *creek* and *small* and *still* modify *pool.*]

17d Commas set off nonrestrictive and other parenthetical elements, contrasted elements, items in dates, and so on.

Nonrestrictive clauses or phrases give nonessential information about a noun or pronoun. They can be omitted without changing the meaning. To set off a nonrestrictive word or word group, use two commas, unless the element is at the beginning or the end of the sentence.

Restrictive clauses or phrases follow and limit the words they modify. They are essential to the clear identification of the word or words they refer to.

(1) Adjective clauses

Adjective clauses that describe the noun they modify are nonrestrictive, but those that limit the noun are restrictive. In the first example below, the proper name "Marilyn Greer" identifies which woman the sentence is describing. As a result, the sentence requires no additional information. "The woman," however, could be any woman and so needs a modifier that limits it to someone in particular.

Nonrestrictive Clauses	Restrictive or Essential Clauses
I spoke with Marilyn Greer, who manages the bank.	I spoke to the woman who manages the bank.
We climbed Mt. Rainier, which is over 15,000 feet high.	We climbed a mountain that is over 15,000 feet high.

Sometimes only the omission or use of commas indicates whether a modifier is restrictive or nonrestrictive and thus signals the writer's exact meaning.

(2) Appositives

Appositives can supply additional but nonessential details about a noun or pronoun (nonrestrictive), or else they limit the meaning of a noun or pronoun by indicating which one—or ones—is meant (restrictive).

Nonrestrictive	Restrictive or Essential
Even Zeke Thornbush, **my friend,** let me down.	Even my friend **Zeke Thornbush** let me down.
Voyager photographed Saturn, **the ringed planet.**	Voyager photographed the planet **Saturn.**

Abbreviations after names are treated as nonrestrictive appositives: "Was the letter from Frances Evans, **Ph.D.,** or from F. H. Evans, **M.D.?**"

(3) Contrasted elements

Human beings, **unlike oysters,** frequently reveal their emotions.   —GEORGE F. WILL

Some writers put a comma before *but* and *not* in such sentences as the following, while others do not.

Other citizens who disagree with me base their disagreement, not on facts different from the ones I know, but on a different set of values.   —RENÉ DUBOS

Today the Black Hills are being invaded again, not for gold but for uranium.   —PETER MATTHIESSEN

(4) Geographical names, items in dates, and addresses

Nashville, Tennessee, is the country and western music center.

I had to write to Ms. Melanie Hobson, 2873 Central Avenue, Orange Park, FL 32065. [no comma between the state abbreviation and the ZIP code]

Hunter applied for the job on Wednesday, June 12, 1996, but turned it down on June 14.

OR

Hunter applied for the job on Wednesday 12 June and turned it down on Friday 14 June. [Commas are omitted when the day of the month precedes the month.]

(5) Parenthetical expressions

Language, **then,** sets the tone of our society.

—EDWIN NEWMAN

When they cause little or no pause in reading, expressions such as *also, too, of course, perhaps, at least, therefore,* and *likewise* need not be set off by commas.

Our ideas about gender roles have **perhaps** changed in recent decades.   —LAWRENCE SACHS

(6) Mild interjections and words used in direct address

Ah, that's my idea of a good meal. [interjection]

Now is the time, **animal lovers,** to protest. [direct address]

(7) Absolute phrases

His temper being what it is, I don't want a confrontation.

He was thumping at a book, **his voice growing louder and louder.**   —JOYCE CAROL OATES

17e   Commas are occasionally needed for ease in reading.

Without commas the following sentences would confuse the reader, if only temporarily.

Still, water must be transported to dry areas. [COMPARE "Still water. . . ."]

The day before, I had talked with her on the phone. [COMPARE "I had talked with her the day before."]

17f Unnecessary (or misplaced) commas send false signals.

To avoid using unnecessary commas, observe the following guidelines.

(1) Commas do not separate the subject from its verb or the verb from its object.

Remove the circled commas.

Most older, married students⊙ must hold a job in addition to going to school. [separation of subject and verb]

The lawyer said⊙ that I could appeal the speeding ticket. [separation of verb and direct object (a noun clause)]

(2) Commas do not follow coordinating conjunctions, and they precede them only when they link independent clauses. (See chapter 3 and 17a.)

Remove the circled commas.

I fed the dog⊙ and put it out for the night. [separation of compound verbs]

For three decades the Surgeon General's office has warned us about the dangers of smoking, but⊙ millions of people still smoke. [separation of the conjunction and the subject of the clause]

(3) Commas set off only those words and phrases that are clearly parenthetical.

Remove the circled commas.

> Martha was born(,) in Miami(,) in 1976.
>
> Perhaps(,) the valve is not correctly calibrated.

(4) Commas do not set off restrictive (necessary) clauses, phrases, or appositives. (See 17d.)

Remove the circled commas.

> Everyone(,) who owns an automobile(,) needs to have collision insurance.

(5) Commas do not precede the first or follow the last item of a series (including a series of coordinate adjectives).

Remove the circled commas.

> Field trips were required in a few courses, such as(,) botany, geology, and sociology.
>
> I've always wanted a low-slung, fast, elegant(,) convertible.

Chapter 18

The Semicolon

The semicolon has two uses: First, it links closely related independent clauses.

> Luverne walked slowly; Hugh ran as fast as he could.

Second, it separates sentence elements that contain internal commas.

> Watching stupid, sentimental, dull soap operas; eating junk food like french fries, cheeseburgers, and milkshakes; and just doing nothing are my favorite vices.

 18a **Semicolons connect independent clauses not linked by a coordinating conjunction.**

Related independent clauses can be linked by a semicolon, connected by coordinating conjunctions, or punctuated as separate sentences.

> Some french fries are greasy; others are not; I like them all.
>
> Some french fries are greasy, **and** others are not, **but** I like them all.
>
> Some french fries are greasy. Others are not. I like them all.

The semicolons indicate a close connection between the ideas, the conjunctions indicate a less close connection, and the periods separate the ideas.

Sometimes a semicolon (instead of the usual comma)

precedes a coordinating conjunction when a sharp division between the two independent clauses is desired.

> Politicians may refrain from negative campaigning for a time; but when the race gets close, they can't seem to resist trying to dredge up personal dirt to use on their opponents.

A semicolon precedes conjunctive adverbs only when they come between independent clauses. (See **3b** and the list on p. 22.)

> Some french fries are greasy; **however,** others are not.

The semicolon is characteristic of formal writing. It is often better to revise compound sentences using a subordinate construction or sentence punctuation. (See chapter **9.**)

Semicolons separate elements that themselves contain commas.

> I subscribe to several computer magazines that include reviews of new, better-designed hardware; descriptions of inexpensive commercial software programs; and actual utility programs that make keeping track of my files easier.

Semicolons do not connect parts of unequal grammatical rank.

Semicolons do not connect clauses and phrases.

> We drove two cars to Colorado; it being perhaps the most spectacular state in the country.

Semicolons do not connect a main clause and a subordinate clause.

> I learned that she had lost her job; which really surprised me.

Chapter 19

The Apostrophe

Apostrophes show possession, mark omissions in contractions, and form certain plurals.

19a The apostrophe shows possession for nouns and indefinite pronouns (*everyone, everybody*).

The possessive case shows ownership: *Tonya's car*. A possessive can follow the word it modifies:

Is that new computer Ana's or Kim's?

(1) Singular nouns, indefinite pronouns, and acronyms add the apostrophe and -s.

Nona's house   anyone's computer   NASA's goal

When the 's results in the awkward repetition of an s, x, or z sound, the -s is omitted: *Moses' city*.

(2) Plural nouns ending in -s add only the apostrophe.

the boys' game   the babies' toys

Plurals not ending in -s add the apostrophe and -s.

men's lives   women's cars

(3) Compounds and expressions that show joint ownership add the apostrophe and *-s* to the last word only.

Olga and Nadia's house [COMPARE Olga and Nadia's houses—they jointly own more than one house.]

her mother-in-law's telephone

(4) Sometimes a relationship comparable to ownership adds the apostrophe, especially in time relationships, in academic titles, or before gerunds. (See **1d(2)**.)

an hour's delay   in a week's time
Bachelor's degree   Asa's dancing
Luverne's having to be there seemed unnecessary.

19b The apostrophe marks omissions in contractions and numbers.

don't   they'll   class of '98

ESL   Since contractions are seldom used in academic writing, you can safely write out the words and omit contractions altogether.

19c The apostrophe and *-s* form certain plurals.

The apostrophe and *-s* are used for the plural forms of lowercase letters and of abbreviations followed by periods.

his *p*'s and *q*'s

When needed to prevent confusion, 's shows the plural of capital letters and of words referred to as words.

too many A's   three minus's

When no confusion would result, either 's or -s forms such plurals as the following:

the 1900's OR the 1990s   his 7's OR his 7s
her and's OR her ands   the &'s OR the &s

! **CAUTION** An 's is not used to indicate plurals of words: The Smiths are home.

19d Personal pronouns and plural nouns that are not possessive do not take an apostrophe.

A personal pronoun (*I, we, you, he, she, it, they*) has its own form to show possession (*my, mine, our, ours, your, yours, his, her, hers, its, their, theirs*).

A friend of **theirs** knows a cousin of **yours**.

Used with a personal pronoun, 's always indicates a contraction.

! **CAUTION** Do not confuse *it's* with *its*. *It's* is a contraction for *it is*. *Its* is the possessive form of *it*.

Its motor is small.   **It's** [it is] a small motor.

Who's is the contraction of *who is*. *Whose* is the possessive form of the relative pronoun *who*.

Who's [Who is] responsible?   **Whose** responsibility is it?

Chapter 20

Quotation Marks

Quotation marks enclose direct quotations (except those in indented blocks), some titles, and words used in a special sense. Any other marks associated with the quotation follow the rules explained below.

20a Quotation marks set off direct quotations and dialogue.

Double quotation marks set off direct quotations, but not indirect ones. Single quotation marks enclose a quotation within a quotation.

(1) Direct quotations

"People are trapped in history," writes James Baldwin, "and history is trapped in them."

(2) Indirect quotations

James Baldwin claims that people cannot escape history and that history cannot exist without people.

(3) Quotations within quotations

"Jennifer keeps telling me to 'get a life,' " Mark complained.

E S L British English and some other languages reverse the use of single (') and double (") quotation marks. It is important to learn the correct system to use in American writing. (See also **20f**.)

(4) Dialogue

Dialogue is directly quoted conversation. When quoting conversation, write what each person says, no matter how short, as if it were a separate paragraph. When quoting more than one paragraph by a single speaker, put quotation marks at the beginning of each new paragraph. There is only one set of closing quotation marks, at the end of the last paragraph.

20b Long quotations are indented.

When using the Modern Language Association (MLA) style of documentation (**34a**), set off any quotation consisting of more than four lines by indenting all lines ten spaces. When using the American Psychological Association (APA) style (**34d**), set off quotations of more than forty words by indenting all lines five spaces.

Except for very special emphasis, enclose a quotation of three (or fewer) lines of poetry in quotation marks and run it into the text. (See **21h**.) Passages of more than three lines should be set off—double-spaced and indented ten spaces unless unusual spacing is part of the poem.

20c Quotation marks enclose the titles of short works such as stories, essays, poems, songs, episodes of a radio or television series, articles in periodicals, and subdivisions of books.

Lon Otto's *Cover Me* contains such wonderful stories as "Winners" and "How I Got Rid of That Stump." [short stories]

"Nani" is my favorite poem by Alberto Rios. [poem]

Did you read William Gibson's "Disneyland with the Death Penalty" when it appeared in *Wired*? [article in a periodical]

Use single marks for a title within a longer title enclosed in double quotation marks.

"Cynicism in Hardy's 'Ah, Are You Digging on My Grave?'"

20d Used sparingly, quotation marks may enclose words intended in a special or ironic sense.

His "gourmet dinner" tasted as if it had come out of a grocer's freezer. [COMPARE His so-called gourmet dinner. The use of *so-called* eliminates the need for quotation marks.]

Quotation marks can be used in definitions.

Ploy means "a strategy used to gain an advantage."

20e Overusing quotation marks detracts from readability.

Quotation marks are not needed in the following cases:

(1) To call attention to a cliché (See 14c.)

A good debater does not beat around the bush.

(2) To enclose *yes* or *no* in indirect discourse

I have to learn to say no to people.

20f Follow American printing conventions for using various marks of punctuation with quoted material.

(1) Comma and period

Generally speaking, commas go inside the closing quotation marks; so do periods if the quotation ends the sentence.

"Lou," she said, "let's go someplace after class."

The period goes at the end of the sentence if other words follow the end of the quotation.

"I don't know why my CD player doesn't work," she said.

(2) Semicolon and colon

Semicolons and colons always go outside the quotation marks.

She spoke of "the gothic tale"; I immediately thought of "The Dunwich Horror": H. P. Lovecraft's masterpiece is the epitome of "gothic."

(3) Question mark and exclamation point

When a question mark or an exclamation point applies only to the quoted matter, it goes inside the quotation marks. When it does not, it goes outside.

Inside the quotation marks:

Pilate asked, "What is truth?"

Gordon replied, "No way!"

Outside the quotation marks:

What is the meaning of the term "half-truth"?

Stop whistling "All I Do Is Dream of You"!

Chapter 21

The Period and Other Marks

Periods, question marks, exclamation points, colons, dashes, parentheses, brackets, slashes, and ellipsis points are important to signal meaning and intonation. Current practice allows for only one space following all punctuation marks.

21a Periods punctuate certain sentences and abbreviations.

(1) Use the period to mark the end of a declarative or a mildly imperative sentence.

We are first and foremost fellow human beings. [declarative]

Respect your ethnic heritage. (mild imperative)

(2) Use periods after some abbreviations.

Dr., Jr.   a.m., p.m.   vs., etc., et al.

Periods are not used with all abbreviations (for example, *MVP, mph, FM*—see **25a**).

Use only one period after an abbreviation that ends a sentence:

The study was performed by Ben Werthman et al.

21b The question mark occurs after direct (but not indirect) questions.

What in the world is Jennifer doing? [direct question]

They want to know what Jennifer is doing. [indirect question]

When we ask ourselves, Why does evil happen? we seek a logical explanation for the irrational.

A question mark in parentheses expresses uncertainty about the preceding word, figure, or date.

Chaucer was born in 1340 (?) and died in 1400.

21c The exclamation point occurs after an emphatic interjection and after other expressions to show strong emotion.

Wow!   That was so cool!   Amazing!

Use the exclamation point sparingly.

21d The colon calls attention to what follows and separates time and scriptural references and titles and subtitles.

(1) A colon directs attention to what follows: an explanation or summary, a series, or a quotation.

Surprisingly enough, my first impression of Nairobi was that it was just like any American city: skyscrapers, movie theaters, discos, and crime. —JAY FORD

The colon can introduce a second independent clause that explains or amplifies the first independent one.

The sorrow was laced with violence: In the first week of demolition, vandals struck every night. —*SMITHSONIAN*

Style manuals vary in their instructions on whether to capitalize a complete sentence after a colon. MLA permits the use of a lowercase letter, but APA does not.

Be careful not to use an unnecessary colon between a verb and its complement or object, between a preposition and its object, or after *such as.*

Unnecessary Colon The winners were: Asa, Vanna, and Jack.

Unnecessary Colon Many vegetarians do not eat dairy products, such as: butter and cheese.

(2) **Use the colon between figures in time references and between titles and subtitles.**

We are to be there by 11:30 a.m.

I just read *Women's Ways of Knowing: The Development of Self, Voice and Mind.*

(3) **Use a colon after the salutation of a business letter.**

Dear Dr. D'Angelo: Dear Faustine:

The colon also appears in bibliographic data. (See chapter 34.)

21e   The dash marks a break in thought, sets off a parenthetical element, and sets off an introductory series.

On a keyboard, indicate a dash by two hyphens with no spaces.

■ **CAUTION** Use dashes sparingly, not as easy or automatic substitutes for commas, semicolons, or end marks.

(1) A dash marks a sudden break in thought or faltering speech.

A hypocrite is a person who——but who isn't?

—DON MARQUIS

But perhaps Miss——Miss——oh, I can't remember her name——she taught English, I think——Miss Milross? She was one of them.   —GARRISON KEILLOR

(2) A dash sets off a parenthetical element for emphasis or (if it contains commas) for clarity.

Local governments——with the encouragement of cable operators——have thrown up nearly insurmountable barriers to the entry of more than one firm into each market.

—JOHN MERLINE

Sentiments that human shyness will not always allow one to convey in conversation——sentiments of gratitude, of apology, of love——can often be more easily conveyed in a letter.

—ARISTIDES

(3) A dash occurs after an introductory list or series.

Keen, calculating, perspicacious, acute and astute——I was all of these.   —MAX SHULMAN

21f Parentheses set off nonessential matter and enclose characters used for enumeration.

Through the use of the Thematic Apperception Test (TAT) they were able to isolate the psychological characteristic of a *need to achieve*.   —MATINA HORNER

Bernard Shaw once demonstrated that, by following the rules (up to a point), we could spell fish this way: ghoti.

—JOHN IRVING

In contrast, a judgment is subject to doubt if there is any possibility at all (1) of its being challenged in the light of additional or more accurate observations or (2) of its being criticized on the basis of more cogent or more comprehensive reasoning.   —MORTIMER J. ADLER

In the next example the entire sentence is parenthetical.

If we refuse to talk "like a lady," we are ridiculed and criticized for being unfeminine. ("She thinks like a man" is, at best, a left-handed compliment.)   —ROBIN LAKOFF

Dashes, parentheses, commas are all used to set off parenthetical matter, but they express varying degrees of emphasis. Dashes set off parenthetical elements sharply and usually emphasize them. Parentheses usually deemphasize the elements they enclose. Commas separate elements, usually without emphasizing them.

21g Brackets set off interpolations in quoted matter and replace parentheses within parentheses. (See also 20a(4).)

The *Home Herald* printed the beginning of the mayor's speech "My dear fiends [sic] and fellow citizens." [A bracketed *sic*—

meaning "thus"—tells the reader that the error appears in the original.]

Not every expert agrees. (See, for example, Malachi Martin's *Rich Church, Poor Church* [New York: Putnam's, 1984].)

21h   The slash occurs between terms to indicate that either term is applicable and also marks line divisions in poetry.

A slash is used unspaced between terms, but with a space before and after it between lines of poetry.

> Equally rare is a first-rate adventure story designed for those who enjoy a smartly told tale that isn't steeped in blood and/or sex.   —JUDITH CHRIST

> When in "Mr. Flood's Party" the hero sets down his jug at his feet "as a mother lays her sleeping child / Down tenderly, fearing it may awake," one feels Robinson's heart to be quite simply on his sleeve.   —WILLIAM H. PITCHARD

Extensive use of the slash to indicate that either of two terms is applicable can make writing choppy.

21i   Ellipsis points (three equally spaced periods) mark an omission from a quoted passage or a reflective pause.

(1) Ellipsis points mark an omission within a quoted passage.

Omission within a quoted sentence

> Noting that "programs spent . . . energy keeping minorities out of rowing," Tina Fisher Forde explains one reason for the small numbers of minorities in rowing.

Omission at the beginning or end of a quoted sentence

Neither ellipsis points (nor capitals) are used at the beginning of a quotation, whether it is run in to the text or set off in a block.

An omission at the end of the quoted sentence that coincides with the end of your sentence requires a period in addition to the three ellipsis points, with no space immediately after the last word in the sentence. In a parenthetical reference, the period comes after the parenthesis.

> Tina Fisher Forde claims that in the past rowing programs worked hard at "keeping minorities out of rowing. . . ." [OR rowing . . ." (19).]

If the quoted material ends with a question mark or exclamation point, three ellipsis points are added and the mark is retained.

To indicate the omission of a full line or more in quoted poetry, use spaced periods covering the length either of the line above it or of the omitted line.

> I love people who harness themselves, an ox to a heavy cart,
> who pull like water buffalo, with massive patience,
> . . . .
> who do what has to be done, again and again.
> —MARGE PIERCY

(2) **Although ellipsis points can mark a reflective pause or hesitation, they should not be overused.**

> Love, like other emotions, has causes . . . and consequences. —LAWRENCE CASTER

Mechanics

Mechanics

Chapter 22

Spelling, the Spell Checker, and Hyphenation

Misspellings may make a reader doubt whether the writer can present information correctly. Therefore, always proofread to detect misspellings or typographic errors.

People often feel that they no longer need to worry about spelling since computers have spell checkers to correct errors. While a spell checker can be helpful, it does not solve all spelling problems. For example, the computer cannot tell when you confuse such words as *principal* and *principle* because it cannot know which meaning is called for.

One way to improve spelling is to record the words you have misspelled and study them. Another way is to develop your own tricks to help you remember. For example, you might remember the spelling of "separate" by reminding yourself that it has "a rat" in it.

If you have doubts about spelling, consult your dictionary. If your dictionary lists two alternatives, the first option listed is usually the more common form.

22a Spelling often does not reflect pronunciation.

Many words in English are not spelled as they are pronounced. One trick is to be aware of how the word would sound if it were pronounced as it is spelled.

accidentally	congratulations	government
athlete	February	
candidate	generally	

It is sometimes helpful to think of the spelling of the root word as a guide to correct spelling.

| confidence, confide | exultation, exult |
| different, differ | indomitable, dominate |

CAUTION Words like *and, than,* and *have* are often not stressed in speech and are thus misspelled. A spell checker will not catch these misspellings.

I would ~~of~~ *have* preferred fish rather ~~then~~ *than* soup ~~an~~ *and* salad.

22b When words sound alike but have different meanings, the spelling determines the meaning.

Words such as *sole* and *soul* are homophones: They sound alike but have different meanings and spellings.

(1) Contractions and possessive pronouns

It's my turn next.   Each group waits its turn.
You're next.   Your turn is next.

(See **19b** and **19d**.)

(2) Single words and two-word phrases

He wore everyday clothes.   He wears them every day.
Maybe we will go.   We may be going.

! **CAUTION** *A lot* and *all right* are still spelled as two words; *alot* and *alright* are considered incorrect, although *alright* is often used in journalistic and business writing.

 The following list contains words that sound exactly alike (*break/brake*) and ones that are similar in sound, especially in rapid speech (*believe/belief*). The spell checker cannot identify words that are correctly spelled but wrongly used. If you are unsure about the difference in meaning between any pair of words, consult the **Glossary of Usage** or your dictionary.

WORDS WHOSE SPELLINGS ARE FREQUENTLY CONFUSED

accept, except	altogether, all together
access, excess	always, all ways
advice, advise	amoral, immoral
affect, effect	angel, angle
aisles, isles	ask, ax
alley, ally	assistance, assistants
allude, elude	baring, barring, bearing
already, all ready	began, begin
altar, alter	believe, belief

board, bored
break, brake
breath, breathe
buy, by, bye
capital, capitol
censor, censure, sensor
choose, chose
cite, site, sight
clothes, cloths
coarse, course
complement, compliment
conscience, conscious
council, counsel
cursor, curser
dairy, diary
decent, descent, dissent
desert, dessert
device, devise
discreet, discrete
dyeing, dying
elicit, illicit
emigrate, immigrate
envelop, envelope
fair, fare
faze, phase
fine, find
formerly, formally
forth, fourth
forward, foreword
gorilla, guerrilla

have, of
hear, here
heard, herd
heroin, heroine
hole, whole
holy, wholly
horse, hoarse
human, humane
its, it's
knew, new
later, latter
lay, lie (see **13c(3)**)
lead, led
lessen, lesson
lightning, lightening
lose, loose
marital, martial
maybe, may be
minor, miner
moral, morale
of, off
passed, past
patience, patients
peace, piece
personal, personnel
perspective, prospective
plain, plane
pray, prey
precede, proceed
presence, presents

principle, principal

prophecy, prophesy

purpose, propose

quiet, quit, quite

raise, rise (see **13c(3)**)

right, rite, write

road, rode

sat, set (see **13c(3)**)

sense, since

shown, shone

stationary, stationery

straight, strait

than, then

their, there, they're, there're

threw, through, thorough

throne, thrown

to, too, two

waist, waste

weak, week

weather, whether

were, wear, where, we're

which, witch

who's, whose

your, you're

22c Adding a prefix to a base word changes the meaning.

Prefixes are added to the beginning of the base word, called the root.

necessary, unnecessary   moral, immoral

No letter is added or dropped when a prefix is added.

22d Adding a suffix may require changing the spelling of the base word.

Suffixes are added to the end of the base word.

resist, resistant   beauty, beautiful

Spelling, however, is irregular and follows certain conventions.

(1) Dropping or retaining a final unpronounced *e*

A word ending in an unpronounced *e* drops the final *e* before a suffix beginning with a vowel.

bride, bridal   combine, combination

A word ending in an unpronounced *e* retains the final *e* before a suffix beginning with a consonant.

rude, rudeness   entire, entirely

Some exceptions are *ninth, truly, duly, wholly.*

To keep the /s/ sound in *ce* or the /j/ sound in *ge*, do not drop the final *e* before *-able* or *-ous*:

noticeable   manageable   courageous

(2) Doubling a final consonant before a suffix

Double the final consonant before a suffix beginning with a vowel if (a) the consonant ends a one-syllable word or a stressed syllable and (b) the consonant is preceded by a single vowel.

drop, dropping BUT droop, drooping
admit, admitted BUT figure, figured

(3) Changing or retaining a final *y* before a suffix

Change the *y* to *i* before suffixes—except *-ing.*

defy: defies, defied, defiance BUT defying

Most verbs ending in *y* preceded by a vowel do not change the *y* before *-s* or *-ed*: *stay, stays, stayed*. The following irregularities in spelling are especially troublesome: *lays, laid; pays, paid; says, said.*

(4) Retaining a final *l* before *-ly*

usual, usually   real, really   cool, coolly

(5) Adding *-s* or *-es* to form the plural of nouns

Form the plural of most nouns by adding *-s* to the singular.

toys   scientists   tables   the Smiths

For nouns ending in an *f* or *fe*, change the ending to *ve* before adding *-s* when the plural changes from an *f* sound to a *v* sound: *thief, thieves; life, lives;* BUT *roof, roofs.*

For nouns ending in *s, z, ch, sh,* or *x,* add *-es* when the plural adds another syllable.

box, boxes   peach, peaches   crash, crashes

Usage varies for nouns ending in *o* preceded by a consonant. Consult a dictionary if you have a question.

echoes   heroes   potatoes   vetoes   [-es only]
autos   memos   pimentos   pros   [-s only]

Certain irregular nouns do not add *-s* or *-es* to form the plural.

Singular	woman	goose	analysis	datum	species
Plural	women	geese	analyses	data	species

22e   *Ei* and *ie* are often confused.

When the sound is /ē/ (as in *me*), write *ie* except after *c,* in which case write *ei.*

chief   yield   priest
[BUT after *c*] receive   perceive   conceit

When the sound is other than /ē/, you should usually write *ei*:

eight   heir   rein   their   weight   foreign

Some exceptions include *either, neither, friend,* and *species.*

22f   Hyphens both link and divide words.

Hyphens link, or make a compound of, two or more words and divide words at the end of a line.

(1) Linking two or more words to form a compound

Nouns   We planted forget-me-nots and Johnny-jump-ups.

Verbs   He speed-read the paper.   I double-checked.

Some compounds are connected with hyphens, others are written separately (*eye chart*), and still others are written as one word (*eyewitness*). When in doubt, consult your dictionary.

Hyphenate two or more words serving as a single adjective before a noun. (See also **1e(2)**.)

a well-built house [COMPARE a house that is well built]

In a series, hyphens can carry over from one item to the next.

eighteenth- and nineteenth-century houses

Omit the hyphen in the following cases.

(a) after an adverb ending in *-ly* (*quickly frozen foods*)
(b) in chemical terms (*sodium chloride solution*)

Hyphenate spelled-out fractions and compound numbers.

one–eighth   eighty–four   twenty–third

Also hyphenate combinations of figures and letters (*mid-1990s*).

Hyphenate to avoid ambiguity.

re–sign the petition [COMPARE "resign the position"]

Hyphenate the prefixes *ex-* ("former"), *self-*, and *all-*; the suffix *-elect*; and a prefix with a capitalized word.

president–elect   ex–husband   all–important   mid–August

(2) Breaking a word at the end of a line with a hyphen

If you must divide a word at the end of a line, use a hyphen to separate syllables. Not every division between syllables is an appropriate place for dividing a word.

Do not create one-letter syllables by putting the first or last letter of a word at the end or beginning of a line. Do not put the last two letters of a word at the beginning of a line.

Chapter 23

Capitals

When special problems arise, consult a good, recent dictionary. When capitalizing something is optional, be consistent:

sunbelt OR Sunbelt, blacks OR Blacks, a.m. OR A.M.

23a **Proper names are capitalized and so usually are their abbreviations and acronyms.**

Common nouns like *college* and *street* are capitalized when they are essential parts of proper names.

(1) Names, nicknames, and trademarks

Zora Neale Hurston, Skylab, Scotch tape

(2) Peoples and their languages

African Americans, Asians, English, Korean

(3) Geographical names

China, Ellis Island, Lincoln Memorial, Middle West, Seventh St.

(4) Organizations, government agencies, institutions, and companies

B'nai B'rith, Congress for Racial Equality, International Red Cross, Phi Beta Kappa, Internal Revenue Service, Howard University, Museum of Modern Art, Ford Motor Company

(5) Days of the week, months, and holidays

Wednesday, August, Thanksgiving

The names of the seasons—spring, summer, fall, winter— are not capitalized.

(6) Historical documents, periods, events, and movements

Declaration of Independence, Stone Age, Gulf War, Impressionism

(7) Religions and their adherents, holy books, holy days, and words denoting the Supreme Being

Christianity, Muslim, Bible, Koran, Yom Kippur, God, Vishnu

(8) Personifications

Then into the room walked Death.

(See also page 340.)

(9) Words derived from proper names

Americanize [verb]; Marxism [noun]; Orwellian [adjective]

(10) **Abbreviations and acronyms of capitalized words**

　　AT&T, B.A., CBS, JFK, NFL, OPEC

(See also chapter 25 and 21a(2).)

23b ## Titles of persons that precede the name are capitalized but not those that follow it or stand alone.

　　Governor Christine Todd Whitman, Uncle Verne

　　Christine Todd Whitman, the governor; Verne, my uncle

Words denoting family relationships are usually capitalized when serving as substitutes for proper names:

　　Tell Mother I'll write soon. [COMPARE "My mother wants me to write."]

23c ## In titles and subtitles of books, plays, essays, and other titled works, first and last words are capitalized, as well as most other words.

All words in titles and subtitles are capitalized, except articles, coordinating conjunctions, prepositions, and the *to* in infinitives (unless they are the first or last word). The articles are *a, an, the;* the coordinating conjunctions are *and, but, or, nor, for, so, yet.* (Formerly, longer prepositions like *before, between,* or *through* in titles were capitalized; MLA style, however, favors lowercasing prepositions, whatever the length.) (See **34a**.)

　　"What It Takes to Be a Leader"
　　Autobiography of a Face

23d The pronoun *I* and the interjection *O* are capitalized.

If **I** forget thee, **O** Jerusalem, let my right hand forget her cunning. —PSALMS

The interjection *oh* is not capitalized except when it begins a sentence.

23e The first word of every sentence (or of any other unit written as a sentence) and of directly quoted speech is capitalized.

Oh, really! Do you want to become more efficient?
Beth got out of the car and shouted, "Home at last!"

23f Unnecessary capitals are distracting.

Do not capitalize common nouns preceded by the articles *a* and *an* or by such modifiers as *several*.

a speech course in theater and television
[COMPARE   Speech 324: Theater and Television]

a university, **several** high schools
[COMPARE   University of Michigan, Hickman High School]

Chapter 24

Italics

When using a word processing program, you can use italics to indicate certain titles and for other purposes. In handwritten or typewritten papers, you can indicate italics by underlining.

24a Italics identify the titles of separate publications.

A separate publication is a work published as a whole rather than as part of a larger work. A newspaper, for example, is a separate publication. In addition to newspapers, the titles of books, magazines, pamphlets, plays, and films are usually italicized. Italics also indicate the titles of television and radio programs, entire recordings, works of art, long poems, comic strips, genera, species, and software programs.

Books	*Beloved*	*The Journey Home*
Magazines	*Wired*	*National Geographic*
Newspapers	*USA Today*	*Wall Street Journal*
Plays, Films	*Othello*	*Forrest Gump*
Recordings	*Unforgettable*	*Great Verdi Overtures*

Works of Art	*Mona Lisa*	*The Last Supper*
Long Poems	*Paradise Lost*	*The Divine Comedy*
Comic Strips	*Peanuts*	*Doonesbury*
Genera, Species	*Homo sapiens*	*Rosa setigera*
Software	*VirusScan*	*WordPerfect*

Neither italics nor quotation marks are used in references to major historical documents or religious texts.

> The Magna Carta marked a turning point in English history.
>
> Matthew, Mark, Luke, and John are the first four books of the New Testament.

The title of a paper (unless it includes the title of a book) should not be italicized. (See also **23c**.)

24b   Italics identify foreign words and phrases in an English sentence.

> I tell her I know Chinese. "*Beyeh fa-foon,*" I say. "*Shee-veh, Ji nu,*" meaning "Stop acting crazy. Rice gruel, Soy sauce."
> —GISH JEN

Countless words from other languages are a part of the English vocabulary and are therefore not italicized.

| cliché (French) | pizza (Italian) |
| patio (Spanish) | karate (Japanese) |

24c   Italics identify the names of legal cases.

Andrews v. City of Philadelphia

24d Italics identify the names of specific ships, satellites, and spacecraft.

U.S.S. *Picking*   the space shuttle *Challenger*

The names of trains and the names of a general class or a trademark are not italicized: Orient Express, Boeing 747.

24e Italics indicate words, letters, or figures used as illustrations, statistical symbols, or the variables in algebraic expressions.

Finally he told my mother to put an *H* in that blank. "For *human* race," he said.   —ELIZABETH GORDON

$c = r^2$

24f When used sparingly, italics indicate emphasis.

If they take offense, then that's *their* problem.

These *are* the right files.

Chapter 25

Abbreviations, Acronyms, and Numbers

Abbreviations and numbers are used in tables, notes, and bibliographies and in some kinds of special or technical writing. The first time abbreviations or acronyms are used in a paper, they should be spelled out.

> Behaviors that rate high on the Sensation Seeking Scale (SSS) include engaging in risky sports, occupations, or hobbies.

Traditionally abbreviations are marked with periods; acronyms are not.

 Designations such as *Ms., Mr., Mrs., Dr.,* and *St.* appear before a proper name, and those such as *Jr., Sr.,* and *II* appear after.

Dr. Sonya Allen   Mark Ngo, Sr.

P.T. Lawrence, III   St. Paul

Avoid redundant titles.

> Dr. Carol Ballou or Carol Ballou, M.D. [NOT Dr. Carol Ballou, M.D.]

Most abbreviations form plurals by adding *-s* alone, without an apostrophe: *IRAs, CODs.*

Use abbreviations such as *Prof., Sen.,* or *Capt.* only before initials or full names.

ESL Other cultures sometimes use *the* before titles. American English omits *the* except when using *Reverend* or *Honorable.*

~~the~~ Dr. Sonya Allen   ~~the~~ Professor Rodriguez

25b **The names of states, countries, continents, months, days of the week, and units of measurement are not abbreviated when they appear in a sentence.**

On a Tuesday in June, we drove to Columbia, Missouri.

For addresses in correspondence, however, use appropriate postal abbreviations. No period follows the abbreviation: AL, DC, NJ.

25c **Words such as *Street, Park,* and *Company* are abbreviated only when they appear in addresses.**

Thompson Avenue is south of Hollywood Park.

25d The words *volume, chapter,* and *page* are written out when they appear in sentences but abbreviated when they appear in bibliographies and reference lists.

I read pages 82–89 of chapter 10 in volume 3 for my sociology course.

The following kinds of abbreviations and acronyms are commonly used in writing.

(1) Certain words used with dates or figures

82 B.C. [OR B.C.E.]   A.D. 95 [OR 95 C.E.]
7:40 a.m. [OR A.M.]   4:52 EST [OR E.S.T.]
No. 19   85 mpg

(2) The abbreviations DC and U.S. when used as adjectives

Washington, DC; the U.S. Navy

(3) Certain common Latin expressions

vs. OR v. [versus]   etc. [and so forth]
e.g.   [for example]   i.e. [that is]

25e When unfamiliar with an acronym, readers benefit from seeing it spelled out the first time it is used.

FEMA (the Federal Emergency Management Administration) was criticized for its slow response to the victims of Hurricane Andrew.

25f Numbers are written in different ways depending on the size of the numbers and the frequency with which they appear.

When you use numbers infrequently in a piece of writing, you can spell out those that can be expressed in one or two words and use figures for the others. When you use numbers frequently, spell out those from one to nine and use figures for all others. Very large numbers can be expressed by a combination of words and figures.

Always   after three days
But   after thirty-three days   OR   after 33 days

Always   758 students
But   seven hundred students   OR   700 students

If a sentence begins with a number, spell out the number.

Two hundred twenty-five contestants competed.

Specific time of day

4 p.m.   OR   4:00 p.m.   OR   four o'clock in the afternoon

Dates

November 8, 1962   OR   8 November 1962
December fourth   OR   December 4
the fifties   OR   the 1950s
the fourteenth century
in 1362   in 1320–21   from 1330 to 1335

Addresses

25 Arrow Dr., Apt. 1, Columbia, MO 78209

Identification numbers

Channel 10   Interstate 40   Edward III   Room 222

Pages and divisions of books and plays

page 15   chapter 8   part 2
in act 2, scene 1   OR   in Act II, Scene I

Decimals and percentages

a 2.5 average   12½ percent   0.853 metric tons

ESL   American English marks any amount smaller than one with a decimal point (period) and uses a comma to divide larger numbers into more understandable units.

10,000   (ten thousand)

7.65   (seven and sixty-five one hundredths)

In some other cultures, the decimal and the comma are reversed.

Chapter 26

Document Design

This chapter contains information on presenting your writing so that it is as readable as possible. Because the way you design your documents tells a reader much about you, a well-designed letter of application and résumé can mean the difference between being hired and not being hired. Similarly, a well-designed term paper can make a difference in how favorably a professor regards the quality of your work.

 Using the proper materials enhances readability.

(1) Paper and binding

Use good 20-pound white 8½-by-11-inch paper (neither onionskin nor erasable bond). If your printer requires continuous sheets, choose paper that allows clean removal of pin-feed strips and separation of sheets. If you write your papers by hand, use regular 8½-by-11-inch lined white notebook paper.

Use a paper clip or a staple to fasten pages. Unless your instructor tells you differently, do not use folders.

(2) Electronic documents

If you submit your work electronically (by electronic or e-mail, on a bulletin board, in a Web document, or on disk), follow your instructor's directions exactly. Whatever the

147

requirements, the computing facilities to meet them are likely to be available on campus at no cost.

(3) Type, fonts, and justification

Most academic papers should be printed using a font that looks like typewriter type. Using a variety of fonts detracts from the content. Resist the impulse to justify your right margins. The irregular spacing within the line can be distracting and at times misleading to readers.

Pages from a good ink jet or laser printer are always acceptable. If you have a dot-matrix printer, set the printer for near-letter-quality print. If you use a typewriter, the ribbon must type clear, dark characters. If your instructor accepts handwritten papers, write in blue or black ink on one side of the paper only.

26b   Clear and orderly arrangement contributes to ease in reading.

The advice here follows the guidelines in the *MLA Handbook for Writers of Research Papers,* fourth edition.

(1) Layout

Unless your instructor agrees to different spacing, double-space all papers except those you write by hand. Generally, leave margins of one or one and one-half inches on all sides of the text.The ruled vertical line on notebook paper marks the left margin for handwritten papers.

(2) Indention

The first lines of paragraphs should be uniformly indented. You can set your word processing software to indent one-half inch. (Indent five spaces on a typewriter, or one inch if writing by hand.)

(3) Paging

Place Arabic numerals at the right margin, one-half inch from the top of each page. Unless you are using a format that requires running titles (e.g., APA), put your last name immediately before the page number.

Unless your instructor requests a title page, place your name, your instructor's name, the course and section number, and the date in the top left-hand corner (one inch from the top and one inch from the left edge), double-spacing after each line. Center the title and double-space between the lines.

Begin your first paragraph on the second line below the title, double-spaced. (See the model in chapter 29.)

(4) Headings

Headings can make a long document easier to read. If you use headings, make them consistent throughout your document, and if you have two levels of headings, treat all occurrences of each level alike.

 26c **The appropriate form for electronic documents can vary.**

Electronic documents may be published on the Internet, on your campus network, or on an electronic bulletin board.

(1) Electronic mail

Using e-mail requires special care to communicate ideas clearly. Some standard advice appears below. (See also 35b(1).)

Checklist for Bulletin Board Postings and Electronic Mail

1. Keep line length short. Some users have monitors that display only 40 characters in a line.
2. Make the subject line descriptive of your message so your reader(s) can find and file your message easily.
3. A signature line at the end of each message should include your name, your position and affiliation (if any), and your e-mail address.
4. Use capitals as you would in an ordinary typewritten document; that is, use mixed upper- and lowercase letters.
5. Use good sense regarding what you write about others. It is possible that a recipient might forward your message without your knowledge, embarrassing you—or even making you liable.
6. Similarly, respect the privacy of others. Don't forward personal messages without the writer's permission.
7. Sarcasm and irony are frequently misunderstood. These strategies depend in large part on facial expression and tone of voice, so your joke may be seen as criticism.

---

(2) The World Wide Web

The World Wide Web contains **pages** that a reader can view using a program that fetches the text and graphic images. Instructors increasingly ask students to construct Web pages in lieu of submitting papers. While the details of such construction are beyond the scope of this handbook, a few tips might be helpful.

Checklist for Designing Web Pages
1. Write the page so that it can be viewed with or without pictures. Many people lack a connection that will allow them to receive graphics.
2. Use graphics sparingly. Graphic files typically take a long time to transfer.
3. Don't crowd your page with text. Set pages up so that they can be read on a single screen and provide a link to other screens.

26d Proofreading provides quality control.

Proofreading is different from revising or editing. **Proofreading** checks for and corrects errors of layout, spelling, punctuation, and mechanics. Proofreading can be done manually or with a word processing program; doing both is insurance against error.

If you are using a word processing program, print out a draft so that you can check it carefully on paper and make any changes before you print the final copy. If you have typed or handwritten your document, make any necessary corrections by neatly drawing a single line through the incorrect material, placing a caret (∧) where the correct material is to be inserted, and writing the information above the line or, if long, to the side with a line drawn to the caret.

To use the proofreading checklist that follows, you might read your paper backward, sentence by sentence, out loud. Read the words slowly, looking at and pronouncing each syllable carefully. Refer to the chapters and sections cross-referenced in this handbook and also keep your dictionary handy to look up any words you are uncertain about.

Checklist for Proofreading   ☑

Layout
- Have you used proper margins? Are paragraphs formatted consistently?
- Is each page numbered?
- Does the first page have title and heading?
- Is the first line of each paragraph indented?
- Is the print (or type or handwriting) dark and legible?
- Are the lines double-spaced?

Spelling (22)
- Are all words spelled correctly?
- Have you double-checked words you frequently misspell or the spell checker might miss (e.g., homonyms or misspellings that form words, such as *form* for *from*)?

Punctuation (17, 18, 19, 20, 21)
- Does each sentence have appropriate closing punctuation and only one space after each period (21a)?
- Is punctuation within sentences appropriately used and placed (comma, 17; semicolon, 18; apostrophe, 19; other internal marks, 21; hyphen, 22f)?
- Are quotations correctly punctuated (20, 33h)?

Capitalization and italics (23 and 24)
- Does each sentence begin with a capital letter (23e)?
- Are all proper names, people's titles, and titles of published works correctly capitalized (23a–c)?
- Are quotations capitalized properly (20a, 33h(2))?
- Are italics used properly (24)?

Larger Elements

Larger Elements

Chapter 27

Working with Paragraphs

Although paragraphs rarely stand alone, it is occasionally useful to view them separately to observe how a single paragraph is organized and why it is or is not effective. Furthermore, many of the development patterns described in this chapter as paragraph strategies also apply to writing the whole essay. The beginning of a paragraph is indented. Paragraphs typically range from 50 to 250 words. Although one-sentence paragraphs are occasionally used for emphasis, short paragraphs often indicate inadequate development. Long paragraphs, too, can reveal problems in your writing, especially if they exhaust one point or combine too many points.

27a Paragraphs should be unified.

In a unified paragraph, each sentence helps develop the main idea.

(1) Main idea and topic sentences

Writers usually convey the main idea of a paragraph in a topic sentence. For example, the topic sentence of paragraph 1 announces that the paragraph will explain two categories of rumors.

1   *Rumors basically deal with people's anxieties and uncertainties, Rosnow says, and he divides them into two types:*

wish rumors that we hope are true, and dread rumors that we pray are false. Your company is giving a year-end bonus, property taxes are going down, there's not going to be a final exam. These are examples of wish rumors. Dread rumors are on the darker side: there are going to be layoffs at work, a fare increase is on the way, your company is going to be moving. —ROBIN WESTEN,
"The Real Slant on Gossip" *Psychology Today*

The main idea of a paragraph is frequently stated at or near the beginning. It is sometimes also restated at the end to emphasize its importance.

Occasionally, the topic sentence is stated near the end of the paragraph, especially when the writer progresses from specific examples to a generalization.

2   Sisters have been taking in other people's children since the days when Pharaoh's daughter had a maiden scoop Moses out of the bullrushes. *In modern times, as efforts to recruit Black adoptive parents have accelerated, Black single women and men have heeded the call.*   —CHERYL EVERETTE,
"Going Solo: Singles Open Their Lives to Adoption" *Emerge*

A single topic sentence can serve for a sequence of two or more paragraphs.

3   *The world has always been divided into two camps: those who love garlic and onions and those who detest them.* The first camp would include the Egyptian pharaohs who were entombed with clay and wood carvings of garlic and onions to ensure that meals in the afterlife would be well seasoned. It would include the Jews who wandered for 40 years in the Sinai wilderness, fondly remembering "the fish which we did eat in Egypt so freely, and the pumpkins and melons, and the leeks, onions and garlic." It would include Sydney Smith, the 19th-century essayist, whose "Recipe for Salad" includes this couplet: "Let onion atoms lurk within the bowl, / And, scarce-suspected, animate the whole."

4   The camp of the garlic and onion haters would include the Egyptian priests who, according to Plutarch, "kept themselves clear of the onion. . . . It is suitable neither for fasting nor festival, because in the one case it causes thirst, and in the other tears for those who partake it." The camp would include the ancient Greeks, who considered the odor of garlic and onions vulgar and prohibited garlic and onion eaters from worshiping at the Temple of Cybele. It would include Bottom, who in *A Midsummer Night's Dream* instructs his troupe of actors to "eat no onions nor garlic, for we are to utter sweet breath."

              —ERIC BLOCK, "The Chemistry of Garlic and Onions"

Occasionally, a paragraph contains no topic sentence because the details unmistakably imply the main idea.

(2) Main idea and paragraph unity

The most common way to unify a paragraph is to make each sentence support the main idea. In paragraph 5, each sentence shows exactly what the writer means by the curious experiences referred to in the topic sentence.

5   The beat spirit was wry, lighthearted and macabre at the same time. Beats celebrated the breaking down of barriers between life and art. Beats celebrated the everyday, down-and-out and ephemeral. They embraced be-bop music and other inventions of black culture. They were early performance artists. They crossed over from one art form to another. They experimented with collage, assemblage and stream of consciousness.   —MICHAEL KIMMELMAN,
    "Celebration of Beat Culture (Sandals and All)"
    New York Times

As you check your paragraphs for unity, revise or eliminate any information that does not clearly relate to the main idea. If more than one major idea appears in a paragraph, either refocus your main idea or develop each idea in a separate paragraph.

27b Clearly arranged ideas and effective transitions foster paragraph coherence.

A paragraph is coherent when the relationship among the ideas is clear and the progression from one sentence to the next is easy for the reader to follow.

(1) Patterns of coherence

Different kinds of writing use different patterns to establish coherence. In the humanities, the primary pattern establishes links between the subject of the topic sentence and all subsequent sentences in the paragraph.

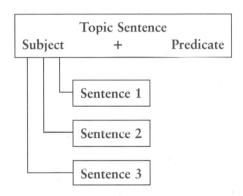

6   Women from all classes protested these abusive and discriminating practices. These protesters banded together and marched through the streets of their country demanding equality with men. And these women were labeled feminists. They wanted the right to vote, they wanted the right to fair working conditions and fair wages, and they wanted the right to live their lives in the manner they chose without ostracism from society. Yes, these women (and a few like-minded men) were called feminists.

—CAROL JOHNSON, "What Is a Feminist?"

The pattern that dominates in the natural and social sciences links each sentence, chain-like, to the predicate of the preceding one, as in paragraph 7.

7　A spider's muscles can curl its legs. But to straighten their legs, spiders have to pump fluids into them. If the spider hasn't gotten enough water, its legs will curl up and cannot be straightened.　　　—MARRIETTA DICHRISTINA,
"Come into My Parlor" *Popular Science*

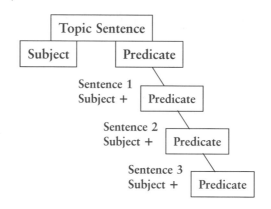

But writers generally match the pattern they see to the writing they do.

(2) Order of ideas

One way to arrange ideas in a paragraph is **order of importance** (climactic), from most to least important or from least to most important. In paragraph 8, the author focuses on a hierarchy of intelligence.

8　An ant cannot purposefully try anything new, and any ant that accidentally did so would be murdered by his colleagues.

It is the ant colony as a whole that slowly learns over the ages. In contrast, even an earthworm has enough flexibility of brain to enable it to be taught to turn toward the left or right for food. Though rats are not able to reason to any considerable degree, they can solve such problems as separating round objects from triangular ones when these have to do with health or appetite. Cats, with better brains, can be taught somewhat more, and young dogs a great deal. The higher apes can learn by insight as well as by trial and error.

—GEORGE RUSSELL HARRISON, *What Man May Be*

Sometimes the movement within the paragraph is from **general to specific** or from **specific to general**. A paragraph may begin with a general statement or idea, which is then supported by particular details, as in paragraph 8 above, or a series of details, or a summarizing statement as in paragraph 9.

9   To bring back some excitement to concertgoing—and some emotions other than nostalgia and/or pity—the music industry has turned to festivals. Not stationary, one-time events like Woodstocks I and II, but massive, carnival-like musical tours that feature at least half a dozen acts as well as food booths, souvenir stands and more. This summer several festivals are touring the land, each with a distinct character vying for a hold on the pop-culture imagination and wallet.

—CHRISTOPHER FARLEY, *"Where the Moshers Are"*

Another common paragraph arrangement is the **problem-solution** pattern, in which the first sentence or two state the problem and the rest of the paragraph suggests the solution, as illustrated by paragraph 10.

10   That many women would be happier not pursuing careers or intellectual adventures is only part of the truth. The whole truth is that many people would be. If society had the clear sight to assure men as well as women that there is no shame in preferring to stay non-competitively and non-aggressively at home, many masculine neuroses and ulcers would be

avoided, and many children would enjoy the benefit of being brought up by a father with a talent for the job instead of by a mother with no talent for it but a sense of guilt about the lack. —BRIGID BROPHY, "Women"

(3) Transitional devices: pronouns, repetition, transition, and parallel structures

Many of the same kinds of transitions link sentences within paragraphs and paragraphs within a paper. (See also chapters 8 and 10.)

Pronouns

In paragraph 11, the writer links sentences by using the pronouns *their* and *they*.

11   Several movements characterize easy victims: their strides were either very long or very short; they moved awkwardly, raising their left legs with their left arms (instead of alternating them); on each step, they tended to lift their whole foot up and then place it down (less muggable sorts took steps in which their feet rocked from heel to toe). Overall, the people rated most muggable walked as if they were in conflict with themselves; they seemed to make each move in the most difficult way possible.   —CARIN RUBENSTEIN,
"Body Language That Speaks to Muggers"

Repetition of words, phrases, or ideas

In paragraph 12, the repetition of the key word *wave* links the sentences.

12   The weekend is over, and we drive down the country road from the cottage to the pier, passing out our last supply of waves. We wave at people walking and wave at people riding. We wave at people we know and wave at people who are strangers.

—ELLEN GOODMAN, "Waving Goodbye to the Country"

Conjunctions and other transitions

Conjunctions and transitional phrases demonstrate the logical relationship between ideas. Here is a checklist of some frequently used transitional connections.

Checklist of Transitional Connections ✔	
• Alternative and Addition	or, nor, and, and then, besides, further, furthermore, likewise, also, too, in addition, next, first, second
• Comparison	similarly, likewise, in like manner
• Contrast	but, yet, or, however, still, nevertheless, on the other hand, even so, in contrast, at the same time, although
• Place	here, beyond, nearby, opposite to
• Purpose	to this end, for this purpose
• Result or Cause	so, for, therefore, accordingly, consequently, thus, as a result, because
• Summary	to sum up, in sum, in short
• Repetition	in other words, that is, to be sure
• Exemplification	for example, for instance, in any event
• Intensification	in fact, indeed, to tell the truth
• Time	meanwhile, soon, after a few days, later, now, then, while

Parallel structures

Parallelism is the repetition of a sentence pattern or structure. (See also chapter **10**.) In paragraph 13, the first three sentences are structured the same way. Repeating this pattern emphasizes the close relationship of the ideas.

13   When you're three years old and stick mashed potatoes up your nose, that's expected. When you're six and make your bed but it looks like you're still in it, you deserve some credit for trying. When you're nine and prepare the family meal but

the casserole looks worse than the kitchen, you should be applauded for your effort. But somewhere along the line, some responsible adult should say, "You're too old for this nonsense."　—DAN KILEY, *The Peter Pan Syndrome: Men Who Have Never Grown Up*

(4) Transitions between paragraphs

Transitions between paragraphs are as important as transitions between sentences. You can repeat a word or idea from the last paragraph in the first sentence of the new one, as in paragraphs 14 and 15.

14　For those who pray or chant with great perseverance, there is the suggestion that their *waiting* has been converted into purposefulness.

15　Of course, we do not just *wait* for love; we *wait* for money, we *wait* for the weather to get warmer, colder; we *wait* for the plumber to come and fix the washing machine. . . .
　　　　　　　　　　　　　　　　—EDNA O'BRIEN, "Waiting"

Paragraphs 16 and 17 show how you can use transitional words or phrases to connect paragraphs.

16　. . . America Online even banned the word "breast," leaving users with more colorful synonyms free to chat but making any discussions of breast cancer or breast exams impossible.

17　Another frightening aspect of the Decency Act is the imposition of the "community standards" clause concerning on-line communication. Given the right equipment, any site is reachable from any place on earth. . . .
　　　　　　　　　　　—SANDY M. FERNANDEZ, "The Cybercops"

Sometimes a transitional paragraph serves as a bridge between two paragraphs. Ordinarily, such a paragraph is short (often consisting of only one sentence) because the writer intends it to be merely a signpost.

18   Now you are expecting me to describe how I saw the folly of my ways and came back to the warm nest, where prejudices are so often called loyalties, where pointless actions are hallowed into custom by repetition, where we are content to say we think when all we do is feel.

19   But you would be wrong. I dropped my hobby and turned professional.

20   If I were to go back to the headmaster's study and find the dusty statuettes still there, I would arrange them differently. I would dust Venus and put her aside, for I have come to love her and know her for the fair thing she is. But I would put the Thinker, sunk in his desperate thought, where there were shadows before him—and at his back, I would put the leopard, crouched and ready to spring.

—WILLIAM GOLDING, "Thinking as a Hobby"

27c Details and examples can develop paragraphs.

Many short paragraphs are adequately developed and supply enough information in context to satisfy the reader. Often, however, short paragraphs need to be developed with more specific details or examples.

(1) Developing with specific details

The details in paragraph 21 support the topic sentence (italicized).

21   *I still go around tasting and smelling things the way I did when I was assaying the palatability of sheep feed; a handy skill, it turns out.* There's the funky tang of sage-like rotted lavender—beautiful or foul depending; and the tarry marvel of creosote bush in the summer after a rain, in the darkness, thunder still drumming the air, while the snakes are emerging, and the spadefoot toads come out to ring and blurt from tran-

sient pools. A thousand scents: the sweet headiness of desert
mistletoe in dry Mojave canyons in January, the piss smell of
the tiny white night-blooming flower called desert snow, the
cactus blooms that have a tang of tangerine or horehound,
the mucilaginous beany taste of young nopales, and the scent
of a salt spring, which is a little like death.

—DIANA KAPPEL-SMITH, "Salt"

(2) Developing with examples

Paragraph 22 uses several closely related examples to explain why violence is both impractical and immoral.

22   Violence as a way of achieving racial justice is both impractical and immoral. It is impractical because it is a de-
scending spiral ending in destruction for all. The old law of
an eye for an eye leaves everybody blind. It is immoral because
it seeks to humiliate the opponent rather than win his understanding; it seeks to annihilate rather than to convert. Violence is immoral because it thrives on hatred rather than love.
It destroys community and makes brotherhood impossible. It
leaves society in monologue rather than dialogue. Violence
ends by defeating itself. It creates bitterness in the survivors
and brutality in the destroyers. A voice echoes through time
saying to every potential Peter, "Put up your sword." History
is cluttered with the wreckage of nations that failed to follow
this command.   —MARTIN LUTHER KING, JR.,
                    "Three Types of Resistance to Oppression"

You can also use one striking example to clarify your idea.

23   Glamour's lethal effect on the psyche is also caught in the
language that commonly describes its impact: "dressed to
kill," "devastating," "shattering," "stunning," "knockout,"
"to die." Perhaps it's not surprising that Rita Hayworth's famous pinup pose in which she's kneeling in a silk negligee on
satin sheets was taped to the bomb that was dropped on
Hiroshima.

—JOHN LAHR, "The Voodoo of Glamour" *New Yorker*

27d Writers use various strategies to develop paragraphs.

All the strategies for developing paragraphs discussed in the following pages are useful for developing whole compositions. Because these development strategies reflect the ways people think, we tend to use them in combination with each other. The important consideration is that the development is clear, complete, and appropriate.

(1) Narrating a series of events

A narrative discusses a sequence of events, normally in the order they occur, that develop the point you are making. This form often uses time markers such as *then, later,* or *at a later date.* The writer in paragraph 24 uses narrative to develop the main idea stated in the last sentence.

24   Contrary to popular opinion, it is not easy to write country songs. One guy who never made it is Robin Dorsey from Matador, Texas. He went to Tech and had a girlfriend from Muleshoe about whom he wrote the love song "Her Teeth Was Stained but Her Heart Was Pure." She took offense and quit him over it, which caused him to write the tragedy-love song "I Don't Know Whether to Commit Suicide Tonight or Go Bowlin'."   —MOLLY IVINS, "Honky Tonking"

(2) Describing to make a point

Descriptive details should be clearly ordered—from near to far, right to left, top to bottom. In paragraph 25, Thomas Merton uses a near-far perspective to enable the reader to share his experience as he approached the monastery that was to become his home.

25   I looked at the rolling country, and at the pale ribbon of road in front of us stretching out as gray as lead in the light of the moon. Then suddenly I saw a steeple that shone like silver in the moonlight, growing into sight from behind a rounded knoll. The tires sang on the empty road and breathless I looked at the monastery that was revealed before me as we came over the rise. At the end of an avenue of trees was a big rectangular block of buildings, all dark, with a church crowned by a tower and a steeple and a cross: and the steeple was as bright as platinum and the whole place was as quiet as midnight and lost in the all-absorbing silence and solitude of the fields. Behind the monastery was a dark curtain of woods and over to the west was a wooded valley and beyond that a rampart of wooded hills, a barrier and a defense against the world.   —THOMAS MERTON, *The Seven Storey Mountain*

(3) Explaining a process

Process paragraphs explain how something is done or made. You might describe the items used and then narrate the steps chronologically, as in paragraph 26.

26   The best of all scientific tricks with an egg is the well-known one in which air pressure forces a peeled hard-boiled egg into a glass milk bottle and then forces it out again undamaged. The mouth of the bottle must be only slightly smaller than the egg, and so you must be careful not to use too large an egg or too small a bottle. It is impossible to push the egg into the bottle. To get the egg though the mouth you must heat the air in the bottle. That is best done by standing the bottle in boiling water for a few minutes. Put the egg upright on the mouth and take the bottle off the stove. As the air in the bottle cools it contracts, creating a partial vacuum that draws the peeled egg inside. To get the egg out again invert the bottle so the egg falls into the neck. Place the opening of the bottle against your mouth and blow vigorously. This will compress the air in the bottle. When you stop blow-

ing, the air expands, pushing the egg through the neck of the bottle and into your waiting hands.

—MARTIN GARDNER, "Mathematical Games"

(4) Showing cause and effect

A paragraph that explores a cause raises the question Why? and must answer that question to the satisfaction of the reader. Paragraph 27 provides several reasons for the development of machismo.

27   Where did machismo come from? From 500 years of total suppression by a dominant culture that spoke of honor but which extended no honor to the colonized people of South and Central America, and which acted dishonorably toward them. Caught between survival realities and powerlessness, further constricted by the dictates of the church, the Latino male became a silent cauldron of unexpressed, justifiable anger. As literal colonialism gave way to economic imperialism, the difficulties of meeting family responsibilities in concert with race hatred turned Latino men inward to internalized self-hatred. Activist poet and former gangsta Luis J. Rodriguez describes it like this: "The patriarchal Mexican culture helped build a wide breach between my father and me. The silent and strong man—vestiges of deceit—was revered. Waited on. Accepted." This persona is lethal.

—RAY GONZALEZ, "Machismo: Silence, the Lethal Weapon" *Sí*

Paragraphs can also demonstrate effects, as in paragraph 28, which discusses some results of protecting the endangered alligator.

28   The alligator's turnaround since that time has made national news. Protection and strict controls on interstate shipment of gator hides have worked: the animals have come back strong. Every so often, one will eat a poodle or take up residence in the water hazard on the sixteenth hole. Fish-and-

game people are then called out to lasso the uncomprehending reptile and move it to an out-of-the-way place. There is even some limited commerce again in the skins. At least one entrepreneur is ranching alligators, just as though they were cattle or mink. Not long ago, someone in Florida was killed by an alligator in what I suspect must have been a well-deserved attack.   —GEOFFREY NORMAN, "Gators"

(5) Comparing and contrasting to develop an idea

A **comparison** points out similarities; a **contrast** points out differences. A comparison or a contrast can be organized in either of two ways, depending on the writer's purpose. Arthur L. Campa uses the **part-by-part method** in paragraph 29.

29   Cultural differences are implicit in the conceptual content of the languages of these two civilizations, and their value systems stem from a long series of historical circumstances. Therefore, it may be well to consider some of the English and Spanish cultural configurations before these Europeans set foot on American soil. English culture was basically insular, geographically and ideologically; was more integrated on the whole, except for some strong theological differences; and was particularly zealous of its racial purity. Spanish culture was peninsular, a geographical circumstance that made it a catchall of Mediterranean, central European, and north African peoples. The composite nature of the population produced a market regionalism that prevented close integration, except for religion, and led to a strong sense of individualism. These differences were reflected in the colonizing enterprise of the two cultures. The English isolated themselves from the Indians physically and culturally; the Spanish, who had strong notions about *pureza de sangre* [purity of blood] among the nobility, were not collectively averse to adding one more strain to their racial cocktail. Cortés led the way by siring the first *mestizo* in North America, and the rest of the conquis-

tadores followed suit. The ultimate products of these two orientations meet today in the Southwest.

Campa switches in the next paragraph (30) to the **unit-by-unit method,** developing first the Anglo and then the Hispanic values.

30   Anglo-American culture was absolutist at the onset; that is, all the dominant values were considered identical for all, regardless of time and place. Such values as justice, charity, and honesty were considered the superior social order for all men and were later embodied in the American Constitution. The Spaniard brought with him a relativistic viewpoint and saw fewer moral implications in man's actions. Values were looked upon as the result of social and economic conditions.
     —ARTHUR L. CAMPA, "Anglo vs. Chicano: Why?"

(6) Classifying and dividing to develop an idea

Classification is a way to understand or explain a diverse subject and discover the relationships within it. When you classify chocolate pudding as a dessert, you tell your reader that, like most desserts, it is sweet and high in calories. **Division,** in contrast, breaks objects and ideas into parts that are smaller and examines the relationships among them. A store manager might group books according to types—biography, science fiction, mystery, and so forth.

   Classification and division often work together because once you have placed something in a class, the next logical step is to explain the characteristics of that class, which is division. Notice how Russell Baker first establishes his classifications in paragraph 31 and then explains them in paragraph 32.

31   Inanimate objects are classified scientifically into three major categories—those that break down, those that get lost, and those that don't work.

32   The goal of all inanimate objects is to resist man and ultimately to defeat him, and the three major classifications are
based on the method each object uses to achieve its purpose.
As a general rule, any object capable of breaking down at the
moment when it is most needed will do so. The automobile
is typical of the category.

—RUSSELL BAKER, "The Plot against People"

(7) Formulating a definition

Paragraphs of definition explain the meaning of a concept,
a term, or an object. The effect of definition is to put a
concept, a term, or an object into a class and then differ-
entiate it from other members of the class: "A concerto
[the term] is a symphonic piece [the class] performed by
one or more solo instruments and orchestra [the differ-
ence]." Paragraph 33 defines volcanos by putting them in
a class ("landforms") and by distinguishing them ("built
of molten material") from other members of that class.
The definition is then clarified by examples.

33   Volcanos are landforms built of molten material that has
spewed out onto the earth's surface. Such molten rock is
called *lava*. Volcanos may be no larger than small hills, or
thousands of feet high. All have a characteristic cone shape.
Some well-known mountains are actually volcanos. Examples
are Mt. Fuji (Japan), Mt. Lassen (California), Mt. Hood (Oregon), Mt. Etna and Mt. Vesuvius (Italy), and Paricutín (Mexico). The Hawaiian Islands are all immense volcanos whose
summits rise above the ocean, and these volcanos are still
quite active.   —JOEL AREM, *Rocks and Minerals*

Definitions can be extended by details, examples, synonyms, or etymology (the history of the word).

27e Editing can improve paragraph logic and effectiveness.

When you rework paragraphs, you should consider the points in the following checklist.

> **Checklist for Revising Paragraphs**
> - Do all the ideas in the paragraph belong?
> - Are any necessary ideas left out?
> - Is the paragraph coherent? Do the sentences focus on the topic? Do they link to previous sentences? Is the order of sentences logical?
> - Are sentences connected to each other with easy, effective, and natural transitions? Is the paragraph linked to the preceding and following paragraphs?
> - Is the paragraph adequately developed? If there are problems, can analyzing the strategy used to develop the paragraph help solve the problem?

Chapter 28

Planning and Drafting Essays

Whenever you write an essay, you engage in a process of developing an appropriate topic (**28b**). You often need to discover what you want to write (**28c(1)**), how to focus your subject (**28c(2)**), how to form a thesis (**28d**), and how to develop a plan of organization (**28e**). Your writing will benefit if you write more than one draft, rethinking and restructuring what you have written.

As you move through this process, you may need to return to a specific activity several times. Rather than seeing repeated effort as a sign of failure, experienced writers consider it an indication of commitment. Writing effective essays requires serious work, but the effort is worthwhile.

28a Writers must understand their purpose, audience, and occasion.

Effective writers have a clear sense of purpose, audience, and occasion.

Purpose   What a writer hopes to achieve in a piece of writing

Audience   Who will read the piece in question

Occasion   Where and when the exchange between writer and audience takes place

172

Your purpose should be appropriate for both the audience and the occasion. The combination of purpose, audience, and occasion is called your **rhetorical situation**.

(1) Purpose means why you are writing.

To clarify your purpose, or why you are writing, it helps to ask yourself if you want to

- express how you feel about something
- report information to readers
- persuade readers to agree with you

Expressive writing emphasizes the writer's feelings and reactions to the world—to people, objects, events, and ideas. Personal letters and journals are often expressive, as are many essays.

Expository writing focuses on the objective world—objects, events, and ideas—rather than on the writer's feelings about them. Textbooks, news accounts, scientific reports, and encyclopedia articles are often expository, as are many of the essays students write in college. When you report, explain, clarify, or evaluate, you are practicing exposition.

Persuasive writing is intended to influence the reader's attitudes and actions. Most writing is to some extent persuasive; through the choice and arrangement of material, even something as apparently straightforward as a résumé can be persuasive. However, writing is usually called persuasive if it is clearly arguing for or against a position. When you write persuasively, you need the critical and rhetorical skills discussed in chapters **31** and **32**.

Writers frequently have more than one purpose. If you have more than one purpose, you should be using one to help you achieve another—which is very different from writing without a purpose or simply losing sight of your original purpose.

(2) Audience means who will read your writing.

Understanding your audience will help you decide on the length and depth of your essay, the kind of language to use, and the examples that will be the most effective.

Specialized audiences

A **specialized audience** has considerable knowledge of the subject you are writing about and a keen interest in it. When writing for specialized audiences, you need to consider how much and what kinds of information, as well as what methods of presentation, are called for.

Many of the papers you write in college are for a specialized audience. You assume that your instructor is already well informed about the material.

General audiences

A **general audience** consists of readers not expert on your topic but presumably willing to learn about new material if it is presented clearly and respectfully. Sometimes you may not know much about your audience. When this is the case, you can often benefit from imagining a thoughtful audience of educated adults. Such an audience is likely to include people with different backgrounds and cultural values, so be careful not to assume that you are writing for readers who are exactly like you.

(3) Occasion means the circumstances under which writers and readers communicate.

Occasion is the context in which the writing occurs, the time, place, and climate. An essay written outside class may be very different from an essay written in a classroom even if both are written for the same audience and with the same purpose. Moreover, your instructor may have higher expectations for your final essay in a course than for your first. The occasion is different because the time and climate are different.

 28b **By exploring subjects, you can focus on a topic.**

When you are free to choose your own subject, you can use a number of different methods to discover the best subject for your essay. If you already have one in mind, the same methods can be used to explore possibilities for focusing and developing it.

(1) There are several ways to search for a subject.

If you have a hard time finding subjects to write about, try journaling or freewriting. If you have a subject in mind but are unsure of how to develop it, try listing, questioning, and applying perspectives. Sometimes you may need to try several methods.

Journaling

Students often benefit from writing daily in a personal journal or a writer's notebook. In a **personal journal**, you reflect on how you feel about what is happening in your life. You might focus on external events, such as what you think about a book or a film, or focus on your inner life by exploring changes in mood or attitude. A **writer's notebook** also includes responses to experience. In this case, however, the emphasis is on sorting through what you are learning. Students often benefit from keeping a writer's notebook in which they record quotations, evaluate the strengths and weaknesses of a particular text, summarize the material, and jot down questions they would like to raise in class or pursue in an essay. In any case, students should feel free to write quickly without worrying about spelling, grammar, or organization.

Freewriting

When freewriting, writers put down on paper without stopping whatever occurs to them during a limited period of time—often no more than ten minutes or so. They do not worry about whether they are repeating themselves or getting off the track; they simply write to see what comes out.

In directed freewriting, writers begin with a general subject area and record whatever occurs to them during the time available. When asked to write about what he remembered about high school, Peter Geske wrote the following directed freewriting during five minutes of class time. This was the first step toward drafting the essay that appears later in this chapter, the final version of which appears in chapter **29**.

Write about high school? I can't believe this topic. Does he think we're all eighteen? I can hardly remember high school and what I remember isn't too good. That's why I didn't go to college right away. Now look at me. A good five years older than anyone in the class and stuck in a dead-end job. Working forty hours a week and borrowing money so that I can go back to school part time and write about some of the worst years in my life. All those <u>stupid cliques</u> and <u>teachers who were real losers. Rodriguez</u> <u>was o.k. At least he listened and didn't</u> <u>treat us like convicts. Maybe that's why I'm</u> <u>still interested in history. But forget the</u> rest of them. <u>Kleinberg had so little control that</u> <u>the kids were flashing knives right in front of</u> <u>him and he never said a thing. No wonder</u> <u>I'm lousy in math. And that zombie who taught</u> <u>chemistry. All she ever did was read from the</u> <u>book. She never even looked at us. Maybe she</u> <u>was afraid to see how many kids were strung</u> <u>out. I don't see how I would've made it except for</u> <u>football. Reynolds wouldn't let us get away</u> <u>with anything. A real tough guy but he really</u> <u>cared about us.</u>

As the color coding shows, this freewrite generated at least four possible writing topics about high school: cliques, unqualified teachers, the importance of football, and positive influences. Within a few minutes, this writer has discovered that he has more to say than can be addressed in a single essay.

Listing

One way to gather ideas about your writing topic is to make an informal list. Jot down any ideas that come to you while you are thinking about your subject. Do not worry if the ideas come without any kind of order, and do not worry about the form in which you write them down. Devote as much time as necessary to making your list—perhaps five minutes, perhaps an entire evening. The point is to collect as many ideas as you can.

Peter made the following list after he had decided to focus his essay on the quality of the education he received at his high school.

geometry with Kleinberg

sophomore English with Mrs. Sullivan

American history with Mr. Rodriguez

out-of-date books

a terrible library

out-of-control classes

failing chemistry

good grades in English and history

blow-off courses
    social problems
    sex education
    speech

partying throughout senior year

too many students in each class

useless computers

As you look through the list, you will find some ideas that are closely related and might be grouped together. For instance, items about school facilities can easily be grouped together, as can items concerning specific courses. Toward the end of his list, Peter began to establish some relationships by developing a sublisting of courses he found useless. Order and direction are beginning to emerge.

Questioning

There are two structured questioning strategies—journalists' questions and the pentad. The **journalists' questions** ask *Who? What? When? Where? Why?* and *How?* Using journalists' questions to explore the subject of high school education could lead you to think about *who* goes to public high school and *who* teaches there, *what* courses are offered, *when* education improved or deteriorated, *why* some classes get overcrowded, *where* funding comes from, and *how* education stimulates or *how* it fails.

The **pentad** considers the five dramatic aspects of a subject: the *act* (what happens), the *actor* (who does it), the *scene* (the time, place, and conditions under which the event occurred), the *agency* (the method or circumstances facilitating the act), and the *purpose* (the intent or reasons surrounding the act). This method differs from journalists' questions by suggesting relationships. For instance, relationships can be explored between failing chemistry (the act) and the actors, in this case the student and the teacher, or between the act and the scene, overcrowded classes and out-of-date equipment.

Applying perspectives

Sometimes it is helpful to consider a subject as static, dynamic, and relative. A **static perspective** would focus on what a high school education is. You might describe the standard curriculum and school year or use a specific school to provide an example. The **dynamic perspective** focuses on action and change. You might examine how your education changed you. The **relative perspective** focuses on systems and relationships. You could examine the relationship between a public and private high school education or between funding for public education and economic conditions in your area.

(2) Writers need to focus on specific material.

Exploring the subject will suggest not only productive strategies for development but also a direction and focus for your writing. Some ideas will seem worth pursuing; others will seem inappropriate. You will find yourself focusing and directing your ideas and moving from a general subject to a more specific one. When you compare the draft of Peter Geske's essay on high school education (page 193) and the final version of it (page 205), you will see how drafting and revising can sharpen a writer's focus.

Strategies for development, which are discussed in **27d** as ways to develop paragraphs, are natural thinking processes that are especially useful for shaping ideas about a subject.

a. *Narration*   What happened to me in high school? What is the story of my high school education?
b. *Process*   How do teachers teach? How do students spend their days?
c. *Cause and effect*   Why did I hate high school? Would I have done better in a different school district?
d. *Description*   What did a typical class look like? What was it like to be in study hall, the cafeteria, or the gym?
e. *Definition*   What is education? What is a good school?
f. *Classification and division*   How could I classify the students or teachers in my high school? What group did I belong to?
g. *Example*   What was a typical day like? Who was my best teacher and who was my worst?

h. *Comparison and contrast* How did my school compare with a rival school? What did my two best teachers have in common?

The following introductory sentence suggests a focus on comparison and contrast:

> When I think of my last two English teachers, I can see how a teacher who cares about students differs from someone who is bored by them.

This sentence suggests cause and effect:

> The poor quality of the high school I attended can be traced to a shrinking tax base and an administrative failure to hold the school accountable to state standards.

Essays frequently combine several of these strategies. The exact focus you finally choose will be determined by your purpose, your audience, and the time and space available.

28c A clearly stated thesis conveys your main idea.

If you have limited and focused your subject, you have gone a long way toward developing a controlling idea, or thesis.

(1) Essays usually include a thesis statement.

Your **thesis statement** contains a single idea, clearly focused and specifically stated, that grows out of your exploration of a subject. A thesis statement can be thought of as a central idea phrased in the form of an assertion that indicates what you claim to be true, interesting, or valuable about your subject. An explicitly stated thesis statement identifies the topic you are writing about, the approach you are taking, and in some cases the plan of development you are using. Note how the thesis statements below do all of these. The first is from an expressive essay:

> By the time that his children were growing up the great days of my father's life were over.
>
> —VIRGINIA WOOLF, "Leslie Stephen"

With this apparently simple statement, the author has established that the topic is her father and indicated that she will discuss both early accomplishments and later decline while focusing primarily on his life within the family.

> A child, in growing up, may meet and learn from three different kinds of disciplines.
>
> —JOHN HOLT, "Kinds of Discipline"

> Nothing better illustrates the low regard that the NCAA has often had for the rights of student-athletes than its random drug-testing policy.
>
> —ALLEN L. SACK, "Random Tests Abuse Dignity"

A clear, precise thesis statement will help unify your paper; it will guide many decisions about what details to keep and what to toss out. But it is important to allow your essay to remain flexible in the early stages. If you have information about your subject that is interesting but does not really help you make your point, including it in your early drafts might lead you to a better essay by indicating a more profitable focus. As you write, check your thesis statement frequently to see if you have drifted away from it. Do not hesitate to change your thesis, however, if you find a more productive path or one you would rather pursue.

Beware of vague qualifiers such as *interesting, important,* and *unusual*. In a thesis statement such as "My education has been very unusual," the vague word *unusual* may indicate that the idea itself is weak and that the writer needs to find a stronger subject. However, this kind of vague thesis may disguise an idea of real interest that simply needs to be made specific: "Our family grew closer after my parents decided to teach me at home." The following examples show ways to focus, clarify, and sharpen vague thesis statements.

Vague   I have trouble making decisions.

Better   Making decisions is difficult for me, especially when money is involved and most of all when such decisions affect other people.

Vague   Summer is an interesting season.

Better   Summer is the best season for losing weight.

Thesis statements appear most often in the introductory paragraph, although you can put them anywhere that suits your purpose—occasionally even in the conclusion. The advantage of putting the thesis statement in the first paragraph, however, is that your reader knows from the beginning what you are writing about and where the essay is going.

ESL   American readers are accustomed to finding a clearly stated thesis statement early in an essay. If you introduce your ideas more gradually—which is the custom in some cultures—you may confuse American readers. Stating your main idea early will help Americans understand what you write in English.

(2) **A main idea is necessary even when a thesis statement is not required.**

Some kinds of writing do not require a formulated thesis statement, but they do contain a main, or controlling, idea. Writing without a thesis statement is especially common when the main thrust of the development is narrative or descriptive. And business documents frequently do not require a thesis. Yet, even when your thesis is implied, your readers should be able to sense a clear direction and focus in your paper.

 CAUTION Many college teachers expect every essay to have a clear thesis statement.

28d Arranging ideas requires choosing an appropriate method.

Many writers need a working plan to direct their ideas and keep their writing on course. Some use informal written lists or formal topic or sentence outlines.

(1) Informal working plans

An informal working plan need be little more than an ordered list that grows out of a collection of ideas. Look at the informal working plan that Peter Geske made as he prepared to write on the quality of his high school education.

Before he started to write his first draft, Peter reexamined his freewriting (page 177) and his first list of ideas (page 178). He decided that he was right to focus on evaluating the quality of the education he had received—passing over other topics such as cliques and football. Reviewing the items on his list, he noticed that his concerns could be grouped into three categories: facilities and supplies, curriculum, and teachers. He then formulated a tentative thesis and made an ordered list to chart the direction of his essay:

THESIS: Academic facilities and standards were so low at my high school that I learned very little while I was there and became discouraged about school.

1. Physical description of the school
2. Textbooks, computers, and other supplies
3. Class size
4. Courses that were a waste of time
5. Bad teachers
6. A few bright spots

When you make such a list, some ideas may drop out, and others may occur as you draft. But you have the beginning of a plan that can guide you.

(2) Outlines

Some writers can develop a plan early in their writing process, turning a working list into a formal outline. Others discover that they need to rethink their original plan after they have actually done some writing. But whether it is written before the first draft or after it, a formal outline is often helpful when analyzing a draft and preparing to revise it. For example, if an outline shows only one subgroup under a heading, that section of the draft might need rethinking.

A structured outline uses indention and numbers to indicate various levels of subordination. The main points form the major headings, and the supporting ideas for each point form the subheadings. An outline of Peter's paper might begin as follows:

```
THESIS: Academic facilities and standards were
so low at my high school that I learned very
little while I was there and became
discouraged about school.
  I. Physical description of the school
     A. The building itself
        1. Run-down
           a. Exterior
           b. Interior
        2. Overcrowded
           a. Hallways
           b. Classrooms
     B. Facilities
        1. Terrible library
           a. Few books
           b. Useless computers
        2. Inadequate labs
           a. Chemistry lab
           b. Biology lab
 II. Courses I took
```

The types of outlines most commonly used are the topic outline and the sentence outline. The headings in a **topic outline** are expressed in grammatically parallel phrases, while a **sentence outline** presents headings in complete sentences. Here is how a sentence outline for Peter's essay might begin:

```
THESIS: Academic facilities and standards were
so low at my high school that I learned very
```

little while I was there and became
discouraged about school.

I. The school building hindered learning.
  A. The building was an eyesore.
    1. It was run-down and covered with
      graffiti.
    2. It was so overcrowded that it
      couldn't be kept clean.
  B. Facilities were inadequate.
    1. The library was terrible.
    2. Laboratories lacked equipment.

The headings in a sentence outline can often serve as topic sentences when you draft.

When drafting an essay, do not let your outline become a straitjacket. If new ideas occur to you as you are writing, put them down as they occur. You may find that these ideas enrich your paper even though they did not appear in the outline.

28e Your first draft will not be your final draft.

Put your ideas on paper quickly. Matters such as spelling, punctuation, and usage are not as important in the first draft as they are in the final draft. Your first draft may be sloppy and tentative, but it gives you something you can improve on in another draft. If you are stuck, referring to your plan can help.

You may prefer to write chunks of your essay without worrying about the final order of those chunks. For example, if you have trouble writing the introduction, start with a supporting idea you feel sure of, and write until you reach a stopping point. You can then move on to another part that will be easy to write. What is important is to begin writing, to write as quickly as you can, and to save your early work so that you can refer to it during revision.

(1) Introductions must be effective.

An effective introduction arouses the reader's interest and indicates the subject and tone of the essay. For complex essays, a good introduction charts the direction the essay will follow so readers know what to expect.

The introduction often contains the thesis statement. (See **28d**.) Introductions have no set length; they can be as brief as a couple of sentences or as long as a couple of paragraphs. Experienced writers may compose them at any time during the writing process—even after they have drafted the rest of the paper.

You can arouse the interest of your audience by writing introductions in a number of ways.

a. Start with an interesting fact or unusual detail that catches the reader's attention.

> A new Census Bureau report predicts that there will be 383 million Americans in the year 2050. That's 128 million more than there are now, and 83 million more than the bureau was predicting just four years ago, when it appeared that the U.S. population would peak and stabilize at around 300 million.   —MICHAEL KINSLEY, "Gatecrashers"

b. Use an intriguing statement to lure the reader into continuing.

> After smiling brilliantly for nearly four decades, I now find myself trying to quit. Or, at the very least, seeking to lower the wattage a bit.
>
> —AMY CUNNINGHAM, "Why Women Smile"

c. Engage the reader's attention with an anecdote.

As I walked out the street entrance to my newly rented apartment, a guy in maroon high-tops and a skateboard haircut approached, making kissing noises and saying, "Hi, gorgeous." Three weeks earlier, I would have assessed the degree of malice and made ready to run or tell him to bug off, depending. But now, instead, I smiled, and so did my four-year-old daughter, because after dozens of similar encounters I understood he didn't mean me but *her*.

—BARBARA KINGSOLVER, "Somebody's Baby"

d. Begin with a question your essay will answer.

In a series of futuristic commercials, AT&T paints a liberating picture of your not-too-distant life, when the information superhighway will be an instrument of personal freedom and a servant to your worldly needs and desires. But is the future of cyberspace really so elegant, so convenient? Or does it represent a serious threat to your privacy and your freedom?   —ERIK NESS, "BigBrother@cyberspace"

e. Start with an appropriate quotation.

When the Reverend Jerry Falwell learned that the Supreme Court had reversed his $200,000 judgment against *Hustler* magazine for the emotional distress he had suffered from an outrageous parody, his response was typical of those who seek to censor speech: "Just as no person may scream 'Fire!' in a crowded theater when there is no fire, and find cover under the First Amendment, likewise, no sleazy merchant like Larry Flynt should be able to use the First Amendment as an excuse for maliciously and dishonestly attacking public figures, as he has so often done."

—ALAN DERSHOWITZ, "Shouting 'Fire!'"

f. Open with an illustration.

Libby Smith knows what it is like to be a victim of gay bashing. First, there were the harassing telephone calls to her home. Then, one evening last March as she went to get her book bag out of a locker at the University of Wisconsin at Eau Claire, she was attacked by two men.

—MARY CRYSTAL CAGE, "Gay Bashing on Campus"

g. Begin with general information about the subject or show how you came to choose it.

Anyone new to the experience of owning a lawn, as I am, soon figures out that there is more at stake here than a patch of grass. A lawn immediately establishes a certain relationship with one's neighbors and, by extension, the larger American landscape. Mowing the lawn, I realized the first time I gazed into my neighbor's yard and imagined him gazing back into mine, is a civic responsibility.

—MICHAEL POLLAN, "Why Mow? The Case Against Lawns"

(2) An essay needs an effective conclusion.

The conclusion often summarizes the main points and may also encourage the reader to action or further thought on the subject. An essay should not merely stop; it should finish. Some suggestions follow.

a. Conclude by rephrasing the thesis.

Such considerations make it clear that it's time for schools to choose between real amateurism and real professionalism. They can't have a little of both. From now on, in college sports, it's got to be poetry or pros.

—LOUIS BARBASH, "Clean Up or Pay Up"

b. Direct the reader's attention to larger issues.

My antibody status does not matter to you. Certainly it matters—with absolute enormity—to me. But what I'd like you to remember is the blood on the subway, the click of the refrigerator door, the woman in black so elegant and uneasy, First Avenue at gritty, gorgeous dusk, the brilliance of that bad art in the examining room, the pores of the doctor's face—all of them declaring, by their very existence: As long and as well as you can, live, live.

—DAVID GROFF, "Taking the Test"

c. Encourage your readers to change their attitudes or to alter their actions.

Our medical care system is in trouble and getting worse. While the experts try to figure out how to achieve utopian goals at affordable prices, let's do something practical about the suffering on our doorsteps. Primary care is the most affordable safety net we can offer our citizens. By all means, let's continue the debate about universal, comprehensive insurance to cover all medical costs, but, in the meantime, let's provide primary health care to all uninsured Americans—now!

—GORDON T. MOORE,
"Caring for the Uninsured and Underinsured"

d. Conclude with a summary of the main points covered.

All our giving carries with it messages about ourselves, our feelings about those to whom we give, how we see them as people and how we phrase the ties of relationship. Christmas giving, in which love and hope and trust play such an intrinsic part, can be an annual way of telling our children that we think of each of them as a person, as we also hope they will come to think of us.

—MARGARET MEAD and RHODA METRAUX,
"The Gift of Autonomy"

e. Clinch or stress the importance of the central idea by referring in some way to the introduction.

Introduction I read *The National Enquirer* when I want to feel exhilarated about life's possibilities. It tells me of a world where miracles still occur. In the world of *The National Enquirer,* UFOs flash over the Bermuda Triangle, cancer cures are imminent, ancient film stars at last find love that is for keeps. Reached on The Other Side by spiritualists, Clark Gable urges America to keep its chin up. Of all possible worlds, I like the world of *The National Enquirer* best. . . .

Conclusion   So I whoop with glee when a new edition of *The National Enquirer* hits the newsstands and step into the world where Gable can cheer me up from The Other Side.

—RUSSELL BAKER, "Magazine Rack"

(3) A good title fits the subject and tone of an essay.

The title is the reader's first impression and, like the introduction, should fit the subject and tone of the paper. Sometimes the title announces the subject simply and directly: "Grant and Lee" or "Civil Disobedience." Often a title uses alliteration to reflect the writer's humorous approach, as in "A Pepsi Person in the Perrier Generation," or a twisted cliché, as in "The Right Wrong Stuff." A good title may also arouse the reader's curiosity by asking a question, as does "Who Killed the Bog Men of Denmark? And Why?"

28f   Studying a first draft helps writers to see how it can be improved.

As you read the following draft, remember that it is only the first draft. Two later drafts—including the final draft—are reprinted in chapter **29**.

Peter Geske
English 101

School Daze

In today's society education is becoming
more and more important. Nobody ever explained
this to my teachers though. High school was
the worst. The teachers at my school were
losers and didn't know what they were doing.
The building was falling apart also and their
was alot of violence in it.

Central was built about a hundred years
ago and that's probably the last time it got a
coat of paint. The walls were cracked and we
used to flick off loose paint chips all the
time. On the outside it looked like a prison.
It used to have big windows but they got
bricked up to save energy. There was also
graffiti all over the place. No trees anywhere
but plenty of broken cement and crumbling
asphalt.

The school had at least twice as many
kids squeezed into it than it was designed
for. Even with plenty of people cutting to
party, every classroom was crowded. Sometimes
at the beginning of the year there wasn't even
a desk for everyone. Computers were a joke. We
had about three for two thousand students and
they were these old machines that you couldn't
run good games or programs on.

Science equipment was also bad. I really
hated my chemistry teacher but maybe she
wouldn't of been so bad if we had a decent
lab.

The teachers were the worst. They couldn't control their classes and everybody took advantage of that. Mr. Kleinberg was my geometry teacher. He wore these green socks everyday and I swear it was always the same pair. When you got close to him it was really gross he smelled so bad. Kids never paid attention to him and he would usually start screaming at one person while knives were being pulled in another corner and other kids were strung out on drugs. My chemistry teacher was just as bad. Her name was Mrs. Fiorelli and she was real skinny. All she would ever do was read from the text book. Her class was out of control also and when somebody would try to ask a question she would just keep on reading. She gave these killer tests though and I ended up flunking her course not that I need to know chemistry for anything.

It wasn't all bad though. Mr. Rodriguez taught American history and he was cool. My English teacher sophomore year was also ok.

This is just my opinion. There might be other kids who had a good experience at Central and maybe someday I'll laugh about it.

⚠ **CAUTION** The preceding paper is an early draft. Do not consider it a model essay. It is reprinted here so that you can see how it improved through revision. For later versions of this paper, see pages 202–5 and 205–7.

Here are some of the comments Peter received when he distributed this draft in a writing group.

Good paper! I think you should say more about science equipment though because that paragraph is so short. Also you mention your chemistry teacher in that paragraph and then talk about her again later on. Maybe you should keep the chemistry stuff together.

The only thing that bothered me about your paper is how you mention teachers first and then the building in your first paragraph, but then you talk about the building first in your paper. Why not be consistent?

I loved your paper, except for the long paragraph about teachers. You make the important point that your math and chemistry teachers were poor, but when you pick on their personal appearance it makes you sound sarcastic. Also, I think you should add a thesis statement to the end of paragraph 1.

I was surprised by how angry you sound in this paper because you always seem so laid back in class. Does this paper sound the way you want it to sound? And if you really are angry, why back off in your conclusion? The last paragraph doesn't work for me because it sounds like you're apologizing for writing the paper.

Before revising this draft, Peter had to weigh these comments and decide for himself which were the most useful.

Chapter 29

Revising and Editing Essays

To **revise** means to take a fresh look at your draft—re-thinking what you have written and what you still need to write. To **edit** means to polish a piece of writing by making word choice more precise (**14a**), prose more concise (chapter **15**), and sentence structure more effective (chapters **11** and **12**), in addition to eliminating any errors in grammar, punctuation, and mechanics. Inexperienced writers sometimes think they are revising when they are really editing. You need to be willing to rearrange paragraphs and make significant cuts and additions as you revise.

29a Your tone reveals your attitude.

Tone reflects your attitude toward your subject and must be appropriate to your purpose, audience, and occasion. When Peter Geske revised the draft essay reprinted in chapter **28** (pages 193–94), he decided to change his tone after one of his readers commented that he sounded sarcastic. Although sounding sarcastic might be appropriate in some rhetorical situations, Peter felt that he sounded harsher than he intended.

29b Revision is essential to writing well.

In one way or another you revise throughout the writing process. Nevertheless, experienced writers usually revise after they have completed a draft—no matter how much they may have revised while planning and drafting. They not only revise and develop paragraphs (chapter 27), they review the draft *as a whole*. Writers usually benefit from setting drafts aside for a time so that later they can see their work more objectively. Whenever possible, plan your writing process so that you can put a draft aside, at least overnight, and then see it later with fresh eyes.

(1) Everything benefits from reconsideration.

When you review your essay, ask yourself if the point of your essay comes through clearly and if you ever digress from it. Now is the time to eliminate side trips. It is also wise to make sure that you develop a point rather than simply repeat the same thing in different words—or, as sometimes happens, contradict yourself by saying two very different things.

Revising also demands reconsidering your rhetorical situation (page 173). Have you provided details that will interest your audience? Is your tone (29a) appropriate for this occasion?

Examine your paragraphs to make sure that they are unified, coherent, and well developed (chapter 27). Assess whether you need to rearrange any, and whether your transitions are effective. See 27b(4).)

! **CAUTION** When you move paragraphs, check to see if you need to write new transitions.

(2) What is not on the page can be even more important than what is there.

One of the most challenging tasks in revision is to look for what you have left out. No matter how good a draft looks, ask yourself if something is missing.

Inexperienced writers sometimes end an essay prematurely because they cannot think of anything else to say. One way to get past this block is to use such strategies as questioning (page 179), listing (pages 178–79), and applying perspectives (pages 179–80). Another way is to share your work with other readers and ask them to let you know if there is anything they find confusing or want to know more about.

Checklist for Revising Essays
- Is the purpose of the work clear (28a(1))? Does the work stick to its purpose?
- Does the essay address the appropriate audience (28a(2))?
- Is the tone (29a) appropriate for the purpose, audience, and occasion?
- Is the subject focused (28c(2))?
- Does the essay make a clear point (28d)? Is this point well supported? Do the relationships expressed in the essay clearly relate to this point?
- Is each paragraph unified and coherent (27a–b)? Are the paragraphs arranged in a logical, effective order (28c)? (See the paragraph checklist on page 171.)
- Does the essay follow an effective method or combination of methods of development (28e)?
- Is the introduction effective (28f(1))?
- Is the conclusion appropriate (28f(2))?

29c   Editing improves your writing.

After you are satisfied with the revised structure and content, edit individual sentences for clarity, effectiveness, and variety. (See chapters 8 through 16.) Consider combining choppy sentences and rework overly complicated ones. Eliminate any needless shifts in grammatical structures, tone, style, or point of view.

Make sure the words you have used are the best choices. If any leap out as more formal or informal than your language as a whole, replace them. If you have experimented with words new to your vocabulary, make sure that you have used them accurately.

 Check whether your punctuation is correct and whether you have followed standard conventions for mechanics. Use a spell checker (**22a**) again because new errors may have been introduced. Remember that such programs are never foolproof. Double-check that you are correctly using words like *there* and *their,* which might be the wrong words in a specific context.

Checklist for Editing   ☑

Sentences

- Are ideas related effectively through subordination and coordination (**9**)?
- Are all sentences unified (**8**)?
- Do any sentences contain misplaced parts or dangling modifiers (**5**)?
- Is there any faulty parallelism (**10**)?
- Are there any needless shifts in grammatical structures, in tone or style, or in viewpoint (**8e**)?
- Are ideas given appropriate emphasis (**11**)?
- Are the sentences varied in length and in type (**12**)?
- Are there any fragments (**2**)? Are there any comma splices or fused sentences (**3**)?
- Do all verbs agree with their subjects (**7a**)? Do all pronouns agree with their antecedents (**6a**)?
- Are all verb forms appropriate (**7**)?

continued

continued from previous page

✓

Diction

- Are any words overused, imprecise, or vague (**14c, 14a**)? Are all words idiomatic (**14b**)?
- Have all **unnecessary** words and phrases been eliminated (**15**)? Have any **necessary** words been left out (**16**)?
- Is the vocabulary appropriate for the audience, purpose, and occasion (**13, 28a**)?
- Have all technical words that might be unfamiliar to the audience been eliminated or defined (**13c(1)**)?

Punctuation and mechanics

- Is all punctuation correct? Are any marks missing?
- Are all words spelled correctly (**22**)?
- Is capitalization correct (**23**)?
- Are titles identified by quotation marks (**20c**) or italics (**24a**)?
- Are abbreviations (**25**) appropriate and correct?

29d Proofreading can help make your papers error-free.

Once you have revised and edited your essay, carefully format it (chapter **26**). Then proofread it, making sure that the product you submit is error-free.

Be alert for minor errors—a misspelled word, a missing comma, a book title not italicized. Also watch for two common errors: accidentally leaving a word out or writing the same word twice.

It is wise to proofread more than once, and many writers benefit from reading aloud as they proofread. An extra pair of eyes can also be helpful, so you might ask a friend to help you. However, this check should be in addition to your own.

Use the Proofreading Checklist in chapter **26**, page 152, to check your paper.

29e   You can benefit from studying how other writers work.

After Peter Geske had time to reconsider the first draft of his essay and to think about the responses he received from readers, he made a number of changes. Here is his second draft.

Peter Geske   *I need to add date and teacher's name*

English 100

School Daze

In ~~today's~~ society education is becoming more and more important. Nobody ever explained this to my teachers though. High school was the worst. The teachers at my school were losers and didn't know what they were doing. The building was falling apart also and their was alot of violence in it. Standards and facilities were so low that I learned very little and became discouraged about school.

I ne a new intro

Central was built about a hundred years ago and ~~that's probably the last time it got a coat of paint~~. The walls were cracked and we used to flick off loose paint chips all the time. ~~On the outside~~ it looked like a prison. It used to have big windows but they got bricked up to save energy. There was also graffiti all over the place. *there were* No trees anywhere *there was* but plenty of broken cement and crumbling asphalt. *Inside,*

The school had at least twice as many kids squeezed into it than it was designed for. ~~Even with plenty of people cutting to party~~, every classroom was *over* crowded, *because* Sometimes at the beginning of the year there wasn't even a desk for everyone. Computers were a joke. We had about three for two thousand students and they were these old machines that you couldn't run good games or programs on.

Science equipment was also bad. I really hated my chemistry teacher but maybe she would not have been so bad if we had a decent lab.

say more

move to p. 2

Many
~~The~~ teachers ~~were the worst. They~~
couldn't control their classes and everybody
took advantage of that. Mr. Kleinberg was my
geometry teacher. ~~He wore these green socks~~
~~everyday and I swear it was always the same~~
~~pair. When you got close to him it was really~~
~~gross he smelled so bad.~~ Kids never paid
attention to him, and he would usually start
screaming at one person while knives were
being pulled in another corner and other kids
were strung out on drugs. My chemistry teacher,
~~was just as bad.~~ Her name was Mrs. Fiorelli,
never did anything except
and ~~she was~~ real skinny. ~~All~~ she would ever do
was read from the textbook. ~~Her class was out~~
w
~~of control also~~ and ∧hen somebody would try to
ask a question she would just keep on reading.
But
∧She gave these killer tests ~~though~~ and I ended
failing   because I learned so little in it.
up ~~flunking~~ her course ~~not that I need to know~~
~~chemistry for anything.~~

move up
and
link
with
line
from p!

It wasn't all bad though. Mr. Rodriguez
taught American history and he was cool. My
English teacher senior year was also ok.

say more
about my
good teachers
earlier on
so I don't
sound like
I'm whining

o apologetic.
that's the
ost important
ing I still
nt to say?

~~This is just my opinion. There might be~~
~~other kids who had a good experience at~~
~~Central and maybe someday I'll laugh about~~ it.

 29f The final draft reflects the care the
writer took.

Peter Geske
English 101, Section 2
Professor Henrikson
12 March 1997

School Daze

Picture a run-down building that looks
like a warehouse and feels like a prison. You
approach through a sea of broken cement and
crumbling asphalt. There are no trees near the
building, although a few tufts of uncut grass
struggle to grow in a yard of baked-down dirt.
Many of the windows have been bricked in, and
the ground floor is covered with graffiti.
Inside, inadequate lights reveal old tiles,
broken lockers, and flaking paint. The school
is empty because it is only seven o'clock.
Within an hour, however, it will be
overcrowded with students who are running wild
and teachers who don't know how to respond.
You have entered Central High School, the
institution where my education suffered
because of poor facilities and low standards.

Built a hundred years ago, Central had a
good reputation when the neighborhoods around
it were prosperous. Now it is the worst high

school in the city, and the school board seems to have given up on it. The more run-down it gets, the worse the morale gets, and as morale gets lower, the school goes further downhill.

After the condition of the building itself, the most obvious problem at Central is the overcrowding. Almost every classroom is filled to capacity. You can't even count on finding a desk--especially at the beginning of the school year when most people still show up for school. The situation gets a little better by Columbus Day. That's when kids have figured out that one of the advantages of Central is that you can skip school without anybody caring.

Our textbooks were usually ten years out of date. And if more expensive supplies ever made it through the door, they didn't last long. We had only three or four computers for two thousand students, and they were old machines that couldn't run many programs. In the chemistry lab, there was never enough equipment for individual experiments even when we were teamed with a lab partner. We were put in groups of four. What usually happened is that one person would do the work, and the rest of the team would coast on those results.

My chemistry teacher, Mrs. Fiorelli, is a good example of another problem at Central: bad teachers. All she would ever do is read from the textbook. When somebody would try to ask a question, she would just keep reading. Then she would turn around every few weeks and give killer tests. It was like she hated us and wanted to punish us when she couldn't ignore us any longer.

I had many other teachers who were just as bad. Mr. Kleinberg, my geometry teacher, couldn't control the class. When we got out of control--which was every day--he would start screaming at one person (usually a girl who wasn't doing anything) while other students were flashing knives and plenty were nodding off from drugs. Would you be surprised to hear that I now have a problem with both science and math?

To be fair, I did have some good teachers at Central: Mr. Rodriguez, who taught American history; Mrs. Sullivan, who taught English composition; and Bob "The Ram" Reynolds, who coached the football team and taught Lifetime Fitness. But they were the exceptions. For every good teacher, there were at least three you wouldn't want to trust your children with.

As I look back at the four years I spent at Central, I am amazed that I learned anything at all. By the time I reached senior year, all I wanted to do was party. I'd lost interest in school--and that's one of the reasons why I've been working in a warehouse the past five years instead of having gone straight on to college. Now that I am here, I sure wish I were better prepared.

Chapter 30 | Writing under Pressure

It is not always possible to engage in a writing process that stretches over a period of weeks or even days. The key to succeeding in such situations is to use whatever time you have as efficiently as possible.

30a Preparing ahead of time helps.

If a specific task must be completed in a relatively short time, invest a few minutes in making a schedule. Give yourself time to study the assignment, plan your response, draft your essay, revise, and proofread.

30b There are ways to overcome writer's block.

If you fear that pressure will lead to writer's block, several strategies can help reduce the risk.

Checklist for Overcoming Writer's Block
- Wear comfortable clothes.
- Use writing implements that work best for you.

continued

continued from previous page

✓

- Keep near you anything you are likely to need. (Even if you do not use your dictionary, knowing that it is close at hand can help you avoid unnecessary stress.)
- Position yourself carefully. (If you are in a classroom with open seating, choose a seat that suits you. Some people feel safest when tucked in a corner; others like to sit in the front row so they can shut out the rest of the class.)

Follow an abridged version of your regular writing process. You can revise even when writing a fifty-minute in-class essay. By planning to save ten minutes at the end for eliminating irrelevant points, clarifying others, and correcting errors, you can draft without becoming obsessed with making mistakes.

30c Essay tests require special preparation.

(1) Read instructions and questions carefully.

When writing in-class essays and essay exams, read the instructions carefully and note specific directions. If you are responsible for more than one question, note how many points each is worth. Pace yourself with this fact in mind.

Be alert for words like *compare, define,* and *cause* that identify your task. Other terms like *discuss* or *explain* are less specific, but they may be linked to words like *similar* or *differ* (which signal a comparison or contrast) or *why* (which signals the need to identify causes). Words like *think, defend,* and *opinion* signal that you are expected to frame a thesis (**28d**) and support it.

(2) Decide how to organize your response.

You should always be able to find time to draft a working plan (28e). Identify the thesis, then list the most important points you plan to cover. When you have finished the list, you can review it: Delete any points that seem irrelevant or not important enough to discuss. Then number the remaining points in a logical sequence.

The language of an assignment sometimes tells you how to organize it. For example:

> Consider the concept of the unconscious as defined by Freud and by Jung. On what points did they agree? How did they disagree?

The reference to two psychoanalysts, coupled with words like *agree* and *disagree,* indicates that your task is to compare and contrast. You could organize your response by first discussing Freud's ideas and then Jung's. Or you could begin by establishing similarities and then move on to differences. Devoting at least a few minutes to planning your organization can help you demonstrate what you know.

(3) State main points clearly.

Make your main points stand out from the rest of the essay by identifying them somehow. For instance, you can use transitional expressions such as *first, second, third;* you can underline each main point; or you can create headings to guide the reader. Use your conclusion to summarize your main points.

(4) Stick to the question.

Sometimes you may know more about a related question than the one assigned. Do not wander from the question being asked to answer the question you wish had been asked.

(5) Revise and proofread.

Make whatever deletions and corrections you think are necessary. If time allows, think about what is not on the page by asking yourself if there is anything you have left out that you can still manage to include. Make sure that your instructor will be able to read your changes. Clarify any illegible scribbles. Finally, check spelling, punctuation, and sentence structure (**29d**).

Chapter 31

Reading and Thinking Critically

To read and think critically means to distinguish between ideas that are credible and those that are less so, to understand that different writers drawing on the same evidence can reach significantly different conclusions. Instead of routinely agreeing with the writer who seems to reinforce reassuringly familiar beliefs, critical readers identify which ideas make more sense than others and determine the extent to which those ideas are reliable and useful. These skills are among the most valuable you can acquire.

31a Previewing can help you read critically.

To **preview** means to orient yourself to a text by assessing what you are likely to learn from it. When you understand what a task demands, you are more likely to complete it successfully.

Checklist for Previewing a Text
- What do I already know about this subject? Can I establish some immediate connections with this text?
- Do I have any feelings about this subject that could interfere with my ability to comprehend how it is treated?

---

continued

continued from previous page

✓

- If this author is familiar to me, can I trust what he or she writes? If this author is unfamiliar to me, is there any information that will help me assess his or her credibility? (See **31d**.)
- What can I learn from the title? The subtitle? If there are subheadings, what do they reveal about the organization?
- Does this book include a table of contents or an index? Does this article include an abstract? Are there graphs, figures, or other visual aids?
- Is there a bibliography that will indicate how extensive and current the research is?
- Does the introduction or conclusion reveal the thesis?
- Has the author included a summary near the conclusion or at the end of any of the subsections?

You can also benefit from scanning. The central idea of a paragraph often appears in the first or last sentence. By reading these, you can get a sense of a work's content and organization. You can also scan for key phrases. The phrase *in other words,* for example, signals that a writer is about to paraphrase a point just made—probably because it is important.

31b Critical readers distinguish between fact and opinion.

Facts—reliable pieces of information that can be verified through independent sources—are valued because they are believed to be true. **Opinions** are assertions that may or may not be based on facts. Accepting opinions unsupported by facts can lead you to faulty conclusions.

To distinguish between fact and opinion, ask yourself questions: Can it be proved? Can it be challenged? How often is the same result achieved? If a statement can consistently be proved true, then it is a fact. If it can be disputed, then it is an opinion.

31c   Critical readers look for evidence.

Critical readers expect writers to support their claims with facts and other data. When a work makes a specific point, ask yourself if the writer has provided evidence that is accurate, representative, and sufficient. Recognize, however, that a writer may provide data that are accurate but unreliable. An argument about the death penalty that draws all its information from material distributed by a police association is unlikely to represent the full range of data available on this topic.

Similarly, examine polls and other statistics carefully. How recent is the information, and how was it gathered? Statistics can be manipulated. Do not accept them uncritically.

31d   Readers must evaluate a writer's credibility.

Critical readers determine if an author is well-informed and fair-minded.

Checklist for Evaluating Credibility
- Does the writer reveal how evidence was obtained?
- Does the writer recognize that other points of view may be legitimate?

continued

continued from previous page

- Does the writer use sarcasm or make personal attacks? ✓
- Does the writer reach a conclusion that is in proportion to the amount of evidence provided?
- Does the writer have credentials that invest the work with authority?

Question any writer who seems entirely one-sided, but also question any writer who seems overly anxious to please.

31e Critical thinkers understand inductive reasoning.

When writers use **inductive reasoning**, they begin with a number of facts or observations and use them to draw a general conclusion. This use of evidence to form a generalization is called an **inductive leap**, and the leap should be in proportion to the amount of evidence gathered.

Because it involves leaping from evidence to interpreting it, inductive reasoning can help writers reach probable, believable conclusions, but not some absolute truth that will endure forever. Making a small leap from evidence to a conclusion that seems probable is not the same as jumping to a sweeping conclusion that could easily be challenged.

When used in persuasive writing (chapter 32), inductive reasoning often employs examples. In the following inductively organized paragraph, a number of examples support the last sentence.

In Chicago last month, a nine-year-old boy died of an asthma attack while waiting for emergency aid. After their ambulance was pelted by rocks in an earlier incident, city paramedics wouldn't risk entering the Dearborn Homes project [where the boy lived] without a police escort. In Atlanta, residents of the Bankhead Courts project had their mail service suspended for two days last month after a postman nearly lost his life in the cross fire of a gun battle. Mail carriers wouldn't resume service until police accompanied them on their rounds. This is the day-to-day reality of life now in America's urban ghettos. Their residents, under siege by what are essentially organized drug terrorists, deserve the benefit of an unapologetic assault on drug-driven crime.

—"Hot Towns," *Wall Street Journal*

31f Critical thinkers understand deductive reasoning.

When writers use **deductive reasoning**, they begin with generalizations (premises) and apply them to a specific instance to draw a conclusion. This argument can be expressed in a structure called a **syllogism**.

Major Premise   All soldiers must complete basic training.

Minor Premise   Martha is a soldier.

Conclusion   Martha must complete basic training.

Sometimes premises are not stated.

Martha has enlisted in the army, so she must complete basic training.

In this sentence, the unstated premise is that all soldiers must complete basic training. A syllogism with an unstated premise can be very effective, but it should be examined with care since the omitted statement may be inaccurate. "Samuel is from Louisiana, so he must like Cajun food" contains the unstated premise that "Everyone from Louisiana likes Cajun food." This premise is unacceptable because there is no reason to assume that everyone from a particular region shares the same taste in food.

The following deductively organized paragraph, from an argument on the welfare of children, draws on the premise stated in the first sentence.

> America cannot afford to waste resources by failing to prevent and curb the national human deficit, which cripples our children's welfare today and costs billions in later remedial and custodial dollars. Each dollar we invest in preventive health care for mothers and children saves more than $3 later. Every dollar put into quality preschool education like Head Start saves $4.75 later. It costs more than twice as much to place a child in foster care as to provide family preservation services. The question is not whether we can afford to invest in every child; it is whether we can afford not to. At a time when future demographic trends guarantee a shortage of young adults who will be workers, soldiers, leaders, and parents, America cannot afford to waste a single child. With unprecedented economic competition from abroad and changing patterns of production at home that demand higher basic educational skills, America cannot wait another minute to do whatever is needed to ensure that today's and tomorrow's workers are well prepared rather than useless and alienated—whatever their color.
>
> —MARIAN WRIGHT EDELMAN, *The Measure of Our Success*

31g The Toulmin method is an alternative approach to reasoning.

Another way of using logic is through the method devised by Stephen Toulmin in *The Uses of Argument*. His approach sees argument as the progression from accepted facts or evidence (**data**) to a conclusion (**claim**) by way of a statement (**warrant**) that establishes a reasonable relationship between the two. For example, in the argument,

> Since soldiers are required to complete basic training, and since Martha is a soldier, Martha must complete basic training,

the claim is that Martha must complete basic training, and the data consists of the fact she is a soldier. The warrant, that soldiers are required to complete basic training, ties the two statements together. The warrant is often implied in arguments and, like the unstated premise in the syllogism, needs careful examination to be acceptable.

31h Critical thinkers recognize logical fallacies.

Fallacies are lapses in logic. They can be the result of poor thinking, but they can also be a deliberate attempt to manipulate. Here are some of the major fallacies.

(1) **Ad hominem:** A personal attack on an opponent that draws attention away from the issues under consideration.

   Faulty He is unfit to be governor because he drank too much when he was a college student.

(2) **Bandwagon:** An argument saying, in effect, "Everyone's doing or thinking this, so you should too."

   Faulty Everyone else is cheating, so why shouldn't you?

(3) **False analogy:** The assumption that because two things are alike in some ways, they must be alike in other ways.

   Faulty Since the books are about the same length and cover the same material, one is probably as good as the other.

(4) **False cause:** The assumption that because one event follows another, the first is the cause of the second.

Faulty The new tax assessor took office last January, and crime in the streets has already increased 25 percent.

(5) **False dilemma:** Stating that only two alternatives exist when in fact there are more than two.

Faulty We have only two choices: to build more nuclear power plants or to be dependent on foreign oil.

(6) **Hasty generalization:** A generalization based on too little evidence or on exceptional or biased evidence.

Faulty Ellen is a poor student because she failed her quiz.

(7) **Non sequitur:** A conclusion that does not follow from the premises.

Faulty Billy Joe is honest; therefore, he will get a good job.

(8) **Oversimplification:** A statement that leaves out relevant considerations to imply that there is a single cause or solution for a complex problem.

Faulty We can eliminate hunger by growing more food.

(9) **Red herring:** Dodging the real issue by drawing attention to an irrelevant issue.

Faulty Why worry about overcrowded schools when we ought to be trying to attract a professional hockey franchise?

Chapter 32

Writing Arguments

When you write an argument, you should understand the importance of arguing ethically and treating your opponents with respect. Argument is a way to discover truth and negotiate differences, not to ridicule people with whom you disagree.

32a Arguments have different purposes.

When writing an argument, your purpose may be to pursue the truth until you have formed an opinion that seems reasonable. It may be to convince readers that your position has merit. If there is little likelihood that you can convince an audience to change a strongly held opinion, you could be achieving a great deal by simply convincing them that your position deserves to be taken seriously. Or you might seek to persuade your audience to undertake a specific action. Just as important, your purpose could be to establish a consensus that brings people with differing views together.

32b Argument assumes differing views.

If most people already share the same opinion, then there is little point in writing an argument espousing this view.

Behind any effective argument is a question that can generate more than one reasonable answer. If you ask "Is

there poverty in our country?" almost anyone will agree
that there is. But if you ask "Why is there poverty in our
country?" or "What can we do to eliminate poverty?" you
will hear very different answers.

> **Checklist for Evaluating a Subject**
> - Is there more than one possible response? Would anyone
>   be likely to disagree with me?
> - Do I know enough about this subject? Can I find out
>   what I need to know?
> - Have I narrowed the subject so that I can do justice to
>   it in the space I have available?
> - Do I have a purpose in writing about this subject?
> - Are the subject and purpose appropriate for my audi-
>   ence?

32c   Argument requires development.

You should have reasons to support your conclusion and
evidence to support these reasons. In addition, you should
consider reasons why other people might disagree with
you.

(1) Effective arguments are well-supported.

Although it is possible to base your case on a single reason,
doing so is risky. When you show that you have more than
one reason for believing as you do, you increase the likelihood that your audience will find merit in your case.

When exploring your subject, make a list of the reasons
that have led to your belief without trying to edit them.
When you are ready to begin drafting, think critically
about the reasons on your list. Some may need to be eliminated because you would have trouble supporting them
or because they seem trivial compared with the others.

(2) Effective arguments respond to diverse views.

In addition, you should list reasons why people might disagree with you. Good arguments introduce reasons why others believe differently and then show why you do not find these reasons convincing.

Issues are often controversial precisely because good arguments can be made by different sides. When you find yourself agreeing with a point raised on another side of the issue, you can benefit by openly conceding that you agree with opponents on a specific point.

ESL   Although it is considered rude in some cultures to disagree openly with authority or to state your own views frankly, American readers are accustomed to such directness. Write with these expectations in mind.

32d   Different kinds of appeal are often necessary.

Getting a fair hearing is essential. Theories of argument offer advice on how to gain this hearing.

(1) There are three classical appeals.

Aristotle and other thinkers in the ancient world believed that persuasion is achieved through a combination of three appeals. **Ethos** means demonstrating that you are fair-minded and well-informed so that readers can trust you. **Logos** is what you employ when you support your claims, make reasonable conclusions, and avoid logical fallacies (**31h**). **Pathos**, or using language that will stir the feelings of your audience, can be misused by people who wish to obscure thought. Pathos can be effective when used to establish empathy.

(2) Rogerian appeals emphasize showing other people that you understand them.

Rogerian argument derives from the work of Carl R. Rogers, a psychologist who believed that people often fail to understand each other because of a natural tendency to judge and evaluate, agree or disagree. His model calls for having the courage to suspend judgment until you are able to restate fairly and accurately what others believe. This model is especially useful when building consensus. An argument organized along Rogerian principles begins with a careful restatement of other people's views, then offers concessions, and only then introduces the position the rest of the essay will support.

32e There are several ways to organize an argument.

A few basic principles are useful to remember.

(1) Separate reasons are best discussed in separate paragraphs.

You will usually need at least a full paragraph to develop any reason for your opinion, but some reasons could take several paragraphs. If you try to discuss two reasons in the same paragraph, your paragraph may lack unity and coherence (chapter 27).

(2) You can begin a paragraph with a view different from yours.

If you follow this strategy, the rest of the paragraph is available for your response. If you begin a paragraph with your view, then introduce an opponent's view, and then move back to yours, readers may miss the point.

(3) Refutation and concessions are most effective when placed where readers will welcome them.

If you wait until the end of your argument to recognize views that differ from yours, some readers may have already decided that you are too one-sided. Under other circumstances, an audience may react negatively to a writer who responds to opposing arguments before offering any reasons to support his or her own view. It is often best to offer at least one strong reason to support your case before turning to opposing views.

One way to organize your argument is to follow the plan recommended by classical rhetoric:

Introduction	Introduce your issue and capture the attention of your audience.
Statement of Background	Report information the members of your audience need to know.
Exposition	Interpret the information. Define key terms.
Proposition	Introduce the position you are taking.
Proof	Discuss the reasons why you have taken your position.
Refutation	Show why you are not persuaded by the arguments of people who hold a different position.
Conclusion	Summarize your most important points and appeal to your audience's feelings.

Research

Chapter 33 | Research: Finding and Evaluating Sources

Chapter 33
Research: Finding and Evaluating Sources   res

Chapter 33

Research: Finding and Evaluating Sources

A research assignment requires you to draw on outside resources and acknowledge them properly. Writing from research involves many of the same skills that you use to write essays based on familiar information.

33a Information from sources is basic to most writing.

Almost anything you write requires you to acquire and use information. On some occasions, you may need to explore the resources of a library to discover the work of other writers or researchers. No matter how many sources you use, you are the most important presence in a paper. Think of the paper as a **researched** paper—that is, written from research that you have evaluated and then used to advance a **thesis** (28d).

(1) Developing a research problem and analyzing your own knowledge

An important step in doing research is to envision your topic as a research problem and then establish what you already know about it. A **research problem** might be a question or an issue that can be resolved at least partly through research. It may be argumentative, but not a matter of opinion. For example, the thesis "animal experimentation is wrong" is not a research problem because research cannot prove a moral judgment. The thesis "animal experimentation is necessary for medical research" is a hypothesis suitable for research.

Try to write down everything you know about your topic. Try to convince someone else of your thesis and write down all the information you bring to your argument. Think about where you have seen your thesis discussed and search your memory for all the information you can remember about the subject. Use the thinking strategies in chapters **31** and **28** to see if your points are matters of opinion or if they are independently verifiable.

(2) Establishing a research routine

Scheduling your time is especially important because researched papers are usually assigned several weeks before they are due, and the temptation to procrastinate may be strong. Make sure to allow enough time for the long process of choosing a subject (**28b**), preparing a working bibliography (**33b**), reading extensively, taking notes (**33f(2)**), developing a thesis (**28d**), outlining (**28e**), drafting (**28f**), and revising (**29b**). Keep your schedule flexible. As you draft your essay, you may discover that you need to return to the library for further research.

A research log can help you stay on schedule. Here is a sample form that can help you make a realistic schedule. You may need more (or less) time for each of these activities.

Activity	Days Needed	Date Completed
1. Explore the campus library	1	_____ ☐
2. Find a topic and develop a working hypothesis	1	_____ ☐
3. Establish a search strategy	1	_____ ☐
4. Develop a working bibliography	6	_____ ☐
5. Take notes	6	_____ ☐
6. Develop the thesis and outline	2	_____ ☐
7. Draft the paper	4	_____ ☐
8. Seek peer review	2	_____ ☐
9. Revise the paper	1	_____ ☐
10. Prepare the works cited	1	_____ ☐
11. Prepare the final draft	1	_____ ☐
12. Proofread	1	_____ ☐

33b A working bibliography lists sources.

A working bibliography contains information (titles, authors, dates, and so on) about the materials you think you might use. Write down the most promising sources you can find. Some researchers find it convenient to put each entry on a separate index card. Others prefer to use a computer. It is also a good idea to follow the bibliographical form you are instructed to use. The MLA bibliographic style can be found in 34a and APA style in 34d.

Primary and secondary sources Primary sources for topics in literature and the humanities are generally documents and literary works. In the social sciences, primary sources can be field observations, case histories, and survey data. In the sciences, primary sources are generally empirical—measurements, experiments, and the like. Secondary sources are commentaries on primary sources. Learn to evaluate the quality of secondary sources. Many are excellent commentaries, although all involve some degree of interpretation. However, some secondary sources, particularly electronic documents, may not be reliable. Unlike print sources, these are often not peer-reviewed before the information is published.

33c   Library research requires a strategy.

College libraries are organized to make research as efficient as possible. Usually a map shows where various kinds of materials are located. Reference books, encyclopedias, and indexes—materials that cannot usually be checked out of the library—are located in the **reference collection**, which may also include indexing information for electronic databases. Other books are located in the **stacks**. If the stacks are open, it may be useful to browse among the books shelved near those you have located through the catalog. **Periodicals** (in print or microform) are usually stored in a special section. Many colleges participate in an interlibrary loan program, an arrangement among libraries for the exchange of books and periodicals. If you have difficulty locating or using any research materials, do not hesitate to ask a **reference librarian** for help.

Your search does not need to be limited to a library. You might use information drawn from radio, television, and the Internet; from conducting interviews with experts on your topic; or from personal experience.

(1) Books and periodicals

Books

The first place to look is usually the **main catalog**. Some libraries still maintain a **card catalog**, which consists of cards arranged alphabetically in drawers by author, title, and subject. Most libraries, however, have **computerized catalogs**. (See **33e**.)

Although there may be a slight visual difference between the computerized entry and its equivalent on a catalog card, both provide essentially the same information: author, title, place of publication, publisher, date of publication, and call number, which tells you where in the library the book is located. If your library provides you with access to both card and computer catalogs, check with a librarian to see which is more current.

An entry from a computerized catalog   A computerized entry usually reveals the status of the book—information that can save time when a book has been checked out by someone else. Expect to encounter variations on this example.

```
        Online Catalogue—BRIEF DISPLAY (1 of 1 titles)

                                    Number of holdings :1
AUTHOR          :Coursen, Herbert R.
TITLE           :Shakespearean performance as
                 interpretation / H.R. Coursen
PUBLISHER       :Newark :
                 University of Delaware Press ;
                 London :
                 Cranbury, NJ :
                 Associated University Presses,
                 c1992
LANGUAGE        :ENGLISH

   LIBRARY      LOCATION     COLLECTION/           STATUS/
                             CALL NUMBER           DUE DATE
   --------     ---------    ----------------      -----------
1. MAIN         MAIN         PR3091.C69 1992       In Library
  Last Page
Options:                               ⟨ENTER⟩ = scroll options
 FD = Full display    P = Prior screen    E = Extend search
  L = Limit list      O = Output         M = MARC
```

This is an example of an author card.

```
PR
3091 Coursen, Herbert R.
.C69 Shakespearean performance as interpretation / H.R.
     Coursen.—Newark:
1992 University of Deleware Press, 1992.
        Bibliographical references (p. 253-262).
        Includes index.
        ISBN 0-874-13432-3 (alk. Paper)

   1. Shakespeare, William, d 1564-1616--Stage history.
   2. Shakespeare--Film and video adaptations. 3. Shake-
   speare--Criticism and interpretation--History.
   I. Title
```

Library of Congress Subject Headings If your library uses Library of Congress numbers for cataloging books, you can first look for your subject in the **Library of Congress Subject Headings** (*LCSH*). If your subject is indexed by that catalog, you will find a specific catalog number for books on your subject, as well as cross-references to related subject areas.

Periodicals

Periodicals (magazines, journals, newspapers) often contain the most recent information on your subject. A variety of periodical indexes (usually located in the reference section) do for articles what the main catalog does for books. You may need to consult a number of indexes to find the information you need. Most print indexes are also available electronically. See page 233.

Indexes for general-interest periodicals   If you think articles on your subject have appeared in general-interest magazines or newspapers, you might consult the *Readers' Guide to Periodical Literature* and a newspaper index, the best known of which is the *New York Times Index*.

Articles on topic

> Richard III
>> *The American Spectator* v29 p58 Mr '96. J. Bowman
>> *The New Republic* v214 p30 F 12 '96. S. Kauffmann
>> *New York* il v29 p48–9 Ja 15 '96. D. Denby
>> *Newsweek* il v127 p58 Ja 29 '96. J. Kroll

The *Readers' Guide* excerpt above (from the search Katie Frushour conducted for her paper on two film versions of *Richard III,* reprinted in the sample MLA research paper) shows that *Newsweek* published a review of the film and that the review can be found in volume 127, page 58, of the January 29, 1996, issue. If you need help reading an entry, you can find a sample entry as well as a key to abbreviations in the front pages of each issue of the *Readers' Guide*.

New York Times Index entries include a brief summary of the contents and an abbreviation that reveals the article's length.

> **Richard III (Movie)**
>   Ben Brantley article on evil characters portrayed by Ian McKellen and Kenneth Branagh in new films Richard III and Othello: photos (M), Ja 21,II,I:2
>   Correction of Jan 21 article on the films Richard III and Othello, Ja 28,II,4:6

Article summary

Medium length article

Section, page, & column numbers

January 21 and 28 issues
(in year of volume consulted)

Indexes for special-interest periodicals   Virtually every specialized field has its own periodicals, which usually provide much more detailed information than can be found in magazines or newspapers aimed at the general public. Some of the most useful ones are listed below.

Applied Science and Technology Index. 1958–.

Art Index. 1929–.

Biological and Agricultural Index. 1946–.

Business Periodicals Index. 1958–.

Education Index. 1929–.

Humanities Index. 1974–.

Index to Legal Periodicals. 1908–.

Medline. 1985–.

Music Index. 1949–.

Public Affairs Information Service (Bulletin). 1915–.

Social Sciences Index. 1974–.

The print versions of these indexes are organized like the *Readers' Guide*. Consult the front of any volume for a key to the abbreviations used in individual entries. A similar format is also used by the *MLA Bibliography,* which is essential for doing research in literature.

Electronic databases of scholarly materials are much easier to search and update than print versions, so most libraries have switched to them. All the CD-ROM databases in your library can probably be searched using much the same set of commands. A different library, however, may subscribe through a different service, and the commands and the screen designs may differ.

Abstracting services An abstracting service provides short summaries of the articles and books it indexes. Your library may have CD-ROM disks for such abstracts as *Academic Abstracts* and CARL, which contains the tables of contents for most scholarly journals. When using one of these, you can scan the short summaries and decide which seem to be useful. You may also be able to print out a list of citations with abstracts and even the full text of some articles. Here is a citation and abstract from *Academic Abstracts.*

Computerized abstract

```
Subject: RICHARD III     (Motion picture);
   RICHARD III Foundation
  Title: Historical Richards.
 Author: Geier, Thom
Summary: Points at the criticism received by
   the film 'Richard III' for its historical
   inaccuracy. New Jersey based Richard III
   Foundation's complaints; Details of the
```

```
    movie, including Richard III portrayed like
    Hitler.
  Source: (US News & World Report, 1/22/96,
    Vol. 120 Issue 3, p14, 1/5p, 1c)
    ISSN: 0041-5537
Item No: 9601167647

        (We subscribe to this magazine.)

    ** FullTEXT Available — Press F7 **
```

---

(2) Reference works

For a detailed list of reference books and a short description of each, consult *Guide to Reference Books* by Eugene P. Sheehy and *American Reference Books Annual (ARBA)*. For a list of reference books useful when writing about literature, see page 336. A few of the most widely used reference books are listed here. Note that these are reference sources: Refer to them for help, but do not rely on any of them as a principal source for a college paper.

Special dictionaries and encyclopedias

Adams, James T. *Dictionary of American History*. Rev. ed. 8 vols. 1983.

Encyclopedia of Philosophy. Ed. Paul Edwards. 4 vols. 1973.

Encyclopedia of Psychology. Ed. Raymond J. Corsini. 4 vols. 1984.

Encyclopedia of World Art. 15 vols. 1959–68. Supp. 1983, 1987.

International Encyclopedia of the Social Sciences. Ed. D. E. Sills. 8 vols. 1977. Supplements.

McGraw-Hill Encyclopedia of Science and Technology. 15 vols. 6th ed. 1987. Yearbooks.

Biographies

Biography and Genealogy Master Index. CD-ROM. 1996.

Biography Index. 15 vols. 1946–88.

Current Biography Cumulated Index, 1940–1985. 1986.

Dictionary of Scientific Biography. 8 vols. 1970–80.

Notable American Women: 1607–1950. 3 vols. 1972.
   Supplements.

Notable Black American Women. 1990.

Almanacs and yearbooks

Americana Annual. 1924–.

Facts on File. 1940–.

Information Please Almanac. 1985–.

33d Field research requires special skills.

The most common alternative to library research is an **interview.** Faculty members, business and professional people, and even relatives and friends can be appropriate subjects if they have relevant firsthand experience with the subject you are researching.

You should consider an interview only after you have done some reading on your subject. Schedule interviews well ahead, and if you plan to use a tape recorder, ask permission. Have pens and paper ready for taking notes and fresh batteries and blank tapes for your tape recorder. Record the time and date of the interview on tape or, if you do not use a tape recorder, at the beginning of your notes.

Begin with questions that are broad enough to give people room to reveal their own special interests; then follow up with more specific questions. Be prepared to depart from your list of planned questions. After the interview, send a letter thanking the interviewee.

Closely related to the interview is the **survey**, in which you ask a number of people the same set of questions and then analyze the results. You can administer the survey orally, or you can distribute a written questionnaire. You may find the following checklist helpful in constructing a good survey questionnaire.

Checklist for Creating Survey Questions
- Does each question relate to the purpose of the survey?
- Are the questions easy to understand?
- Are the questions designed to elicit specific responses?
- Are the questions designed to collect concrete data?
- Are written questions designed to give respondents enough space for their answers?

You may also have occasion to draw directly on your own **experience** or **observations**. Observation might involve arming yourself with a still or video camera and/or tape recorder, writing out a plan for observing, rehearsing the observation, and taking written notes (in addition to tape) during the actual observation. But check with your instructor to see whether field research is appropriate for your research project and what kind of field research would be most productive.

33e   Electronic resources are fast and efficient.

Electronic research tools require knowing how to evaluate sources as well as how to find them.

(1) Developing a research strategy

Publicly available information is stored electronically in **on-line information storage and retrieval systems** (for example, *Dialog*), on CD-ROM disks, and on the Internet. Like library sources, electronic research demands that you follow a basic search strategy.

BASIC SEARCH STRATEGY TIPS

1. Determine databases to be searched.
2. Identify the keywords.
3. Check the controlled vocabulary thesaurus (if there is one).
4. Apply a basic search logic.
5. Check system documentation on file structure and format information.
6. Log on and perform the search.
7. Identify citations to keep.
8. Refine the search strategy if the first search returned too many, too few, or irrelevant citations.

Selecting a database is similar to deciding whether to consult the *MLA Annual Bibliography* or the *Social Science Index*. Will you use a database stored on a CD-ROM (which has the advantages of being inexpensive and relatively easy to use) or do you need to do an on-line search (which can be expensive and tricky to execute efficiently)? **Identifying keywords** is also not much different from deciding on a list of subject headings.

When you use a database, you must **check your keywords against the database thesaurus**—a list of the controlled vocabulary used for retrieving information. If a keyword is not part of the controlled vocabulary, a database search will turn up no **records**. That means no information can be found using the terms you have tried, not that the database contains no information on that subject. Use the controlled vocabulary for your search terms.

Basic search logic enables you to guard against retrieving too many or too few records. A search result that says, "Found: 2,493,508 records containing the descriptor 'film'" is as useless as one that reports, "Sorry, no records found." You can use certain words to broaden or narrow your search:

or   broadens a search—**young adults or single adults** finds all records that contain information about either category;

and narrows a search—**young adults and single adults** returns only those records that contain both categories;

not excludes specific items—**young adults and single adults not homeless** will exclude any records that mention homeless young single adults.

(2) Your college library as a gateway

Many college libraries offer students access to major electronic information storage and retrieval systems such as *First Search* or *Dialog*, which allow you to search in a large number of databases. If your school does not, check to see if you have access to *Academic Abstracts* or *InfoTrac*. Other databases that may be available are *CARL-Uncover* (which indexes a large number of periodicals) and some full-text search and retrieval databases such as *EBSCO MAGS* for periodicals and *LEXIS-NEXIS* for legal documents and newspapers, respectively.

Sample search: *MLA* (using *First Search* system)

```
+************* List of Records ***************+
DATABASE: MLA              LIMITED TO: /English
SEARCH: su:shakespeare film criticism FOUND 6 Records
NO.        TITLE                        AUTHOR        YEAR
|1 Screening Shakespeare               Pilkington, Ace  1990
|2 Criticism and the Films of          Felheim, Marvin  1986
|  Shakespeare's P...
|3 Shakespeare on Film: Some German    Bies, Werner     1983
|  Appro
|4 The Spiral of Influence: 'One       Kliman, Bernice  1983
|  Defect' in H...
|5 Sight and Space: The Perception     Styan, J. L.
|  of Shakesp
|6 Criticism for the Filmed            Homan, Sidney R  1977
|  Shakespeare
```

HINTS: View a record.................type record number.
    Decrease number of records....type L (to limit) or A (to
    'and').
    Do a new search.................type S or SEARCH.
RECORD NUMBER (or Action): 5
************* Full Record Display ***************

Record 5 of 6
```
|  NUMBER: Accession: 78-1-4052. Record: 78104052.
|  UPDATE CODE: 7801
|  AUTHOR: Styan, J. L.
|  TITLE: Sight and Space: The Perception of Shakespeare on
|       Stage and Screen
|  SOURCE: Bevington, David; Halio, Jay L.; Muir, Kenneth;
|       Mack, Maynard.
|       Shakespeare, Pattern of Excelling Nature:
|       Shakespeare Criticism in Honor of America's
|       Bicentennial from The International Shakespeare
|       Association Congress, Washington, D.C., April 1976.
|       Newark: U of Delaware P, London: Associated UP. 304
|       pp.
|  PAGES: 198-209
|  LANGUAGE: English
|  PUB TYPE: book article
|  DESCRIPTORS: English literature; 1500-1599; Shakespeare,
|       William themes and figures; Film
```

(3) Using the Internet

The Internet, an international network of computers linked through telephone and fiber-optic lines, is one of the most exciting tools available to you. Detailed instructions for gaining access to and using the Internet are beyond the scope of this handbook, but the academic computing center at your school may offer workshops. If not, check out one of the many helpful books, a few of which are below.

Gaffin, Adam. *Big Dummy's Guide to the Internet.* [on-line]

Krol, Ed. *The Whole Internet User's Guide & Catalog,* 2nd ed. 1995.

Reddick, Randy, and Elliot King. *The Online Student: Making the Grade on the Internet.* 1996.

You probably have access to the Internet through your academic computing account, especially if your school charges a computer use fee. If you have a computer with a **modem** (see **Glossary of Terms**) and your school has a data number you can dial, you can also probably do your Internet searching from home. If your room is not wired to the school network or your school does not support dial-up access, you may want to consider a local Internet service provider that offers unlimited access for a flat monthly fee.

Electronic mail or e-mail allows you to send messages in seconds to anyone with an e-mail address anywhere in the world. E-mail can let you ask a question of a well-known scholar (assuming you know the e-mail address) and lets the scholar answer at his or her convenience.

Discussion lists allow you to read messages posted to all members of a group interested in a specific topic and to post messages yourself that those dozens or hundreds of like-minded people will read. You can send e-mail messages to the **listserv address** that will redistribute them. Similarly, you can receive replies from anyone who subscribes to the list, but everyone will be able to read the same replies. Anyone who wants to discuss the topic seriously can join the list.

To find out if there are any lists that might discuss the problems of young adults living with their parents, Adrienne Harton (see 34e) could have sent an e-mail message to listserv@listserv.net, leaving the subject line blank and including this phrase: list global/multiple-generation household. A return message would list all groups listserv can identify with that keyword.

The **World Wide Web** is a huge, mostly unindexed collection of information. The easiest way to find information on the Web is to use one of the available robotic or semi-robotic search systems, such as Yahoo or Lycos. After you type keywords into a text entry box, these engines will return a list of electronic documents (Websites) that meet the searching criteria. Most search engines encourage the use of the logical operators *and, or,* and *not* to make the search as efficient as possible.

One engine may be better for academic information, another for general information, and yet another for business information. You should probably try them all, and you should always read the instructions (help screens). The introductory screen from Yahoo, one of the best-known search engines, shows that they are relatively simple to use.

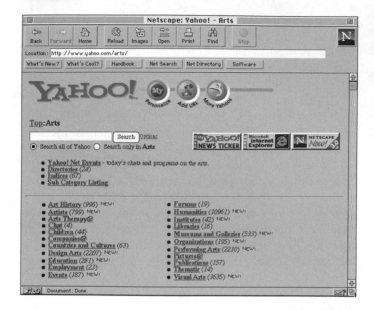

The result of the successful search will be a list of Uniform Resource Locators (URLs, pronounced as "Earls") you can use to access the page(s) you need.

As with any resource that is not moderated, harebrained or tasteless information is readily available. However, a careful researcher will have a sense of what is appropriate and with a little checking and critical thinking can avoid what is unsuitable or unreliable.

Web pages can be accessed only with a browser. Unless you have a fast connection to the Internet, you may need to use a textual browser such as Lynx. A sample page looks much like the one Katie Frushour found.

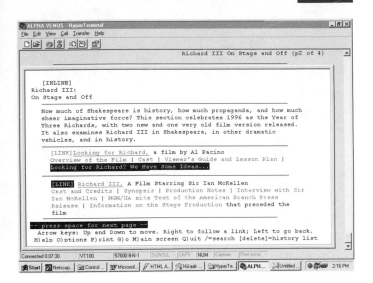

Web pages are best viewed with a graphically capable browser (the one below shows the same page retrieved with Netscape) that retrieves the pictorial elements intended to make Web pages pleasant to look at and easy to read. **Links,** which work somewhat like a floating index, are underlined and usually change color when they have been used.

FTP, Gopher, and Telnet   FTP is a way of getting files from a remote computer to yours (or vice versa). It is especially valuable for getting free software, many kinds of government documents and other text files, and graphic images. You use FTP in one of two ways: You log on using "anonymous" as the user name and your e-mail address as the password, or less frequently, you log on to the remote computer with a user name and password assigned to you. The files you want are generally kept in a large directory (similar to a folder), which is usually called **pub** and which may have many subdirectories. FTP is powerful, but it is not friendly. For help in finding where files on a particular subject might be stored on a remote computer, you can use a keyword searching system called **Archie**. (See the academic computing service at your school to learn how to use it.)

Gopher is a system for finding and accessing files on remote computers. Gopher has two searching programs (**Veronica** and **Jughead**) for finding files in Gopherspace. Once you find the file you want, you generally have the option of printing it at your own location, retrieving it to the file space allotted to you through your college account, or cutting and pasting it into a document in your word processing program.

Telnet allows you to use other tools at remote locations. If, for instance, your school lacks access to Gopher, you could Telnet to a school that has it.

! **CAUTION** Caution #1 **Guard against computer viruses.** They lurk in every part of the Internet and can be extremely destructive. Good virus checkers are available.

Caution #2 **Be conscious of security.** Do not give out your telephone number or address over the Internet. Do not tell anyone your password.

Caution #3 **Pay for what you use** unless the material is clearly freeware or public domain.

Caution #4 **Give proper credit.** *Freeware* and *public domain* mean you do not have to pay, not that you can use images or text as if they were your own.

Caution #5 **Check reliability.** Evaluate the source critically. Are there errors? Is the site monitored? (Many are not.) Is the author identified and are his or her credentials given?

33f   Evaluating sources requires thought; taking notes demands accuracy.

(1) Testing reliability, bias, and integrity

When you are doing research, one important consideration always is the reliability of your sources. (See **33b**.)

> **Checklist for Evaluating Sources**   ✓
> - What are the author's credentials?
> - Do others speak of the writer as an authority?
> - Does the work contain evidence indicating that the author is well informed?
> - Does the work contain evidence that the author is prejudiced in any way?
> - Is the work recent enough to provide up-to-date information?
> - Is the work published by a reputable company?
> - Does the work provide documentation to support important points?
> - Does the work include a bibliography that can help you to identify other sources?

Book Review Digest, which contains summaries of critical opinion on a book, could help you decide which books are most dependable. You can usually assume that university presses demand a high standard of scholarship. An article published in an academic journal has usually been reviewed by experts. Be alert for bias that may be built into a source. An article on malpractice suits in the *Journal of the American Medical Association* is likely to be sympathetic to physicians.

As you read your sources, learn how to find and evaluate useful passages with a minimum of time and effort.

You cannot always take the time to read each book completely. Use the table of contents and the index of a book, and learn to skim the pages until you find the passages you need.

Evaluating electronic sources demands some variations on the questions in the Checklist for Evaluating Sources.

Checklist for Evaluating Electronic Sources
- Is there evidence of frequent maintenance?
- Have the best available resources been used?
- Is there evidence that copyright has been honored?
- Is the author acknowledged?
- Is the source located at an institution respected in the academic community?
- Does the work include citations to other sources or, in the case of hypertext, links to other reliable documents?

(2) Taking notes

Some note takers are more comfortable taking notes on 8½-by-11 paper, others on index cards, and others using the computer. Whatever you use, keep the following points in mind:

Checklist for Taking Notes
- Does every note clearly identify its source?
- Is an author/title code for each source noted in the working bibliography and on every page of your notes?
- Have you put the full bibliographic citation on the first page of every photocopy and a short form on the following pages?

continued

continued from previous page

- Is the bibliographic information for the source of every note accurate?
- Have you taken down verbatim—that is, copied every word, every capital letter, and every punctuation mark exactly as it was in the original—any useful passage that you think you may later quote, being especially careful to put quotation marks around any words you use directly from a source? Failure to do so as you take notes may lead to unintended plagiarism when you draft your paper.
- On photocopies, have you clearly indicated passages you intend to quote directly, passages you intend to paraphrase, and those you plan to summarize?
- Have you used different type-styles or different colors in computer files to make source identification of quoted text easy?

Using a notebook

A ring binder into which you can insert pages of notes as well as photocopies is an excellent organizational tool, particularly if you have a system for sorting notes into the main subject categories your work covers. Use a fresh page for each new source.

Using notecards

Many researchers use larger cards for notes than for bibliographic references. Different sizes of cards help keep the cards' functions separate. Show the author's name (and a short title if the bibliography contains more than one work by that author) on each card, and include the exact page number(s). If you put no more than a single note, however brief, on each card and a heading of keywords at the top, you can easily arrange your cards as you prepare to write.

Using photocopies

On a photocopy you can mark quotable material and jot down your own ideas as you study the source. Make sure you document the source on the photocopy.

Photocopied source with notes

phrase?

Olivier's use of the <u>direct address</u> to the camera, which defies the naturally assumed aesthetic laws of the medium, is *important point!* another of those brilliant strokes whereby he brings a distinctly theatrical action to film and then gives it an impact which only cinema can. <u>The success of its effect depends upon</u> *tried to make film reflect R's char* <u>the fact that it amplifies elements which are implicit in the</u> <u>play in the character of Richard.</u> The boldness with which he affronts the aesthetic laws of the medium is consonant with the assuredness with which Richard challenges the accepted procedures of royal succession and affronts the apparent spiritual order of the real.

Using computer files

If you have good keyboarding skills, you may find it efficient to use your computer for taking notes. One problem with this method is that it is tempting to take down too much information verbatim. Another is that you may go too fast and make mistakes.

TIPS ON USING A COMPUTER TO TAKE NOTES

1. Create a separate master folder (or directory) for your paper.
2. Create folders within the master folder for your bibliography, notes, and portions of drafts.
3. Keep all the notes for each source in a separate file.
4. Use distinctive fonts for notes on different source materials.

Using a computer to take notes makes it easy to copy and paste information into subject files and ultimately from subject files into the finished paper.

⚠ CAUTION Systematically identify the source of each note you cut and paste. As you work the information smoothly into your text, document your sources accurately and responsibly.

33g Plagiarism is a serious offense.

Taking someone else's words or ideas and presenting them as your own is called **plagiarism** or **cheating**. For whatever reason it occurs, it is wrong.

The *MLA Handbook for Writers of Research Papers,* 4th edition (New York: MLA, 1995) advises:

> At all times during research and writing, guard against the possibility of inadvertent plagiarism by keeping careful notes that distinguish between your musings and thoughts and the material you gather from others. A writer who fails to give appropriate acknowledgment when repeating another's wording or particularly apt term, paraphrasing another's argument, or presenting another's line of thinking is guilty of plagiarism. You may certainly use other persons' words and thoughts in your research paper, but the borrowed material must not appear to be your creation. (26)

> **ESL**   In some cultures, anyone who has purchased a book and decides to quote from it can do so without citing the source. The rationale says that the person bought the words when he or she bought the book. In America, you can get in serious trouble with that kind of thinking.

You must give credit for all information you borrow except for common knowledge and your own ideas. Common knowledge includes such information as "December has thirty-one days," and well-known proverbs or historical information such as the date of the Declaration of Independence. After you have read a good deal about a given subject, you will be able to distinguish between common knowledge in that field and the distinctive ideas or interpretations of specific writers. As for your own ideas, if you have been scrupulous in noting your own thoughts as you took notes, you should have no difficulty distinguishing between what you knew to begin with and what you learned in your research and so must give credit for.

Source   (from "Returning Young Adults," in *Psychology and Marketing*, 11, 1994, by J. Burnett and D. Smart, page 254)

> Both generations want their rights. The RYAs want the autonomy they have grown accustomed to and expect their parents to treat them like adults. The parents, meanwhile, have come to recognize their own rights. They may resent that the time, money, and emotional energy they planned to invest in themselves after the child's departure are instead allocated to the RYA.

Undocumented copying

```
They may resent that the time, money, and
emotional energy they planned to invest in
```

themselves after the child's departure are
instead allocated to the RYA.

Appropriate citation

Marketing professors John Burnett and Denise
Smart note that parents "may resent that the
time, money, and emotional energy they planned
to invest in themselves after the child's
departure are instead allocated to the RYA"
(254).

Quotation marks show where the copied words begin and
end, and the number in parentheses tells the reader the
exact page on which it appears. The sentence identifies the
authors and establishes the context for the quotation. If,
after referring to the following checklist, you cannot decide whether you need to cite a source, the safest policy is
to cite it.

Checklist for Kinds of Information to Cite
- Writings, both published and unpublished
    by direct quotation
    by indirect quotation
    by reference to ideas
- Opinions and judgments not your own
- Arguable points and claims
- Facts (unless widely known)
- Images and graphics such as
    works of art   drawings   tables and charts
    film/video   maps   advertisements
    photographs   music   statistics and graphs
- Personal communication
- Electronic media

33h Integrating sources fosters mastery of information.

A research project that is a patchwork of snippets from others (even when meticulously cited) indicates that you are, at the very least, an inexperienced writer. The foundation of researched writing is always the writer's own ideas, which flow from point to point, supported and guided by research.

(1) Integrating sources

When good research writers use borrowed material, they introduce it to readers by establishing the context; for example, in a researched paper about the value of vitamin C, readers might find it useful to know that the author of a quotation praising the vitamin is a Nobel laureate in chemistry. Similarly, you can introduce a paraphrase by making clear why the information is important. An excellent way to introduce research is to use a phrase that indicates the author's attitude or the importance of the information. The following list of verbs can be helpful in deciding how to integrate that information with your own ideas.

THIRTY-TWO LEAD-IN VERBS

acknowledge	complain	explain	refute
admit	concede	express	reject
agree	conclude	interpret	remark
argue	contend	list	report
believe	criticize	note	respond
charge	deny	object	state
claim	disagree	observe	suggest
compare	emphasize	oppose	write

Writers of researched papers borrow information in three ways: quoting, paraphrasing, or summarizing. Whatever option you choose, make sure that you use sources responsibly.

■ **CAUTION** Words or ideas borrowed from other writers must not be distorted in any way, and credit must be given when borrowing occurs.

The following examples show MLA documentation style. For additional information on documentation, see **34a, 34c,** and **34d.**

(2) Using direct quotations

Select quotations only if (a) you want to retain the beauty or clarity of someone else's words or (b) you plan to discuss the implications of the words in question. Keep quotations short and make them an integral part of your text.

Quote **accurately**. Enclose every quoted passage in quotation marks. If a quotation is longer than four lines, set it off as an indented block. (See **20b.**) Cite the exact source for your quotation. If you think your audience might be unfamiliar with a source, identify its author the first time you refer to it. (Note that this citation is in APA style.)

```
Family science researcher Judith S. Peck
(1991) defines the "launching" stage as "one
of the most complex stages of the family's
life cycles" (p. 150).
```

> **Checklist for Direct Quotations** ✓
> - Have I copied all the words accurately?
> - Have I copied all the punctuation accurately? (See **20f**.)
> - Have I used ellipsis points correctly to indicate anything that is left out? (See **21i**.)
> - Have I avoided using ellipsis points *before* quotations that are clearly only parts of sentences?
> - Have I used square brackets around everything I added to the direct quotation? (See **21g**.)
> - Have I used too many quotations?

(3) Paraphrasing

A **paraphrase** is a restatement of a source in about the same number of words. Paraphrase when you (a) use someone else's content but not his or her specific words or (b) simplify difficult material.

Using your own words

Unless you enclose an author's words in quotation marks, do not mix them with your own even if the sentence structure is different. Equally important, do not think that you can substitute synonyms for an author's words while you preserve his or her sentence structure. Both of these are plagiarism, even if you cite the source.

Source (from "Returning Young Adults," *Psychology and Marketing, 11,* 1994, by J. Burnett and D. Smart, pages 253–269)

> In general, contrary to assumptions about RYAs amassing large amounts of disposable income, the findings suggest that economic deprivation is the primary factor distinguishing the RYA from a single cohort. RYAs have an appreciably higher unemployment rate and lower income than a comparable sin-

gles group. Thus, the notion characterizing the modern RYA as a somewhat spoiled individual who wants to maintain his or her earlier lifestyle is not supported in this study.

Inadequate paraphrasing

```
Although many think that RYAs have large
amounts of money to spend, research has shown
that RYAs differ from single young adults
mainly because more RYAs are unemployed or
have lower incomes. Research shows that the
general impression that RYAs are lazy
parasites is not correct. (p. 267)
```

Although this passage ends with a parenthetical reference to the original sources, the reference does not reveal the size of the debt. The author could be giving credit to Burnett and Smart for the whole passage or only the last sentence—it is hard to tell. And when you compare this "paraphrase" with the original source, you will find that the author has followed the same structure. Although the wording has changed, the paraphrase in this case is so close to the original that it could be considered plagiarism.

Adequate paraphrasing

```
Burnett and Smart report research showing
that RYAs, contrary to opinion, have a more
difficult time meeting their bills than other
single young adults. Therefore, attitudes that
view them as lazy parasites are incorrect. (p.
267)
```

In this example, the page reference establishes where the paraphrase ends; the introductory "Burnett and Smart report" establishes where it begins. As a general rule, begin paraphrases with a few words indicating that you are about to restate another writer's words.

⚠ **CAUTION** If you simply change a few words in a passage, you have not adequately restated it. You may be charged with plagiarism if the wording of your version follows the original too closely, even if you provide a page reference to the source you used.

Maintaining accuracy

Any paraphrase must accurately maintain the sense of the original.

Original	Owning a boat is like standing in the shower tearing up $1,000 bills.
Inaccurate	Boat owners would feel comfortable "tearing up $1,000 bills." [Changes the focus.]
Accurate	Owning a boat is an expensive way to get wet. [Changes the language but remains faithful to the sense.]

Of course, deliberately changing the gist of what a source says is unethical.

Unethical	Boat owners are financially irresponsible masochists who enjoy being uncomfortable. [Shifts focus from the experience of boat owning to an indictment of boat owners' personalities.]

(4) Summarizing

When you summarize, you condense the main point(s) of your source as you restate them in your own words. A summary is shorter than the original source and lacks the kind of detail that fleshes out the original. Summarizing enables writers to report the work of others without getting bogged down in unnecessary detail. Summarize whenever you can save space by condensing a passage (or, in some cases, an entire work).

Source (from "Boomerang Age," *American Demographics 12,* 1990, pages 25–30)

> Young adults are also taking longer to finish school. Four years after high school graduation, for example, only 7 percent of the members of the class of 1982 had a bachelor's degree, versus 15 percent of 1972 high school graduates. Only one-fifth of the 1982 graduates had received any postsecondary degree within four years of graduation, compared with one-quarter of 1980 graduates and one-half of 1972 graduates. The gap is not as great seven years after graduation, reports the Department of Education, but is still substantial. (p. 27)

Summary

According to *American Demographics,* the number of students graduating in the traditional four years dropped significantly between 1972 and 1982. (p. 27)

! **CAUTION** When you are summarizing, you may find it useful to retain a key phrase from your source; but if you do, put quotation marks around the words.

Citations
MLA/APA

| Chapter 34 | Research: Using and Citing Sources |

Chapter 34
Research: Using and Citing
Sources cit

Chapter 34

Research: Using and Citing Sources

To document sources accurately demands meticulous attention to details. Different disciplines usually employ different documentation styles. Use the style your instructor specifies. The manuals listed below discuss documentation forms in detail. If you are asked to use one of these, look for it in your library's reference collection.

Style books and manuals

American Chemical Society. *The ACS Style Guide: A Manual for Authors and Editors.* 1997.

American Institute of Physics. *AIP Style Manual.* 4th ed. 1990.

American Mathematical Society. *A Manual for Authors of Mathematical Papers.* Rev. ed. 1990.

American Psychological Association. *Publication Manual of the American Psychological Association.* 4th ed. 1994.

The Chicago Manual of Style. 14th ed. 1993.

Council of Biology Editors. *Scientific Style and Format: The CBE Manual for Authors, Editors, and Publishers.* 6th ed. 1994.

Gibaldi, Joseph. *MLA Handbook for Writers of Research Papers.* 4th ed. 1995.

Turabian, Kate L. *A Manual for Writers of Term Papers, Theses, and Dissertations.* 6th ed. 1996.

The rest of this chapter discusses the two documentation styles most widely used in college writing: MLA style, most frequently used for papers in English (**34a**), and APA style, most often used for papers in psychology and other social sciences (**34d**). Some disciplines prefer to use the footnote or endnote system, so samples of this style are provided in **34c**

34a   MLA style documentation is appropriate for research papers in literary studies and foreign language courses.

(1) Using parenthetical citations

Although some disciplines still use a note system (see **34c**), the MLA recommends placing citations in parentheses directly in the text. These parenthetical citations refer the reader to a list of works cited at the end of the paper. The advantage of this system is that it is easy for both writers and readers to use. The MLA suggests reserving numbered notes for supplementary or explanatory comments. See page 297.

The basic elements of the parenthetical citation are the author's last name and the page number of the source. However, it is not necessary to repeat information that is already clearly provided. In other words, omit the author's name from the parenthetical citation if you have identified it in the text of the paper, shortly before the material being cited.

A work by one author

```
Olivier creates Richard III's "central device
of coherence" by using a cyclical theme of the
crown (Brown 133).
```

In this citation, the author's name is included within the parentheses because it is not mentioned in the text. A page number is included because the reference is to a specific passage. Note how the citation changes if the text includes more information about the source:

```
Constance Brown argues that in Richard III,
Laurence Olivier uses a cyclical theme of the
crown to create "the central device of
coherence" (133).
```

A work by two or three authors

```
High software prices mean that "education must
do without this resource, prices must come
down, or new strategies for development must
be devised" (Holdstein and Selfe 27).
```

Provide the last name of each author, punctuating as you would for items in a series.

A work by more than three authors

Follow the bibliographic entry, giving either the first author's last name followed by *et al.* or all the last names. (Do not italicize or underline the Latin phrase.)

```
In one important study, women graduates
complained more frequently about "excessive
control than about lack of structure" (Belenky
et al. 205).
```

OR

```
In one important study, women graduates
complained more frequently about "excessive
control than about lack of structure"
```

```
(Belenky, Clinchy, Goldberger, and Tarule
205).
```

A multivolume work

When you cite material from a multivolume work, include the volume number (followed by a colon and a space) before the page number.

```
As Katherine Raine has argued, "true poetry
begins where human personality ends" (2: 247).
```

If your list of works cited includes only one volume of a multivolume work, then you do not need to include the volume number in the parenthetical citation.

More than one work by the same author

When your list of works cited includes more than one work by the same author, your parenthetical citations should include a shortened title that reveals which of the author's works is being cited. Use a comma to separate the author's name from the shortened title.

```
According to Gilbert and Gubar, Elizabeth
Barrett Browning and Virginia Woolf considered
poetry by women to be forbidden and
problematic (Shakespeare's Sisters 107). That
attitude was based on the conception that male
sexuality is the "essence of literary power"
(Gilbert and Gubar, Madwoman 4).
```

This passage cites two different books by the same authors, Sandra M. Gilbert and Susan Gubar: *Shakespeare's*

Sisters: Feminist Essays on Women Poets and *The Mad-woman in the Attic: The Woman and the Nineteenth-Century Literary Imagination.* The authors' names are not necessary in the first citation since they are mentioned in the text; they are included in the second because their names are not mentioned in connection with *Madwoman.*

Works by different authors with the same last name

Occasionally your list of works cited will contain sources by two authors with the same last name. In such cases, you must use the first name as well as the last.

```
Richard Enos includes a thirteen-page
bibliography in Greek Rhetoric before
Aristotle (141-54). In Professing the New
Rhetorics, Theresa Enos mentions contemporary
reliance on pre-Aristotelian rhetoric and
includes an essay on the subject by Michael
Halloran (25, 331-43).
```

An indirect source

If you need to include material that one of your sources quoted from another work, but you cannot obtain the original source, use the following form:

```
The critic Susan Hardy Aikens has argued on
behalf of what she calls "canonical
multiplicity" (qtd. in Mayers 677).
```

A reader turning to the list of works cited should find a bibliographic entry for Mayers (which was the source consulted) but not for Aikens.

Poetry, drama, and the Bible

When you refer to poetry, drama, and the Bible, you must often give numbers of lines, acts, and scenes, or of chapters and verses, rather than page numbers. This practice enables a reader to consult an edition other than the one you are using.

Act, scene, and line numbers (all Arabic) are separated by periods. The MLA suggests that biblical chapters and verses be treated similarly, although some writers prefer to use colons. In all cases, the progression is from larger to smaller units.

The following example illustrates a typical citation of lines of poetry.

```
Emily Dickinson concludes "I'm Nobody! Who Are
You?" with a bittersweet stanza:
     How dreary to be somebody!
     How public, like a frog
     To tell your name the livelong June
     To an admiring bog! (5-8)
```

The following citation shows that the famous "To be, or not to be" soliloquy appears in act 3, scene 1, lines 56–89 of *Hamlet*.

```
In Hamlet, Shakespeare presents the most
famous soliloquy in the history of the theater:
"To be, or not to be . . ." (3.1.56-89).
```

Chapter 35 contains additional examples of how to quote and cite literary works.

In the following example, the writer refers to the creation story in Genesis and that the story begins in chapter 1, verse 1 and ends with chapter 2, verse 22.

```
The Old Testament creation story (Gen. 1.1-
2.22), told with remarkable economy,
culminates in the arrival of Eve.
```

Names of books of the Bible are neither italicized—underlined—nor enclosed in quotation marks, and abbreviation is desirable.

Punctuation and mechanics

Punctuation and numbers   Commas separate the authors' names from the titles (Brown, "Olivier's *Richard III: A Reevaluation*") and indicate interruptions in a sequence of pages or lines (44, 47). Hyphens indicate continuous sequences of pages and lines (1–4). Colons separate volume and page numbers (Raine 2: 247); one space follows the colon. Periods separate acts, scenes, and lines in drama (3.1.56–89). Periods (or colons) distinguish chapters from verses in biblical citations (Gen. 1.1 or Gen. 1:1).

Ellipsis points (**21i**) indicate omissions within a quotation: "They lived in an age of increasing complexity and great hope; we in an age of . . . growing despair" (Krutch 2). Brackets (**21g**) indicate interpolations within quotations: "The publication of this novel [*Beloved*] establishes Morrison as one of the most important writers of our time" (Boyle 17).

Placement of citations   Wherever possible, citations should appear just before a mark of punctuation in the text of the paper.

```
Richard Enos provides a bibliography of
sources for the study of Greek rhetoric before
Aristotle (141-54), and Theresa Enos's edited
collection, Professing the New Rhetorics,
```

```
includes Michael Halloran's essay "On the End
of Rhetoric, Classical and Modern" (331-43).
```

In a sentence such as the following, the citations follow the authors' names to keep the references separate.

```
Richard Enos (141-54) and Theresa Enos (25)
address classical rhetoric from very different
perspectives.
```

Lengthy quotations   When a quotation is more than four lines long, set it off from the text by indenting ten spaces from the left margin (**20b**). The citation in this case follows the final punctuation.

```
Ben Brantley further stresses the
effectiveness of Loncraine's setting as a
device to emphasize the image of tyranny. He
says:
            Setting the work in Fascist Europe,
            with Richard's Black Shirt presence
            playing on memories of Oswald Mosley
            and Edward VII's alleged Nazi
            sympathies, always made a certain
            sense. It immediately set up echoes
            of what is still perceived as the
            greatest historical example of evil
            in the 20th century: Hitler's Third
            Reich. (1)
```

When quoting more than one paragraph, indent the first line of each paragraph by three additional spaces. Do not indent if you are quoting only one paragraph (or if the first sentence quoted is not the first sentence in a paragraph).

(2) Listing the works cited—MLA style

For MLA papers, the list of sources from which you have cited information is called the **Works Cited**. When you are ready to produce your final draft, eliminate from your working bibliography items you have not cited. Arrange the list of works alphabetically by author. If a source has more than one author, alphabetize by the first author's last name. Type the first line of each entry flush with the left margin and indent subsequent lines five spaces (a hanging indentation); double-space throughout.

As you study the following MLA style entries, observe both the arrangement of information and the punctuation.

Books

Most book entries consist of three units separated by periods:

Author	Title	Publication data

Lastname, Firstname. Title Underlined. City: Publisher, date.

1. *Author.* Give the last name first, followed by a comma and the first name.
2. *Title.* Underline the title of the book, and capitalize all major words. Always include the book's subtitle. Make the underlining continuous, not separate under each word.
3. *Publication data.* Provide the city of publication, the brief name of the publisher, and the latest copyright date shown on the copyright page. Type a colon after the city and a comma after the publisher. To shorten the name of the publisher, use the principal name: Harcourt Brace becomes Harcourt; Harvard University Press becomes Harvard UP; University of Michigan Press becomes U of Michigan P.

One author

```
Smith, Jeanne Rosier. Writing Tricksters:
     Narrative Strategy and Cultural Identity
     in Maxine Hong Kingston, Louise Erdrich,
     and Toni Morrison. Berkeley: U of
     California P, 1997.
```

More than one work by the same author

```
Angelou, Maya. A Brave and Startling Truth.
     New York: Random, 1995.
---. Kofi and His Magic. New York: Potter,
     1996.
```

Alphabetize by the first *major* word in each title. Substitute three hyphens for the name in subsequent entries.

Two authors

```
Holdstein, Deborah H., and Cynthia L. Selfe,
     eds. Computers and Writing: Theories,
     Research, Practice. New York: MLA, 1990.
```

Invert the name of the first author (or editor) and place a comma after it. Do not invert the second name.

Three authors

```
Tate, Gary, Edward P. J. Corbett, and Nancy
     Myers, eds. The Writing Teacher's
     Sourcebook. 3rd ed. New York: Oxford UP,
     1994.
```

More than three authors

Hawisher, Gail E., et al. <u>Computers and the
    Teaching of Writing in American Higher
    Education, 1979-1994: A History</u>. New
    Directions in Computers and Composition
    Studies. 1. Norwood: Ablex, 1996.

OR

Hawisher, Gail E., Paul LeBlanc, Charles
    Moran, and Cynthia L. Selfe. <u>Computers
    and the Teaching of Writing in American
    Higher Education, 1979-1994: A History</u>.
    New Directions in Computers and
    Composition Studies. 1. Norwood: Ablex,
    1996.

Corporate author

Institute of Medicine. <u>Blood Banking and
    Regulation: Procedures, Problems, and
    Alternatives</u>. Washington: National
    Academy P, 1996.

Anonymous author

<u>You Know You're Anonymous in Washington
    When . . .</u> . New York: St. Martin's, 1996.

Begin the entry with the title.

Editor as author

Warhol, Robyn R., and Diane Price Herndl, eds.
    <u>Feminisms: An Anthology of Literary</u>

Theory and Criticisms. New Brunswick:
    Rutgers UP, 1993.

Edition after the first

Fromkin, Victoria, and Robert Rodman. An
    Introduction to Language. 5th ed. Ft.
    Worth: Harcourt, 1993.

Work from an anthology

Jordan, June. "Ah, Momma." Double Stitch:
    Black Women Write about Mothers &
    Daughters. Eds. Patricia Bell-Scott,
    Beverly Guy-Sheftall, Jacqueline Jones
    Royster, Janet Sims-Wood, Miriam DeCosta-
    Willis, and Lucille P. Fultz. New York:
    Harper, 1993. 117-18.

For an article or essay that was published elsewhere before
being included in an anthology, use the following form:

Chaika, Elaine. "Grammars and Teaching."
    College English 39 (1978): 770-83. Rpt.
    in Linguistics for Teachers. Eds. Linda
    Miller Cleary and Michael D. Linn. New
    York: McGraw, 1993. 490-504.

Note where the essay first appeared and then show where
you read it. Use "Rpt." for "reprinted." Both forms require you to cite the pages where the material can be
found. In the second example, you must cite the pages of
the original publication.

Translation

Duras, Marguerite. <u>The North China Lover</u>.
    Trans. Leigh Hafrey. New York: New Press,
    1992.

Reprint

Alcott, Louisa May. <u>Work: A Story of
    Experience</u>. 1873. Harmondsworth: Penguin,
    1995.

The original work was published over a century before this
paperback version. Use this form for books—even relatively recent ones—that have been reissued in a new
format.

A multivolume work

Odell, George C. D. <u>Annals of the New York
    Stage</u>. 15 vols. New York: Columbia UP,
    1927-49.

Cite the total number of volumes in a work when you have
used more than one volume. If you use only one volume,
include the number (preceded by the abbreviation *Vol.*)
after the title and include the number of volumes in the
complete work at the end of the entry:

Blanco, Richard L., ed. <u>The American
    Revolution, 1775-1783: An Encyclopedia</u>.
    Vol. 1. Hamden: Garland, 1993. 2 vols.

Encyclopedias and almanacs

```
Hopkinson, Ralph G. "Electric Lighting."
    Encyclopedia Americana. 1985 ed.
```

Full publication information is not necessary for a well-known reference work organized alphabetically. For sources that are more unusual, you should reveal more about the source:

```
Dreyer, Edward L. "Inner Mongolia."
    Encyclopedia of Asian History. Ed.
    Ainslee T. Embree. 4 vols. New York:
    Scribner's, 1988.
```

When an author's name is indicated only by initials, check the table of contents for a list of contributors. When an article is anonymous, begin your entry with the article title.

An introduction, foreword, or afterword

```
Morrison, Toni. Afterword. The Bluest Eye. By
    Toni Morrison. New York: Penguin, 1994.
    209-16.
```

Pamphlets and bulletins

```
Safety Data Sheet: Kitchen Machines. Pamphlet
    690. Chicago: Natl. Restaurant Assn.,
    1970.
```

Government publication

```
McDonald, Mike. Amphibian Inventory of the
    Jarbidge Resource Area, Boise District.
```

```
Technical Bulletin. Boise: US Bureau of
Land Management, Idaho State Office,
1995.
```

When citing a government publication, identify the government (e.g., "United States," "Minnesota") followed by the agency that issued the work.

Articles

The documentation format for articles differs slightly from that for books. The three units are the same, and they are still separated by periods, but note the differences in treatment for titles and publication information.

Author	Titles	Publication data
Lastname, Firstname.	"Title of Article." <u>Periodical</u>	day/month/year: pages.
Lastname, Firstname.	"Title of Article." <u>Journal</u>	volume (year): pages.

1. *Author*. Give the last name first, followed by a comma and the first name.
2. *Article title*. Type the article title in regular (Roman) face, and put it in quotation marks with the period inside the final quotation marks. Capitalize all major words in the title.
3. *Publication data*. All references provide the periodical title, the date of publication, and the page numbers on which the article appeared. Continuously underline the periodical title, and capitalize major words. Note that no punctuation follows the periodical title and that a colon introduces the page numbers. If the periodical provides both volume number and date, put the date in parentheses.

Weekly magazine or newspaper

```
Stresser, Stan. "Report from Cambodia." The
New Yorker 18 May 1992: 43-75.
```

MLA style abbreviates the names of months (except for May, June, and July).

Daily newspaper

```
Ibata, David. "Information Highway to the
     Future." Chicago Tribune 17 Nov. 1992,
     final ed., sec. 1: 8.
```

When it is not part of the newspaper's name, the city's name should be given in brackets after the title: *Star Tribune* [Minneapolis]. If a specific edition is not named on the masthead, put a colon after the date and provide the page reference. Insert the section number immediately before the page number. If the section is lettered, simply include the section letter next to the page number as it appears in the newspaper: A7 or 7A.

Editorial

```
Lewis, Anthony. "Black and White." Editorial.
     New York Times 18 June 1992, natl. ed.,
     A19.
```

If the editorial is not signed, begin with the title.

Monthly magazine

A *journal* is a scholarly publication for a specific profession, whereas a *magazine* is written for the general public.

```
Barlow, John Perry. "Is There a There in
     Cyberspace?" Utne Reader March-April 1995:
     53-56.
```

Magazine articles are often interrupted by other articles. Give only the first page number followed by a plus sign: 45+.

Journal with continuous pagination

```
Diaz, Gwendolyn. "Desire and Discourse in
     Maria Luisa Bombal's New Islands."
     Hispanofila 112 (1994): 51-63.
```

Citing a specific issue is not necessary when a journal's pages are numbered continuously throughout the year.

Journal with separate pagination

```
Leroux, Neil. "Frederick Douglass and the
     Attention Shift." Rhetoric Society
     Quarterly 21.2 (1991): 36-46.
```

When an issue is paged separately (each issue begins with page 1), put a period after the volume number and add the issue number.

Nonprint sources

Motion picture

```
Richard III. Dir. Richard Loncraine. MGM/
     United Artists. 1995.
```

When you cite a particular performance, a screenplay, and so on, put the person's name first:

```
McKellen, Ian, perf. Richard III. By William
     Shakespeare. Screenplay by Ian McKellen.
```

```
Dir. by Richard Loncraine. MGM/United
Artists, 1996.
```

Radio or television program

```
"'Barbarian' Forces." Ancient Warriors. Narr.
Colgate Salsbury. Dir. Phil Grabsky. The
Learning Channel. 1 Jan. 1996.
```

Play

```
A Streetcar Named Desire. By Tennessee
Williams. Dir. Gregory Mosher. Barrymore
Theater, New York. 9 Aug. 1992.
```

Recording

```
Moby. Everything Is Wrong. Compact Disc. Mute
Records Limited, 1996.
```

Electronic media

Citations to CD-ROM disks and diskettes should identify the publisher, the place, and the date of publication. Citations for information obtained on-line should state the electronic address and the date of access. The electronic address must be absolutely precise.

The *MLA Handbook for Writers of Research Papers,* 4th edition, does not address sources available through FTP, the World Wide Web, Gopher, Telnet, listserv, or synchronous communication, nor does it indicate how to represent hypertext linkages. Until the *MLA Handbook* is revised to include them, ask whether your instructor will accept the following supplementary citation formats (based on Harnack and Kleppinger's article in *Kairos*).

E-mail

E-mail is treated much the way letters are treated.

```
Mapp, Larry G. "Rhetoric and Hypertext."
     E-mail to Suzanne Webb. 10 Mar. 1996.
```

Harnack and Kleppinger suggest adding the sender's e-mail address, the kind of communication, and the date of access:

```
Mapp, Larry G. ⟨lgmapp@frank.mtsu.edu⟩
     "Rhetoric and Hypertext." 10 Mar. 1996.
     Personal e-mail. (11 Mar. 1996).
```

CD-ROM

```
"About Richard III." Cinemania 96. CD-ROM.
     Redmond: Microsoft, 1996. 20 June 1996.
```

Publication on diskette

```
Hieatt, Constance, Brian Shaw, and Duncan
     Macrae-Gibson. Beginning Old English:
     Exercise Disk. Vers. 6.4. Diskette.
     Binghamton: OEN Subsidia. 1994. DOS.
```

More than one medium

```
English Poetry Plus. CD-ROM, diskette. New
     York: Films for the Humanities &
     Sciences, 1995.
```

Electronic texts

Shakespeare, William. <u>Richard III</u>. <u>The Works
    of William Shakespeare</u>. Ed. Arthur H.
    Bullen. Stratford Town Ed. Stratford-on-
    Avon: Shakespeare Head, 1911. Online.
    Dartmouth Coll. Lib. Internet. 18 June
    1996.

Electronic journal

Harnack, Andrew, and Gene Kleppinger. "Beyond
    the <u>MLA Handbook</u>: Documenting Sources on
    the Internet." <u>Kairos</u> 1.2 (summer 1996):
    n. pag. Online. Internet. 14 Aug. 1996.
    Available: http://www.english.ttu/acw/
    kairos/index.html

Harnack and Kleppinger suggest setting off the electronic
address in angle brackets. Consult your instructor about
which form to use.

World Wide Web

"<u>Richard III</u>: On Stage and Off." <u>Richard III
    Society</u>. 22 Nov. 1995. ⟨http://
    www.webcom.com/~blanchrd/mckellen/
    index.html⟩ (7 July 1996).

Gopher

Page, Melvin E. "Brief Citation Guide for
    Internet Sources in History and the

Humanities." 20 Feb. 1996. 〈gopher://h-
net.msu.edu/00/lists/h-africa/internet-
cit〉 (7 July 1996). [OR command-path
address: gopher h-net.msu.edu/00/lists/
h-africa/internet-cit]

FTP

"Beowulf, fol. 192 verso." The Electronic
Beowulf Project. ftp 〈ftp://
beowulf.engl.uky.edu/ftp/pub/beowulf〉 (27
Aug. 1996). [OR command-path address: ftp
beowulf.engl.uky.edu/ftp/pub/beowulf]

Newsgroup

May, Michaela. "Questions about RYAs." 19 June
1996. Online posting. Newsgroup alt.soc.
generation-x. Usenet. 29 June 1996.

Because newsgroup messages are not usually retrievable
after a few weeks, use information from these sources with
care.

Synchronous communications

Galin, Jeff. "Teaching Writing in the Digital
Age: What Makes Teaching Good These
Days?" Netoric's Tuesday Cafe Discussion.
MediaMOO. telnet purple-crayon.media.mit.
edu/8888. (10 Sep. 1996).

Linkage data

```
Schipper, William.
     ⟨schipper@morgan.ucs.mun.ca⟩ "Re: Quirk
     and Wrenn Grammar." 5 Jan. 1995 ⟨ansax-
     l@wvnvm.wvnet.edu⟩ via gopher
     cwis.ucs.mun.ca (12 Sep. 1996). Lkd.
     ⟨http://www.georgetown.edu/labyrinth⟩.
```

Oral sources

Lecture

```
Thompson, Lou. "Understanding The Turtle
     Diaries." Class lecture. English 3273.
     Texas Woman's University, Denton, TX. 11
     Sep. 1996.
```

Provide a descriptive label for an untitled lecture.

Interview

```
Day, Michael. Personal interview. 31 May 1996.
```

For samples of citations of other nonprint sources, consult Eugene B. Fleischer's *A Style Manual for Citing Microform and Nonprint Media* (Chicago: American Library Association, 1978).

(3) **Final revising, editing, and proofreading**

Refer to chapters **26** and **29** as needed, particularly the revising, editing, and proofreading checklists. If you have questions about final manuscript form, refer to chapter **26** and to the sample research papers in **34b** and **34e**.

Some instructors require a title page and a final outline along with the text of the paper. The MLA recommends using no title page and giving the identification on the first page before the title of the paper. (For a sample title page that can be modified for an MLA style paper, see **34e,** Sample APA research paper.)

34b Sample MLA research paper

When submitted with the text of a research paper, the final outline serves as a table of contents. In this case, a title page is advisable.

Comments

1. The identification, double-spaced, begins one inch from the top of the page and flush with the left margin. A double-spaced line precedes the centered title of the paper. A margin of one inch is provided at the left, right, and bottom.
2. Double-space between the title and the first line of the text. (A title consisting of two or more lines is double-spaced, and each line is centered.)
3. All pages (including the first one) are numbered with Arabic numerals in the upper right-hand corner, one-half inch from the top. The page number is preceded by the author's last name. Notice that no period follows the page numbers.
4. All three quotations in paragraph 2 are cited with only a page number because the authors' names are included in the text.

Katie Frushour
Professor Thompson
English 200, Section 5
8 May 1997
Using Cinematic Techniques to Emphasize Theme:
    Olivier's and Loncraine's <u>Richard III</u>

    Shakespeare's plays are popular targets   1
for film adaptations, and <u>Richard III</u> is no
exception. With his 1995 release of <u>Richard
III</u>, Richard Loncraine is the newest addition
to the field of Shakespearean directors,
joining Laurence Olivier, who directed a
version of the same play in 1955. While the
films are true to the play's central theme of
tyranny, the cinematic techniques of the two
versions of <u>Richard III</u> are dramatically
different. In order to demonstrate the tyranny
of Richard, Olivier uses more traditional
techniques, such as a cyclical theme, artful
use of the shadow, and a careful film
adaptation, while Loncraine relies on an
unusual setting, clever casting, and creative
film adaptation.

    Olivier's traditional cinematic methods   2
bring the complexity of Richard, Duke of
Gloucester, to life by highlighting his malice
and desire to control the crown of England.
Olivier uses the cyclical theme of the crown
being handed from king to king to symbolize
the rise and fall of Richard III, what
Constance Brown justly calls "the central
device of coherence" (133). Jack Jorgens
concurs with Brown's assertion as he states

Comments

1. The second reference to Jorgens includes both a direct quotation and a paraphrase. Both are cited with a reference to page 137.
2. Notice how Frushour integrates the information from Jorgens into her own analysis.
3. Frushour uses her own viewing of Olivier's film for this information, and so nothing need be cited (paragraph 3).

that there "is no question that the theme of
the crown is important to the film" (137).
Jorgens identifies the theme of the film as
the "fall and rise of state" and argues that
the fall and rise are represented by the image
of the crown (137). The film opens with the
crowning of Edward IV, after which the
audience learns of Richard's self-serving lust
for the throne. The audience increasingly
becomes a party to Richard's growing tyranny
in his quest for power, which culminates in
his possession of the crown of England. Soon
after obtaining the throne, however, Richard's
tyrannical methods lead to his death and the
surrender of the crown to Richmond, the
rightful heir. This common cycle of events
creates a sense of balance, which is central
to the theme.

Another technique employed by Olivier is 3
the artful use of the shadow. As Richard
confides his plots to kill Clarence and to
marry Lady Anne, his shadow slowly grows until
it consumes the screen. Likewise, while the
audience watches Clarence describe the
horrible nightmare he sees through the window
of his cell in the Tower, the camera slowly
reveals the shadow of Richard on the cell
door. Through this action, Anthony Davies
suggests, the audience becomes an accomplice
to Richard's eavesdropping and thus a
confidant to his plotting (70). This action is
cinematically advantageous because it involves
the audience in the film, while developing

Comments

1. Because the quotation from Jorgens in paragraph 3 is brief, it can be run in with the text instead of being indented.
2. In paragraph 4, Frushour identifies McKellen's dual roles in the film—as main character and as the writer of the screenplay.
3. The citation to Wilson's article, (83–84), at the end of paragraph 4 indicates that the summarized information appears on two pages.
4. Because Robert Wilson engages in a lengthy discussion about the archetypal clichés in *Richard III,* a summary of the remainder of his thesis is included in the notes and is indicated by a superscript numeral. The discussion is not included in the text because it is not directly relevant to Frushour's analysis.

Richard's tyranny. Finally, the shadow is used
to emphasize the intertwining of Richard with
the Duke of Buckingham, a vital alliance in
Richard's quest for the crown. Jorgens
describes this powerful scene: "Buckingham's
shadow merges with Richard's . . . and the
shadow of the murderers falls upon the crucifix
in Clarence's cell as they enter to kill him"
(146). The shadows of both men are shown side
by side as they exit a room after plotting to
meet the young Prince of Wales' escort. This
visual representation of the alliance of
Richard and Buckingham reinforces their ties
to one another and provides a strong contrast
centered on Richard's tyranny when he and
Buckingham are estranged.

Perhaps the most important of Olivier's 4
cinematic techniques is his adaptation of the
play. Shakespeare plays are never performed in
their entirety, as actor/screenwriter Ian
McKellen states in the "Production Notes" of
Loncraine's version of Richard III. Olivier
uses traditional methods of adaptation, such
as cutting characters and dialogue, which
serve to clarify the plot by eliminating minor
characters. He also maintains the stereotypes
of the characters defined by Shakespeare.
Robert Wilson points out that Olivier uses
Shakespeare's archetypal clichés of Lady Anne
and Richard III (83-84).[1]

However, Olivier also adds scenes to the 5
film that are not in the play. One of these

Comments

1. The long quotation in paragraph 5 from *Magill's Survey of Cinema* is set off as a block, indented one inch from the left margin, because it is longer than four typed lines. Brackets indicate that the information enclosed is not part of the quotation. The ellipsis points that appear at the end of the quotation indicate that the remainder of the quoted sentence is omitted.

2. No page number is cited in the parentheses because *Magill's Survey of Cinema* is an electronic source and has no pages. Instead, the quotation can be found by searching for a distinctive phrase.

3. When using an anonymous source such as *Magill's Survey of Cinema,* use a shortened version of the title. Frushour uses the title of the article in the work: "Richard III."

4. The reference to Brown in paragraph 6 includes Brown's name because the name is not mentioned in the text immediately preceding the reference.

5. The reference to Stark in paragraph 7 acknowledges that Frushour got the idea that there is renewed interest in Shakespeare because of Branagh's productions from Stark's article. No page is cited because Frushour used the online version of the source.

Frushour 4

key additions is described in <u>Magill's Survey of Cinema</u>:

> [Olivier] interpolated the
> coronation of <u>Edward IV</u> from the end
> of <u>Henry VI, Part 3</u> (the play that
> preceded <u>Richard III</u> in
> Shakespeare's history cycle) into
> the beginning of the film. This
> accomplished two things: it gave the
> audience a bit of welcome background
> to the action commencing on screen,
> and it also gave Olivier a framing
> device to use. . . . ("<u>Richard III</u>")

This adaptation is important to the theme 6
of the film because it provides an insight
into the events that lead to Richard's
coronation, and it provides the cyclical theme
of the three crownings. Olivier also adds
Mistress Shore to the opening scenes. Her
brief interaction with Edward IV emphasize
Edward's lasciviousness (Brown 14), which
parallels Richard's lust for power. These
brief scenes work to enforce the image of
Richard as tyrant and are an important part of
the cinematic beauty of Laurence Olivier's
<u>Richard III</u>.

Loncraine's release of <u>Richard III</u> in 7
1995 takes a more contemporary approach to
Shakespeare. Fueled by a renewed interest in
Shakespeare resulting from Kenneth Branagh's
success in bringing the playwright to the big
screen (Stark), the film sparked a controversy
concerning Loncraine's choice of setting.

Comments

1. Kauffmann's complaints about the film are given in a footnote because they are not directly relevant to Frushour's analysis.
2. In paragraph 7, ellipsis points in the quotation from Kersey and from Kroll (see original text below) show that nonessential information is omitted.

   Source: Kroll, Jack. "Richard III—My Kingdom for a Movie." <u>Newsweek</u> 29 Jan. 1996: 58.

   Loncraine gives you true movie visuals and rhythms as Richard rises to power, polishing off all the men, women, and children in his way, in an England of art deco and prewar tensions.
3. The citation to Kersey in paragraph 7 refers to a Newsgroup posting for which no page number is available. The Works Cited list, however, gives the full electronic address for the source.
4. Notice that the page number for the blocked quotation from Brantley in paragraph 7 comes after the final period, whereas for quotations that are run into the text, such as Kroll's, the page number comes before the period.

Loncraine uses a fictional, fascist, art deco London circa 1930, which adds to its cinematic capabilities. Although critics such as Stanley Kauffmann complain that Loncraine's setting is unbelievable,[2] Jack Kroll states, "Loncraine gives you true movie visuals and rhythms as Richard rises to power . . . in an England of art deco and prewar tensions" (58). The setting parallels the tyranny of Richard. Richard's tyranny fuels his rise to power, which "parallels Nazi Germany . . . with his introduction at a Nuremberg-style rally just prior to his coronation" (Kersey). Ben Brantley further stresses the effectiveness of Loncraine's setting to emphasize the image of tyranny:

> Setting the work in Fascist Europe, with Richard's Black Shirt presence playing on memories of Oswald Mosley and Edward VII's alleged Nazi sympathies, always made a certain sense. It immediately set up echoes of what is still perceived as the greatest historical example of evil in the 20th century: Hitler's Third Reich. (1)

This setting, complete with "a wild boar 8 on the flags instead of a swastika" (Kersey) and modeled from the modern image of tyranny and fascism, makes the film more appealing to audiences with a strong mental picture of Hitler's rule. McKellen states, "We weren't

Comments

1. Newspapers are cited by giving both the page number and the section in which the article appears. (Sime 1C) in paragraph 8 is an example.
2. Brackets in the blocked quotation in paragraph 9 indicate that the production notes include only the actor's surname.
3. No page number is necessary for the blocked quotation in paragraph 9 because it is a citation to a Web page. In this instance, a paragraph number is given instead, according to advice (rather than a requirement) in the *MLA Handbook*. However, the full electronic address appears in the Works Cited.

trying to bring the play <u>Richard III</u> to as
many people as possible, but trying to make a
film . . . that would appeal to as many people
as possible" (Sime 1C). The audience relates
Richard to Hitler, enforcing both the theme
and the cinematic appeal of the film.

     Loncraine also makes a few casting   9
decisions that relate the plot and theme of
the film to the audience. The "Production
Notes" from <u>Richard III</u> explain:

> [Robert] Downey [Jr.] and Annette
> Bening play Americans. Their casting
> . . . grew out of the fact that in
> the play Queen Elizabeth and her
> brother, Earl Rivers, are outsiders.
> They are not members of the
> aristocracy and Loncraine and
> McKellen wanted to find a twentieth-
> century equivalent. (Paragraph 15)

Loncraine's choice to cast two Americans in
the small but important roles of Queen
Elizabeth and her brother emphasizes the role
of both characters as outsiders by equating
their exclusion from the aristocracy to an
average American's exclusion from royalty in
Britain today. Thus, a seemingly minor part of
the cinematic production enables Loncraine to
demonstrate a crucial element of the plot.

     Finally, like Olivier's film, the most   10
important technique emphasizing the theme of
Loncraine's film while making it cinematically
favorable is adaptation. Ian McKellen, who
wrote the screenplay in addition to playing

Comments

1. The citations in paragraph 10 refer to the two identically authored and titled films. The director's name is included to distinguish one version from the other.
2. The citation in paragraph 10 to the interview with McKellen includes the title to avoid confusion with other electronic sources that quote McKellen. Since the reference is to a Web page, there is no page number.

Richard, makes numerous character cuts,
rearranges or drops lines, and combines
scenes. Characters like Lords Dorset and
Northumberland and Queen Margaret are
eliminated, and their lines are given to other
characters. To increase the pace of the film,
McKellen combines two scenes between Richard
and Lady Anne (Loncraine, Richard III), so
that she is successfully wooed in one scene
rather than two (Olivier, Richard III). This
reduction in scenes emphasizes the power that
Richard has over Anne. Even in his negative
review of Loncraine's film, Kauffmann
describes the scene between Anne and Richard
as intrinsically interesting (30). Yet,
despite the major alterations that McKellen
makes, he insists on preserving the spirit of
Shakespeare. He says, in an on-line interview,
"I will not betray his words." McKellen
emphasizes the fact that although the
characters are changed, lines rearranged, and
scenes added or dropped, the words remain true
("Richard III: Interview with Sir Ian
McKellen"). This dedication to the spirit of
Shakespeare's Richard III, while making
cinematically advantageous alterations,
enables Loncraine to focus on the tyranny of
Richard.

     In Olivier's version of the play,   11
Richard's tyranny is stressed using
traditional methods that are as cinematically
appealing today as they were in 1955.
Likewise, Loncraine's Richard III introduces a

Comments

1. Notes are usually put at the end of the text and titled *Notes*. They are coordinated with their location in the text by a superscript number that comes before the indented first line of the note and also at the appropriate location in the text.

2. Footnotes fell out of general use because of the difficulty of arranging text around them. Rather, the information was placed on a separate page at the end of the text, which has the additional advantage of making it easy for a reader to set the notes side-by-side with the page being read. In-text citation is even easier to manage, and in an electronic source, a hypertext link (which generally offers fuller information) often accomplishes the same purpose as a note.

dramatic twist to the film, opening it for
cinematic reinterpretation. Both directors
successfully emphasize the tyranny of Richard
III while employing vastly different, yet
equally effective, cinematic techniques.

Notes

[1]Wilson states that Lady Anne continues
to represent the angel image that is set in
opposition to the devil image represented by
the character of Richard III (83-84). He
further explains that as the angel, Lady
Anne's assigned duty is to reform the fallen
man, Richard III. Richard III, the devil, is
defined by his symbolic rape of the weakened
victim, Lady Anne.

[2]Kauffmann argues that by changing the
setting to Fascist times, Loncraine succeeds
only in creating an unbelievable story line
and distorts Shakespeare's original
intentions. Kauffmann says, "Are we to believe
that this power-greedy homicidal malcontent
was a fascist? Nonsense. He had nothing in his
head except schemes for personal advancement"
(30).

Comments

1. All works cited as sources in the paper and only those should be included in the list of works cited.
2. Alphabetize entries according to the author's last name. Works with more than one author are alphabetized under the name of whichever writer is listed first in the source itself.
3. Observe the use and placement of periods and commas, especially in relation to parentheses and quotation marks. A colon separates a title from a subtitle and the place of publication from the publisher's name. A colon also precedes page numbers of articles from periodicals. Some authorities recommend using angle brackets to set off an electronic address in citations to electronic sources as shown in the alternate citations below.
4. Alternate citation for Kersey:

Kersey, Alan. ⟨kersey@aol.com⟩ "Review: Richard III (1995)" ⟨rec.arts.movies.reviews⟩ (9 July 1996).

5. Alternate citation for "Richard III: Interview with Sir Ian McKellen":

"Richard III: Interview with Sir Ian McKellen." Richard III Onstage and Off. 22 Nov. 1995. ⟨http://www.webcom.com/~blanchrd/mckellen/film/mckell.html⟩ (3 July 1996).

Frushour 10

Works Cited

Brantley, Ben. "Mesmerizing Men of Ill Will."
New York Times 21 Jan. 1996, late ed.:
1+.

Brown, Constance. "Olivier's Richard III: A
Reevaluation." Focus on Shakespeare
Films. Ed. Charles W. Eckert. Englewood
Cliffs: Prentice, 1972. 131-45.

Davies, Anthony. Filming Shakespeare's Plays:
The Adaptations of Laurence Olivier,
Orson Welles, Peter Brook, and Akira
Kurosawa. Cambridge: Cambridge UP, 1988.

Jorgens, Jack J. Shakespeare on Film.
Bloomington: Indiana UP, 1977.

Kauffmann, Stanley. "Stanley Kauffmann on
Films: Shrinking Shakespeare." The New
Republic 12 Feb. 1996: 30-31.

Kersey, Alan. "Review: Richard III (1995)." 6
May 1996. Online posting. Newsgroup
rec.arts.movies.reviews. Usenet. 9 July
1996.

Kroll, Jack. "Richard III--My Kingdom for a
Movie." Newsweek 29 Jan. 1996: 58.

Richard III. By William Shakespeare.
Screenplay by Ian McKellen. Dir. Richard
Loncraine. MGM/United Artists, 1995.

Richard III. Dir. Laurence Olivier. British
Broadcasting Company, 1955.

"Richard III: Interview with Sir Ian
McKellen." 20 Dec. 1995. Online.
Internet. 3 July 1996. Available http://
www.webcom.com/~blanchrd/mckellen/film/
mckell.html

Comments

1. An anonymous source (such as <u>Magill's Survey of Cinema</u> or "<u>Richard III</u>: Production Notes") is alphabetized under the first important word in the title.
2. Alternate citation for "<u>Richard III</u>: Production Notes":

"<u>Richard III</u>: Production Notes." <u>Richard III</u>
    <u>Onstage and Off</u>. 20 Dec. 1995. ⟨http://
    www.webcom.com/~blanchrd/mckellen/film/
    notes.html⟩ (3 July 1996).

3. Inclusion of the issue number and date indicates that each issue of this journal is paged separately.

"Richard III." Magill's Survey of Cinema. CD-
     ROM. Salem: Salem Press, Inc., 1996.

"Richard III: Production Notes." 20 Dec. 1995.
     Online. Internet. 3 July 1996. Available
     http://www.webcom.com/~blanchrd/mckellen/
     film/notes.html

Sime, Tom. "Now Is McKellen's Winter of
     Content: Acclaimed Shakespearean Finally
     Wins Film Stardom in Richard III." Dallas
     Morning News 4 Feb. 1996: 1C.

Stark, Susan. "His Naked Villainy: Sir Ian
     McKellen Is No Garden-Variety Richard
     III." The Detroit News 20 Jan. 1996: n.
     pag. Online. Internet. 3 July 1996.
     Available http://www.detnews.com/menu/
     stories/32720.htm

Wilson, Robert F., Jr. "Shakespeare and
     Hollywood: Two Film Clichés." Journal of
     Popular Film and Television 15.2 (1987):
     83-84.

34c   Some disciplines use the note style of documentation.

Both footnotes and endnotes require that a superscript number be placed as near as possible to whatever it refers to, following the punctuation at the end of the direct or indirect quotation. **Footnotes** should be single-spaced four lines below the last line of text on the same page. Double-space between footnotes if more than one appears on any one page. **Endnotes** should be double-spaced on a separate page headed *Notes*.

A book by one author

¹Jeanne Rosier Smith, <u>Writing Tricksters: Narrative Strategy and Cultural Identity in Maxine Hong Kingston, Louise Erdrich, and Toni Morrison</u> (Berkeley: U of California P, 1997) 143.

Indent five spaces.

A book by more than one author

²Deborah H. Holdstein and Cynthia L. Selfe, eds., <u>Computers and Writing: Theories, Research, Practice</u> (New York: MLA, 1990) 124.

³Gail E. Hawisher, Paul LeBlanc, Charles Moran, and Cynthia L. Selfe, <u>Computers and the Teaching of Writing in American Higher Education, 1979-1994: A History</u>. New

Directions in Computers and Composition
Studies. 1 (Norwood: Ablex, 1996) 201.

A multivolume work

[4]George C. D. Odell, Annals of the New
York Stage, vol. 15 (New York: Columbia UP,
1949) 243.
[5]Richard L. Blanco, ed., The American
Revolution, 1775-1783: An Encyclopedia, vol. 1
(Hamden: Garland, 1993) 2 vols. 377.

An edited book

[6]Robyn R. Warhol and Diane Price Herndl,
eds., Feminisms: An Anthology of Literary
Theory and Criticisms (New Brunswick: Rutgers
UP, 1993) 165.

A work in an anthology

[7]June Jordan, "Ah, Momma," Double Stitch:
Black Women Write about Mothers & Daughters,
eds. Patricia Bell-Scott, Beverly Guy-
Sheftall, Jacqueline Jones Royster, Janet Sims-
Wood, Miriam DeCosta-Willis, and Lucille P.
Fultz. 1991 (New York: Harper, 1993) 117-18.

An introduction, preface, foreword, or afterword

[8]Toni Morrison, afterword, The Bluest
Eye, by Toni Morrison (New York: Penguin,
1994) 209-16.

An article from a newspaper

⁹David Ibata, "Information Highway to the Future," <u>Chicago Tribune</u> 17 Nov. 1992, final ed., sec. 1: 8.

An article from a magazine

¹⁰Stan Stresser, "Report from Cambodia," <u>The New Yorker</u> 18 May 1992: 63.

An article from a journal with continuous pagination

¹¹Gwendolyn Diaz, "Desire and Discourse in Maria Luisa Bombal's <u>New Islands</u>" <u>Hispanofila</u> 112 (1994): 51-63.

34d   APA style documentation is appropriate for research papers in psychology and most social sciences.

(1) Using parenthetical citations

In APA style, the basic elements of a parenthetical citation are the author's last name, the year of publication, and the page number if the reference is to a specific passage. If the author's name is mentioned in the text, give the date alone or the date and the page number in parentheses.

A work by one author

One writer has stated, "Prisons can be divided into specific social groups organized by type of crime" (Liptz, 1979, p. 235).

OR

Liptz has stated, "Prisons can be divided into specific social groups organized by type of crime" (1979, p. 235).

OR

Liptz (1979) has stated, "Prisons can be divided into specific social groups organized by type of crime" (p. 235).

APA style requires *p.* (or *pp.* for "pages") before the page reference. Use commas to separate the author's name from the date and the date from the page reference.

A work by two authors

There is evidence that students in second and third grade respond favorably to guidance from elementary school students in higher grades (Bowman & Myrick, 1987).

Use the ampersand (&) to separate the authors' names.

A work by more than two authors

One study has shown that people who fear failure are not susceptible to hypnosis (Manganello, Carlson, Zarillo, & Teeven, 1985).

For works with *three to five authors*, cite all authors in the first reference, but in subsequent references give only the last name of the first followed by *et al.* For works with *more than six authors,* provide only the last name of the first followed by *et al.,* even in the first citation.

Anonymous works

```
Chronic insomnia usually requires medical
intervention ("Sleep," 1993).
```

The author has cited "Sleep disorders: What can be done about them."

Two or more works within the same parentheses

```
Much animal experimentation may be both
unnecessary and cruel (Mayo, 1983; Singer,
1975).
```

Use a semicolon to separate different studies, and arrange them in alphabetical order.

(2) Listing the references—APA style

Format the "References" (alphabetical list of works cited) in the APA style your instructor specifies. As the fourth edition of the *Publication Manual* asserts, **final manuscript style** allows considerable freedom to format documents. Some instructors prefer that the first line of each entry in the references list be typed flush left and that subsequent lines be indented three spaces. Others prefer that you indent the first line of each entry five spaces and type subsequent lines flush left. The reference entries below have a hanging indent, but they could have been formatted with an indented first line—the recommended approach for **copy manuscript** (see page 312).

Books

Most book entries consist of four units separated by periods:

1. *Author.* Give the author's last name and use initials for the first and middle names. For entries that contain more than one author, invert all names and put an ampersand (&) before the last one. (If two authors have the same last name and initials, spell out their first names and list the references in the alphabetical order of their first names.)
2. *Date.* Put the date in parentheses after the author's name.
3. *Title.* Capitalize only the first word in titles and subtitles. Do not capitalize other words (except for proper names that would be capitalized in other contexts). Underline the title and any period immediately following it.
4. *Publication data.* Give only enough of the publisher's name so that it can be identified clearly.

Book by one author

Riordan, C. H. (1997). <u>Equality and
    achievement: An introduction to the
    sociology of education.</u> New York: Longman.

More than one work by the same author

If you use more than one work by the same author, list the works in order of the publication date, with the earliest first. Repeat the author's name for each work.

Gates, H. L. (1995). <u>Colored people: A memoir.</u>
    New York: Vintage.
Gates, H. L. (1997). <u>13 ways to look at a
    black man.</u> New York: Random House.

Book by two or more authors

```
Fish, B. C., & Fish, G. W. (1996). The
    Kalenjiin heritage: Traditional religious
    and sociological practices. Pasadena, CA:
    William Carney Library.
```

Contrast APA style with MLA style, which inverts only the name of the first author in a multiauthor work. (See page 268.)

An edition after the first

```
Kelly, D. H. (1989). Deviant behavior: A text-
    reader in the sociology of deviance (3rd
    ed.). New York: St. Martin's.
```

Translation

```
Freud, S. (1960). Jokes and their relationship
    to the unconscious (J. Strachey, Trans.).
    New York: Norton. (Original work pub-
    lished 1905)
```

Cite the date of the translation and include the date of the original publication at the end of the entry. In text, use the following form: (Freud, 1905/1960).

A government document

```
Department of Transportation. (1996).
    Liability cost and risk analysis studies:
    Bus liability review for six transit
    systems (DOT-T-96-13). Washington, DC:
    Technological Sharing Program.
```

Treat the issuing agency as the author when no author is specified. Include a document or contract number (but not a library call number) if either number is printed on or in the document.

Works with no author

Unless Anonymous is specifically designated as the author of a work, do not use it for the list of references.

Directory of Mental Health Providers in Texas.
    (1996). Austin: State Employees' Insurance
    Agency.

Articles

Capitalize only the first word and any proper nouns in article titles, and do not put quotation marks around titles. (If the article has a subtitle, capitalize the first word.)

The title of a journal is capitalized differently from article or book titles. Underline the volume number and the commas preceding and following it (but not the issue number) so it will be distinct from the page reference (which is not preceded by *p.* or *pp.*).

Journal: Continuous pagination

Lenfant, C. (1996). High blood pressure: Some
    answers, new questions, continuing
    challenges. JAMA, 275, 1605-1606.

Journal: Separate pagination

Kolakowski, L. (1992). Amidst moving ruins.
    Daedalus, 121(2), 43-56.

Place the issue number in parentheses immediately after the volume number but do not underline it.

Monthly or weekly magazine

```
Levy, D. H. (1992, June). A sky watcher
    discovers comets and immortality.
    Smithsonian, 23, 75-82.
```

For a monthly magazine, give the year first, followed by a comma and the full spelling of the month. For a weekly magazine, provide the exact date: (1997, February 18).

Newspaper

```
Baker, R. (1996, July 23). Down with all of
    that! New York Times, p. A119.
```

Work in an anthology

```
Chlad, F. L. (1991). Chemical storage for
    industrial laboratories. In D. A. Pipitone
    (Ed.), Safe storage of laboratory chemicals
    (pp. 175-191). New York: Wiley.
```

Book review

```
Becker, J. G. (1992). The dilemma of choice
    [Review of the book Psychiatric aspects of
    abortion]. Contemporary Psychology, 37, 457-
    458.
```

When a review is titled, place the subject of the review in brackets after the review title. When a review is untitled, use the material in brackets as the title, but retain the brackets to show that this "title" is a description.

Nonprint sources

Film

```
Doran, Lindsay (Producer), & Lee, Ang
    (Director). (1995). Sense and sensibility
    [Film]. London: Mirage.
```

Recording

```
Fellows, W. (Speaker). (1993). Nutritional
    needs for women with AIDS (Cassette
    Recording No. 8294). Madison, WI:
    Nutritionworks.
```

Electronic media

The APA *Publication Manual* suggests the following formats. Note that the final period is omitted for all because trailing periods can cause difficulty in retrieving files:

Lastname, I. (date). Title of article. *Name of Periodical* [On-line], *xx*. Available: Specify path

Lastname, I. (date). Title of article or chapter. In *Title of full work* [On-line]. Available: Specify path

Computer program

```
O'Reilley, R. (1993). Prostyle [Computer
    software]. Bloomington, MN: Wordcorp. (OTR-
    71148).
```

On-line journal

```
Crump, E. (1995, February). RhetNet, a
   cyberjournal for rhetoric and writing
   [30 lines]. ACW Connections [On-line
   serial]. Available E-mail:
   acw-mem@unicorn.acs.ttu.edu or World Wide
   Web: http://prairie_island.ttu.edu/acw/
   acw.html
```

World Wide Web page

```
Salvo, M. (1996, August). Kairos. Available:
   http://acw.english.ttu.edu/acw/kairos/
   index.html
```

Cite e-mail, newsgroup, or bulletin board messages in the text but do not list them in the references.

34e   Sample APA research paper

The APA *Publication Manual* specifies two different styles of manuscripts, the **copy manuscript** and the **final manuscript**. The copy manuscript style is used for a document that will be sent to a publisher and set in type. The final manuscript style should be used for such documents as student papers, lab reports, master's theses, and doctoral dissertations.

Copy manuscripts, the APA *Publication Manual* explains, "must conform to the format and other policies of the journal to which they are submitted" (p. 332). Final manuscript style, however, permits a "number of variations from the requirements described in the *Publication*

Manual" (p. 332) and should conform to the requirements of an individual university, department, or instructor.

Generally speaking, a **title page** includes three elements, all of which are double-spaced. The **running head** is a shortened version of the **title** and appears in the upper left-hand corner of the title page. It will also appear in the upper right-hand corner of every page, including the title page, which is counted as page 1. (If you use this title page as a model for a paper in MLA style, do not include the running head or the page number.) The title appears next in upper- and lowercase letters and is centered. The **author's name** or **byline** appears below the title and is followed by the author's affiliation. If an instructor asks that the course number be included, it will generally appear as the affiliation. Unless the instructor specifically requires it, the instructor's name and the date the paper is due are not included. (A final manuscript may also include an **abstract**, a 100- to 200-word summary of the paper.)

The body of the paper should normally be double-spaced. Variations in spacing to promote readability, however, are encouraged.

A fourth essential component of the final manuscript, the **references**, is a list of all the references cited in the text. It does not usually include any references not cited. However, any material that is especially pertinent or that informs the whole paper may be included if it is considered essential. When that is the case, the reference list becomes a bibliography.

Comments

1. Student papers should be prepared in **final manuscript style** (see page 312), double-spaced with in-text citations as specified in the APA *Publication Manual*. Depending on the particular requirements of your department or instructor, requirements for final copy may differ from those for copy manuscript style described in the body of the *Manual*.

2. A **title page** includes three double-spaced elements: running head, title, and author's full name and affiliation. Center the title and author horizontally (but not necessarily vertically).

3. The **running head** is a shortened version of the title. It appears in the upper right-hand corner of every page and the upper left of the title page, which is counted as page 1.

4. If an instructor asks that the course number be included, it generally appears instead of the affiliation. Unless specifically required, the instructor's name and the date the paper is due are not included.

Running head: GENERATION X

Generation X: Moving Back Home

Adrienne Harton

Texas Woman's University

Comments

1. An abstract is a short summary of a paper. The APA *Publication Manual* requires that an abstract be supplied on the second page of any essay that is to be submitted for publication (copy manuscript style). Check with your instructor to see if an abstract is required for your paper.

2. Harton's abstract is slightly over 60 words, a reasonable length for a short paper. The usual length is 100 to 120 words.

Generation X 2

Abstract

Young adults are returning to their parents'
homes in record numbers. Research indicates
that education, occupation, and personal
lifestyles all contribute to the economic
hardships of young adults. The generation born
between 1964 and 1980 faces financial
difficulties just like previous generations,
but parents of this generation seem more
willing, almost obligated, to support their
adult children.

Comments

1. In her opening paragraph, Adrienne Harton draws on personal experience to catch her audience's interest.
2. At the beginning of paragraph 2, Harton explains what RYA means. Thereafter, she uses the abbreviation without explanation.

Generation X: Moving Back Home

     Jim and Carole Wilson appear to be a 1
comfortable couple in their 50s, married for
30 years. The Wilsons own a home, drive nice
cars, and were able to pay for a college
education for all three of their children. The
Wilsons deviate from the stereotypical couple,
though, because one of their college-educated
children has moved back home. Scott, the
oldest child, quit his temporary job (waiting
tables "while I look for something better")
and resumed residence in his old bedroom.
Unfortunately for parents like the Wilsons,
this syndrome has become increasingly common
in the past 10 years. Grown children are
returning to the nest or sometimes never
leaving at all. The primary impetus for this
phenomenon is economic: Young adults are
moving back home because of educational
opportunities or the lack of them,
occupational difficulties, and personal
lifestyle choices.

     The RYA (Returning Young Adult) 2
phenomenon is a family development syndrome
looked at as circular. The young adult leaves
home to experience adult independent living,
returns home, hopefully to leave again, this
time successfully. The act of emerging from
the core family home and finding a place in
the world can often be unsuccessful
financially for many young adults. Peck (1991)
defines the "launching" stage as "one of the

Comments

1. Paragraph 3 describes RYA by using demographic evidence.
2. Note that the long quotation—a quotation of more than 40 words—in paragraphs 2, 6, 8, and 10 is indented five spaces only, per APA style. (See **20b**.)

Generation X 4

most complex stages of the family's life cycles" (p. 150). According to Natalie Swartzberg (1991)

> American family young adulthood can be defined as usually beginning in the early twenties . . . when the young person is launched from the family of origin, and ending sometime in the early thirties, when the young adult is firmly esconced in a job and is capable of intimacy. (p. 77)

For the most part, the reason for the RYA syndrome is economics.

Before analyzing the financial reasons why people in their 20s are returning to their parents' homes, researchers first determine the characteristics of this group. Burnett and Smart (1994) define RYAs: "To be a true RYA, both the individual and parents expected the child to leave home, the child actually did leave home but, because of the need for economic support, returned" (p. 255). The RYA phenomenon is also called the crowded nest or "boomerang effect." The number of children in the RYA generation who return to live with their parents seems surprisingly high. "About 40 percent of young adults return to their parents' home at least once. Men and women are equally likely to return home until age 25, but men are more likely to return after that age" ("Boomerang age," 1990, p. 26). With almost half of the 20-something generation moving home, a family with two or more children can almost surely anticipate an RYA.

Comment

1. Paragraph 4 includes statistical evidence that will support Harton's analysis. Note that she relies heavily on one source, *American Demographics* (which, however, is a long statistical study). When introducing the Holtz study, Harton works the author's name into the text. Notice also that the page numbers follow the quote.

Generation X 5

Another intriguing statistic is that males are more likely to live with their parents than females: "Men are more than twice as likely as females to live with their parents" (Burnett & Smart, 1994, pp. 257-258). Researchers can typify the RYA as a male in his early 20s with a low-paying job or no job.

Education affects young adults in two 4 ways with regard to moving home. Either the RYA is attending college and cannot afford to live on his or her own, or the RYA chose not to further his or her education and cannot be self-sustaining on the paycheck alone. In the first case, research shows that more young adults are going to college, and almost half of first-year college students have a job ("Boomerang age," 1990, p. 30). Furthermore, many students start at 2-year colleges and so take longer to finish. Such statistics show that young adults are spending more time in college than ever before. Living with one's parents decreases a student's financial burden. Holtz (1995) claims, "The average college undergraduate was taking more than six years to earn a degree; fewer than half graduated after the traditional four years of study" (p. 124). An economic chain reaction exists for college students living at home. "Because people are delaying marriage, they are living with their parents longer. They are delaying marriage because they're going to school. They're going to school because most well-paying jobs now require a college degree" ("Boomerang age," 1990, p. 26).

Comment

1. Paragraph 5 includes a citation to a source with two authors and to a source that is a government document.

APA cit **34e** 32.

But what about the RYAs who are not 5
continuing their education? Some RYAs simply
cannot afford to live away from home on a
small salary. The typical 25-year-old working
man has a median income less than the poverty
level for a single person (Holtz, 1995, p. 158).
Obviously, returning to one's childhood home
makes sense whether the young adult is trying
to save money or to maintain a particular
lifestyle. While long-term prospects for the
educated RYA are more promising, the average
income for males without a college degree has
fallen (Levy & Michel, 1991, p. 45). Many RYAs
do not even have jobs. According to the U.S.
Census (1993), the unemployment rate for young
adults living at home is 30 to 35%.

Jobs obviously affect economic situations 6
of young adults. One study notes, "As the U.S.
economy shifts from manufacturing to services,
it sharply reduces the number of entry-level
jobs available to people who don't have much
schooling" ("Boomerang age," 1991, p. 30). As
the business and technology sectors grow
faster than areas grounded in liberal arts,
college students should plan for long-term job
security by selecting a marketable major.
Although unemployment seems to be an
undesirable predicament, RYAs have a parental
safety net, as illustrated by E. L.
Klingelhofer (1989):

The inability to find appropriate work
has not been as catastrophic a burden as
it once might have been because the

> parents were able to support the child,
> to help out, to tide him or her over.
> And, as the individual quest for work
> wore on and eventually, wore out, what
> had been thought of as a temporary
> arrangement imperceptibly became a
> permanent one. (p. 86)

Whereas unemployment once meant failure,
embarrassment, and perhaps even homelessness,
now it seems to be an opportunity to return
home.

7   Even for young adults with jobs, moving
home can be a solution to financial problems.
RYAs change careers with great frequency. As
research reveals, "Young adults have the
highest rate of occupational mobility. Thirty
percent of employed men aged 16 to 19, and 22
percent of those aged 20 to 24, changed
occupations" compared with 10 percent for all
workers ("Boomerang age," 1990, p. 52).
Apparently, grown children choose to live with
their parents to find some stability during
professional uncertainty. Furthermore, the
jobs that young adults, even when college
educated, obtain may not yield enough money to
survive away from home. Some young adults who
shoulder their entire college debts cannot
afford to live away from home while paying
student loans (Kuttner, 1995, p. M5).
Regardless, the economic sense of moving back
home exceeds the need for independence.

8   The final financial reason why grown
children are returning to the nest encompasses

personal lifestyle decisions: delayed marriage and middle-class comfort. The average age of marriage has steadily increased since the 1970s. Littwin (1986) concludes:

> Commitment to a relationship is just as difficult for them as commitment to a career or point of view. It is one act that might define them and therefore limit their potential. Besides, it is difficult to be in a relationship when you still don't know who you are. (p. 219)

With the option of moving home, young adults do not feel the pressure or the necessity to marry early. Even when people do marry early and divorce, research shows that many young adults return to their parents' homes to recover and stabilize (Klingelhofer, 1989, p. 86). RYAs can opt to live with their families as an alternative to marriage or to reestablish themselves after a divorce.

Some RYAs return to the nest to attain the material comforts of a middle- to upper-class home that they enjoyed and expected as dependents. Adult children now receive allowances, their own rooms, telephones, cars, personal freedom. Why should they leave the nest? For wealthier families, adult children moving home is a particular problem. Littwin (1986) says:

> The affluent, perfect parent is the ideal target for rebellion-and-rescue. . . . The young adult resents that he has been

Comments

1. Harton cites the personal communication from Karl James in paragraph 10 in the text but, as with other nonrecoverable sources such as personal letters, e-mail, and bulletin board postings, does not list it in the references.
2. Harton's concluding paragraph follows the traditional model of summarizing the preceding points and suggesting a direction for future study (**28f(2)**).
3. A strong final statement, the quotation Harton uses to conclude her essay contains an implicit challenge to Generation X. Note also that it is introduced by a colon (**21d(1)**).

Generation X 9

given so much that he cannot give
himself. He has been cared for too well
and too conscientiously. (p. 140)

A potential RYA, still a student at a private
university and for whom his parents pay all
expenses, recently complained about the
constraints his full-time summer job placed on
his lifestyle, "I don't see how you and Dad
get anything done when you have to work 40
hours a week" (K. James, personal
communication, August 15, 1996). In an instant-
gratification-seeking generation, returning to
the nest is just easier than earning comfort.

In conclusion, young adults are moving   11
back home for a variety of reasons. Of course,
people of the 20-something generation would
not be able to return home without parental
acquiescence. Future research will reveal if
RYAs develop a pattern of adult dependence on
their parents, but for now, research proves
that grown children are moving back home for a
myriad of financial considerations. And,
perhaps, as one Gen X'er bemoans: "We us a
generation have yet to produce any defining
traits, except perhaps to show a defeatist
belief that we will do worse than our parents"
(Janoff, 1995, p. 10).

Comments

1. The reference list is organized alphabetically and begins on a new page. The last name is always given first, and initials are provided for first and middle names. The date of publication is always given parenthetically, immediately after the author's name. (See **34d**(2).)

2. Observe the use of periods and commas, the style of capitalization for book and article titles, and the different capitalization style for journal titles. Underline book and journal titles, and carry continuous underlining of periodical titles through the volume number.

3. If Harton's instructor had specified a final manuscript format that called for the first line of each entry to be indented five spaces, the first two entries would look like this:

```
    Boomerang age. (1990). American
Demographics, 12, 25-30.
    Burnett, J., & Smart, D. (1994).
Returning young adults. Psychology and
Marketing, 11, 253-269.
```

4. Notice that the entry for Colligan's electronic article specifies its length as seven paragraphs. Citations for electronic sources sometimes refer to a specific paragraph where citations to print sources would refer to page numbers.

Generation X 10

References

Boomerang age. (1990). American Demographics, 12, 25-30.

Burnett, J., & Smart, D. (1994). Returning young adults. Psychology and Marketing, 11, 253-269.

Cipriano, E. (1996). Who is this generation formerly known as x? Seriously [On-line serial], 6(1). Available FTP: spc.5yr.edu/seriously/generation

Colligan, P. (1996, March 19) Go Pat go? No Pat no? [7 paragraphs]. CGX [On-line serial], 3(4). Available E-mail: conservgenx@teleport.com

Holtz, G. T. (1995). Welcome to the jungle: The why behind "Generation X." New York: St. Martin's Griffin.

Janoff, J. B. (1995, April 24). A gen-x Rip Van Winkle. Newsweek, 127, 10.

Klingelhofer, E. L. (1989). Coping with your grown children. Clifton, NJ: Humana Press.

Kuttner, R. (1995, June 25). The new elite: Living with mom and dad. Los Angeles Times, p. M5.

Levy, F., & Michel, R. C. (1991). The economic future of American families: Income and wealth trends. Washington, DC: Urban Institute.

Littwin, S. (1986). The postponed generation: Why American youth are growing up later. New York: William Morrow.

Generation X 11

Peck, J. S. (1991). Families launching young
    adults. In F. H. Brown (Ed.), Reweaving the
    family tapestry: A multigenerational
    approach to families. (pp. 149-168). New
    York: Norton.

Schwartzberg, N. (1991). Single young adults.
    In F. H. Brown (Ed.), Reweaving the family
    tapestry: A multigenerational approach.
    (pp. 77-93). New York: Norton.

U.S. Department of Commerce, Bureau of the
    Census. (1993). 1990 Census of Population.
    Washington, DC: U.S. Government Printing
    Office.

Chapter 35

Writing for Special Purposes

This chapter will introduce you to principles that govern writing about literature (**35a**) and effective business communication (**35b**).

35a Writing about literature increases understanding of it.

Like all specialized fields, literature has its own vocabulary. When you learn it, you are grasping concepts that will help you write about it effectively.

(1) Prepare for writing by reading, reflecting, and planning.

Begin the process by reading carefully and noting your personal response.

(a) Explore your personal response to literature.

As you read, take notes and jot down ideas. What characters do you admire? Did the work remind you of any experience of your own? Were you amused, moved, or confused? These first impressions can provide the seeds from which strong essays will grow.

(b) **Analyze, interpret, and evaluate.**

Although you may have occasion to write papers in which you simply explore your personal response to a work of literature, writing papers about a literary work usually requires you to focus on the work itself by analyzing it, interpreting it, or evaluating it. A short paper may do only one of these; a long paper may do all three.

Analyze a work of literature by breaking it into elements and examining how such elements as setting, characters, and plot combine to form a whole. How do the elements interact? How does one element contribute to the overall meaning of the work?

Interpret a work by asking what it means, bearing in mind of course that a work may have more than one meaning. Support your interpretation by referring to elements in the work itself. Interpretation is closely related to analysis and allows writers to draw freely on any part of a work that can be used to explain its meaning.

Evaluate a work by asking how successful the author is in communicating its meaning to readers. Like interpretation, evaluation is a type of argument in which a writer cites evidence to persuade readers to accept a clearly formulated thesis. (See chapter 32.) An evaluation of a literary work should consider both strengths and weaknesses if there is evidence of both.

⚠ CAUTION Although **summarizing** a literary work can be a useful way to understand it, do not confuse summary with analysis, interpretation, or evaluation. Do not submit a summary unless your instructor has asked for one.

(c) **Choose a subject and decide how to develop it.**

To choose your subject, you first should reflect on your personal response. Reviewing your response may also enable you to formulate a tentative thesis. Also try some of the methods suggested in **28c** to explore the work.

Apply strategies of development (**27d**). You might **define** why you consider a character heroic, **classify** a play as a comedy of manners, or **describe** a setting that contributes to a work's meaning. Perhaps you could **compare and contrast** two poems on a similar subject or explore **cause-and-effect** relationships in a novel.

(d) Reread carefully.

A literary work can provoke different responses, and you can have a significantly different response when rereading a work. Whenever possible, reread any work that you are planning to write about. If its length makes doing so not feasible, at least reread the chapters or scenes that impressed you as especially important or problematic.

A good way to note evidence, ideas, and concerns is to annotate as you read. Experienced readers often keep a pen or pencil at hand so they can mark passages they may wish to draw on when writing.

(e) Do research when appropriate.

Readers often favor papers that are focused on a person's individual analysis. But by reading criticism that reveals what other readers think, you can engage in a dialogue. When you draw on the ideas of other people, however, remember that you must still advance a position that is clearly your own.

Remember that a work of literature rarely has a single meaning. Three different critics may offer three radically different interpretations. Your responsibility is not to determine who is right but to determine the extent to which you agree or disagree with differing views.

Chapter **33** explains how to do research. To locate material on a specific writer or work, consult your library's catalog and the *MLA Bibliography*, an index of books and articles about literature.

You may also locate useful information in the following:

Davidson, Cathy N., et al., eds. *The Oxford Companion to Women's Writing in the United States*. New York: Oxford UP, 1995.

Drabble, Margaret, ed. *The Oxford Companion to English Literature*. 6th ed. New York: Oxford UP, 1996.

Elder, John, ed. *American Nature Writers*. 2 vols. New York: Scribner's, 1996.

Elliott, Emory, et al., eds. *Columbia Literary History of the United States*. New York: Columbia UP, 1988.

Evory, Ann, et al., eds. *Contemporary Authors*. New Revision Series. Detroit: Gale, 1981–.

Hart, James D., ed. *The Oxford Companion to American Literature*. 6th ed. New York: Oxford UP, 1995.

Hazen, Edith P., ed. *The Columbia Granger's Index to Poetry*. 10th ed. New York: Columbia UP, 1993.

Klein, Leonard. *Encyclopedia of World Literature in the 20th Century*. 2nd ed. 5 vols. New York: Ungar, 1981–84.

Levernier, James A., and Douglas R. Wilms, eds. *American Writers Before 1800*. 3 vols. Westport: Greenwood, 1983.

Preminger, Alex, et al., eds. *The Princeton Handbook of Poetic Terms*. Princeton: Princeton UP, 1986.

CAUTION Research is not appropriate for all assignments. If your instructor has not assigned a researched paper, ask if one would be acceptable.

(2) Write essays about fiction.

Although the events have not happened and the characters may never have existed, serious fiction expresses truth about the human condition through such components as **setting**, **character**, and **plot**.

Setting   **Setting** involves time—not only historical time, but also the length of time covered by the action. It also involves place—not only the physical setting, but also the atmosphere created by the author.

Plot   The sequence of events that make up the story is the **plot**. Unlike a narrative, which simply reports events, a plot establishes how events relate to one another. Narrative asks "What comes next?"; plot asks "Why?" Depending on the author's purpose, a work of fiction may have a complicated plot or almost no plot at all.

Characters   The **characters** usually include a main character, called a **protagonist**, who is in conflict with another character, with an institution, or with himself or herself. By examining a character's conflict, you can often discover a story's **theme**.

Point of view   The position from which the action is observed is the **point of view**. It may be that of a character within the story or of a narrator. Many works of fiction are told from a single point of view, but some shift the point of view from one character to another.

Tone   **Tone** is the author's attitude toward the events and characters in the story. A story could have an ironic, humorous, wry, or bitter tone. By determining a work's tone, you can gain insight into the author's purpose.

Symbolism   A **symbol** is an object, usually concrete, that stands for something else, usually abstract. In writing about a particular symbol, first note the context in which it appears. Then think about what it could mean. When you have an idea, trace the incidents in the story that reinforce that idea.

Theme   The main idea of a literary work is its **theme**. If you can relate the **setting, plot, characterization, tone,** and **symbols** to the idea you are exploring, then that idea can be considered the work's theme.

> **Checklist for Analyzing Fiction** ✓
> • From whose point of view is the story told?
> • What is the narrator's tone?
> • Who is the protagonist? How is his or her character developed?
> • With whom or what is the protagonist in conflict?
> • How does one character compare with another?
> • What symbols does the author use?
> • What is the theme?

(3) Write essays about drama.

Drama has many of the same elements as fiction.

Dialogue   Dialogue is the principal medium through which we see action and characterization when reading a play. Examine dialogue to discover motives, internal conflicts, and relationships among characters.

Characters   Characters are developed largely through what they say and what is said about them and to them. In writing about drama, you might compare characters or analyze their development through their dialogue and their actions.

Plot   Plot in drama is usually advanced by conflict between characters. **Subplots** may reinforce the theme of the main plot. You might examine how dialogue, character-

izations, setting, and stage directions for gestures and
movement further the action.

Checklist for Analyzing Drama

- How are the characters depicted through dialogue?
- What is the primary conflict within the play?
- What motivates the characters to act as they do?
- Are there any parallels between different characters?
- How does setting contribute to the play's action?
- What is the theme of the play?
- If there is more than one story in the play, how do they
  relate to one another?

---

(4) Write essays about poetry.

Poetry may contain a narrator with a point of view, and
narrative poems may have plot, setting, and characters.
But poetry is primarily characterized by its concentrated
use of the following devices.

Speaker   The first-person *I* in a poem may be a character, or **persona**, that the poet has created. Although the
poet may be the speaker, you need to distinguish between
the two.

Diction   The term **diction** means "choice of words," and
the words in poetry convey meanings beyond the obvious
denotative ones. (See **14a**.) As you read, check definitions
and derivations of key words in your dictionary to find
meanings beyond the obvious ones. How do such definitions and derivations reinforce the meaning of the poem?
How do the connotations of these words contribute to the
poem's meaning?

Imagery   The **imagery** in a poem is a word or phrase
describing a sensory experience. In a poem by Robert

Browning about a lover journeying to meet his sweetheart, the smell of the beach, the scratch of a match being lighted, and the sight of the two lovers in the match light, embracing—all are images conveying the excitement and anticipation of lovers meeting in secret.

Allusion   An **allusion** is a brief, unexplained reference to a work or a person, place, event, or thing (real or imaginary) that serves to convey meaning compactly. Writing about her father, Sylvia Plath describes him in "Daddy" as "A man in black with a Meinkampf look. . . ." *Mein Kampf* is the title of Hitler's political manifesto. Plath links her father to Hitler by making an allusion.

Paradox   A **paradox** is a seemingly contradictory statement that makes sense when thoughtfully considered. In a poem about searching for religious salvation, John Donne writes, "That I may rise and stand, o'erthrow me. . . ." The wish to be overthrown seems to contradict the desire to "rise and stand." However, the speaker believes that he will rise spiritually only after he has been overwhelmed by God.

Personification   The attribution to objects, animals, and ideas of characteristics possessed only by humans is called **personification**.

Simile   A **simile** is a comparison using *like* or *as* to link dissimilar things. (See **14a(5)**.)

Metaphor   A comparison that does not use *like* or *as*, **metaphor** is one of the figures of speech most frequently used by poets. (See **14a(5)**.)

Overstatement Also called **hyperbole**, **overstatement** is a deliberate exaggeration used for ironic or humorous effect.

Understatement Like **overstatement**, **understatement** is used for ironic or humorous effect. In this case, however, a serious matter is treated as if it were a small concern.

Sound Sound is an important element of poetry. **Alliteration** is the repetition of initial consonants, **assonance** is the repetition of vowel sounds in a succession of words, and **rhyme** is the repetition of similar sounds either at the end of lines (end rhyme) or within a line (internal rhyme).

Whenever possible, read poetry aloud so you can hear the sound.

Checklist for Analyzing Poetry
- What words have strong connotations?
- What words have multiple meanings?
- What images convey sensation?
- What figures of speech does the poet use?
- How does the poet use sound and rhyme?
- What does the poem mean?

---

(5) Use proper form in writing about literature.

Writing about literature follows certain conventions.

Tense Use the present tense when discussing literature, since the author is communicating to a present reader at the present time. (See 7c.)

Documentation Check with your instructor about the reference format he or she prefers.

Recall from 34a that references to short stories and novels are by page number; references to poetry are by line number; and references to plays are usually by act, scene, and line number.

Poetry　Type quotations of three lines or less within your text and insert a slash (**21h**) with a space on each side to separate the lines. Quotations of more than three lines should be indented one inch (or ten spaces) from the left margin, with double-spacing between lines. (See page 113.)

35b　Effective business communication is necessary in most professions.

Effective business communication requires an understanding of business conventions.

(1) Use e-mail effectively in the workplace.

When first introduced, e-mail was perceived as a vehicle for fast communication that did not need to be as carefully written as a memo or a letter. Businesses now generally use sophisticated messaging programs that make correcting typographical errors in messages easier and, therefore, as important as it would be in any business communication. In business, e-mail tends to be used for brief comments or requests, whereas longer documents are generally still handled by letter or memo. Be aware that e-mail is not really private. Most businesses operate e-mail on their own networks, so the system administrator also has access to what you have written.

　　Take care to spell your recipient's name correctly at the To: prompt, and be sure to enter an accurate and descriptive subject line. Many people find unnecessary e-mail inefficient and time-wasting. Send copies to anyone who has some legitimate reason for being included, but do not send out messages indiscriminately.

(2) Write effective memos.

Although e-mail is ideal for sending brief announcements and requests for information, many business writers prefer the memo when communicating detailed information. A memo begins with essentially the same information provided by the message header of an e-mail. If the memo is long, it sometimes begins with a summary of the discussion.

An example of memo format

To: Regional Sales Managers
From: Alicia Carroll, National Sales Director
Date: January 26, 1997
Re: Performance review

Now that we have final sales figures for 1996, it is clear that sales are growing in the South and West, but declining in the Northeast and Midwest. These results should not be seen as a reflection of individual performance. Each of you will soon receive a confidential evaluation of your work. The purpose of this memo is to outline goals for the coming year.

(3) Write effective business letters.

Standard business stationery is $8\frac{1}{2} \times 11$ inches for paper and 4×10 inches for envelopes. In the workplace, you usually use company letterhead that can be fed right into the office printer. In most cases, business letters should be word processed or typed. The main formats for business letters are block and indented.

A business letter has six parts.

The **heading** gives the writer's full address and the date. Depending on your format, place the date flush left, flush right, or centered just below the letterhead. On plain stationery, place the date below your address.

The **inside address**, placed two to six lines below the heading, gives the name and full address of the recipient.

Place the **salutation** (or greeting) flush with the left margin, two spaces below the inside address, and follow it with a colon.

In the **body** of the letter, single-space inside paragraphs and double-space between them. If you use a block format, do not indent the first line of each paragraph. If you use an indented format, indent first lines five to ten spaces.

The **closing** is double-spaced below the body. If your letter is in block style, type it flush with the left margin; if it is in indented style, align it with the heading. Place your full name four lines below the closing and, if you are writing on company business, your title on the next line.

Notations, flush with the left margin two lines below your title, indicate any materials you have enclosed with or attached to the letter (*enclosure* or *enc., attachment* or *att.*), who will receive copies of the letter (*cc: AAW, PTN* or *c: AAW, PTN*), and the initials of the sender and the typist (*DM/cll*).

Model business letter (block format)

LETTERHEAD
CONTAINING
RETURN ADDRESS

Willcox, Davern, and Smith

529 Lake Side Boulevard   Chicago, IL 60605   312-863-8916

September 1, 1997

Dr. Elizabeth Boroughs
Fairchild Clinic   } **INSIDE ADDRESS**
1710 Sheridan Ave.
Lakewood, IL 60045

Dear Dr. Boroughs: } SALUTATION

I have just given final approval to several organizational
changes designed to ensure closer attention to the individual
needs of our clients. I am writing to advise you of the one
that will affect you most directly.

- BODY

Effective the first of November, our certified public
accountants will specialize in the areas in which they have
the greatest expertise. Although we have always tried to
direct clients to the accountant best suited to their needs,
most staff members have had a diverse workload.
Accountants in our company will henceforth work within one
of three divisions: corporate, small business, and individual.

Richard Henderson, who has prepared your taxes for the past
three years, will now be working exclusively with individual
clients. I have reviewed your tax records with him, and we
agree that Grace Yee will give the Fairchild Clinic the best
help we can offer. She comes to us with twelve years

of experience working mostly with medical groups.

You can expect to hear separately from both Rick and Grace, but I wanted to let you know myself that Willcox, Davern, and Smith remains committed to serving you and your business.

Sincerely,	Complimentary Close	⎫
Ted Willcox	Signature	⎬ CLOSING
Edward Willcox	Typed Name	
President	Title	⎭

EW/nfd   } **NOTATION**

(4) Write effective application letters.

A letter of application usually accompanies a résumé (**35b(5)**) and provides you with the chance to sound articulate, interesting, and professional. Make the most of the opportunity.

Address your letter to a specific person. If you are responding to an advertisement that mentions a department without giving a name, call the company and find out who will be doing the screening. A misspelled name creates a bad impression, so make sure you spell that person's name correctly when you write.

In your opening paragraph, you should state the position you are applying for, how you learned about it, and—in a single sentence—why you believe you are qualified to fill it. Devote the paragraphs that follow to describing the experience that qualifies you for the job. Mention that you are enclosing a résumé, but do not summarize it. Your goal is to get a busy person to read the résumé. In addition to stating your qualifications, you might also indicate why you are interested in this particular company. Demonstrating that you already know something about it will help you appear to be a serious candidate.

In your closing paragraph, offer additional information and make a specific request. Instead of settling for "I hope to hear from you soon," tell your reader how and where you can be reached. At the very least, indicate that you are available for an interview.

A good letter of application should run between one and two pages, depending on your experience. As you revise, delete anything that is nonessential.

Model application letter

> 431 Felton Ave.
> St. Paul, MN 55102
> April 5, 1997

Mr. Thomas Flanagan
Tristate Airlines
2546 Ashton Ave.
Bloomington, MN 55121

Dear Mr. Flanagan:

I am writing to apply for the position of Assistant Director of Employee Benefits in the Human Resources Department of Tristate, as advertised in this morning's Star Tribune. My education and experience are well suited to this position, and I'd welcome the chance to be part of a company that has shown so much growth during a period when other airlines have been operating at a loss.

As you can see from my résumé, I majored in Business Administration with an emphasis in human resources. As an assistant in the Admissions Office at the University of Southern Minnesota, I worked successfully with students, parents, alumni, and faculty. The position required both a knowledge of university regulations and an understanding of people with different needs.

I also benefited from working as an intern last summer in the personnel division of Central Bank & Trust, a department that handles the benefits for almost three thousand employees. I learned procedures for monitoring benefits that are easily transferable.

I am very interested in putting my training to use at Tristate and hope we can schedule an interview sometime during the next few weeks. I will be in St. Paul until May 7, when I leave to spend a week visiting my family in Iowa (515-283-1652). If I haven't heard from you by then, I will telephone to see if the position is still available.

Sincerely,

Marcia Baumeister

Marcia Baumeister

enc.

(5) **Write effective résumés.**

A résumé is made up of four categories of information:

1. Personal data: name, mailing address, telephone number
2. Educational background
3. Work experience
4. References

Like the letter of application, the résumé is a form of persuasion designed to emphasize your qualifications for a job and get you an interview. If you keep your résumé in a computer file, you can easily tailor it to each job you apply for so you can present your qualifications in the best light.

Résumés can be organized in a number of ways. One is to list experience and activities in reverse chronological order, so that your most recent experience comes first. This is a good plan if you have a steady job history. An alternative is to list experience in terms of job skills. This plan is useful when your work history is modest but you know you have the skills for the job in question.

Remember that presentation is important. Use good-quality paper and a laser printer. Use boldface to mark divisions and experiment with different fonts. Resist the impulse to create fancy design features that can make the overall effect too busy to be effective. When in doubt, choose simplicity.

Checklist for Résumé Writing
- Make sure to include your name, address, and telephone number.
- Identify your career objective simply, without elaborating on future goals.
- Mention your degree, college or university, and pertinent areas of special training.

continued

continued from previous page

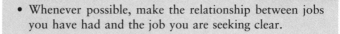

- Whenever possible, make the relationship between jobs you have had and the job you are seeking clear.

Chronological résumé

Marcia Baumeister
431 Felton Ave.
St. Paul, MN 55102
(612) 228-1927

Career Objective: A management position specializing in the administration of employee benefits.

Work Experience:

Intern, Central Bank & Trust, June–August 1996.
Provided information to new employees, helped the personnel department get on-line, and entered data for changes in medical benefits.

Student Assistant, Admissions Office, University of Southern Minnesota, January 1995–May 1997.
Responded to queries from parents and prospective students, conducted campus tours, and wrote reports on recruitment.

Tutor, University Writing Center, September 1994–May 1997.
Tutored students in business writing. Provided computer assistance, including access to the World Wide Web.

Education:

University of Southern Minnesota, B.S. with honors, 1997. Major in Business Administration with an emphasis in human resources. Minors in Economics and Communications. Recipient of the 1997 Grable Award for university service.

Active in Management Club, Yearbook, Alpha Phi Sorority

References available on request.

Glossary of Usage

The following short glossary covers the most common usage problems. It also distinguishes between formal and informal styles. An expression labeled **informal** is usually not acceptable in academic or business writing.

accept, except   *Accept* means "to receive"; *except* means "to exclude": I **accept** your apology. All **except** Joe will go.

adapt, adopt   *Adapt* means "to change for a purpose"; *adopt* means "to take possession": You must **adapt** to extreme cold. The company will **adopt** a new policy.

advice, advise   *Advice* is a noun, and *advise* is a verb: I accept your **advice.** Please **advise** me of the situation.

affect, effect   The verb *affect* means "to influence" or "to touch the emotions." The noun *effect* means "result of an action or antecedent": Smoking **affects** the heart. Drugs have side **effects.** When used as a verb, *effect* means "to produce an effect": The medicine **effected** a complete cure.

ain't   Unacceptable in writing unless used in dialogue or for humorous effect.

allusion, illusion   An *allusion* is a casual or indirect reference. An *illusion* is a false idea or an unreal image: The **allusion** was to Shakespeare. His idea of college is an **illusion.**

alot   A misspelling of the overused and nonspecific phrase *a lot*.

already, all ready   *Already* means "before or by the time specified." *All ready* means "completely prepared."

alright   Not yet a generally accepted spelling of *all right*.

altogether, all together   *Altogether* means "wholly, thoroughly." *All together* means "in a group": That book is **altogether** too difficult, unless the class reads it **all together.**

among, between   Use *among* with objects denoting three or more (a group), and use *between* with those denoting only two (or twos): whispering **among** themselves, just **between** you and me.

amount of, number of Use *amount of* with a singular noncount noun: The **amount of** rain varies. Use *number of* with a plural count noun: The **number of** errors was excessive.

anxious Not to be used as a synonym for "eager."

anyone, any one; everyone, every one *Anyone* means "any person at all"; *any one* refers to one of a group. *Everyone* means "all," and *every one* refers to each one in a group.

> Was **anyone** hurt? Was **any one** of you hurt?
>
> **Everyone** should attend. **Every one** of them should attend.

anyways, anywheres Unacceptable for *anyway, anywhere.*

as 1. As a conjunction, use *as* to express sameness of degree, quantity, or manner: Do **as** I do. As a preposition, use *as* to express equivalence: I think of Tom **as** my brother.
  2. Use *if, that,* or *whether* instead of *as* after such verbs as *feel, know, say,* or *see:* I do not know **if** [NOT as] my adviser is right.
  3. In subordinate clauses, prefer *because* to introduce a causal relationship or *while* to introduce a time relationship: **Because** [NOT as] it was raining, we watched TV.

assure, ensure, insure *Assure* means "to state with confidence." *Ensure* and *insure* are sometimes used interchangeably to mean "make certain": Marlon **assured** me that he would vote for my ticket. I **ensured** (or **insured**) that Vincent had his tickets.

as to Imprecise; use the clearer *about:* He wasn't certain **about** [NOT as to] the time.

awful Unacceptable for the often overused adverb *awfully:* She is **awfully** [NOT awful] intelligent.

awhile, a while *Awhile,* an adverb, is not used as the object of a preposition: We rested **awhile.** We rested for **a while.**

bad Unacceptable as an adverb: Bill danced **badly** [NOT bad].

being as, being that Wordy and imprecise; use *since, because.*

beside, besides Always a preposition, *beside* usually means "next to," sometimes "apart from": The chair was ·**beside** the table. As a preposition, *besides* means "in addition to" or "other than": She has many books **besides** those on the table. As an adverb, *besides* means "also" or "moreover": The library has a fine collection of books; **besides**, it has a number of valuable manuscripts.

better Unacceptable for *had better:* We **had better** [NOT better] run the spell check.

between See **among, between.**

biannual, biennial *Biannual* means twice in one year, while *biennial* means every two years.

bring, take Both words describe the same action but from different standpoints. Someone *brings* something *to* the speaker's location, while someone else *takes* something *away* from the speaker's location: **Bring** your book when you come here. I **take** my notes home with my book.

busted Unacceptable as the past tense of *burst.*

but what, but that Informal after expressions of doubt. Use *that:* I do not doubt **that** [NOT but what] they are correct.

can't hardly, can't scarcely Unacceptable for *can hardly, can scarcely.*

capital, capitol A *capital* is a governing city; it also means "funds." As a modifier, *capital* means "chief" or "principal." A *capitol* is a statehouse; the *Capitol* is the U.S. congressional building in Washington, D.C.

censor, censure *Censor* (verb) means "to remove or suppress because of moral or otherwise objectionable ideas"; a *censor* (noun) is a person who suppresses those ideas. *Censure* (verb) means "to blame or criticize"; a *censure* (noun) is an expression of disapproval or blame.

center around Informal for *to be focused on* or for *to center on.*

cite, site, sight *Cite* means "to mention." *Site* is a locale. *Sight* is a view or the ability to see: Be sure to **cite** your sources in your paper. The president visited the disaster **site**. What a tragic **sight!**

compare to, compare with *Compare to* means "regard as similar" and *compare with* means "examine to discover similarities or differences": The instructor **compared** the diagram **to** [NOT with] the finished product. The student **compared** the first draft **with** [NOT to] the second.

complement, compliment *Complement* means "to complete" or "to supply needs." *Compliment* means "to express praise": Their personalities **complement** each other. Betsy **complimented** Jim on his performance.

continual, continuous *Continual* means recurring at regular intervals: He coughed **continually.** *Continuous* means recurring without interruption: He talked **continuously.**

different than, different from Both are widely used, although *different from* is generally preferred in formal writing.

disinterested, uninterested *Disinterested* means "impartial" or "lacking prejudice": a **disinterested** referee. *Uninterested* means "indifferent, lacking interest."

don't Unacceptable when used for "doesn't": My father **doesn't** [NOT don't] dance.

drug Unacceptable as the past tense of *dragged.*

due to Usually avoided in formal writing when used as a preposition in place of *because* or *on account of*: **Because of** [NOT due to] holiday traffic, we arrived an hour late.

effect See **affect, effect.**

e.g. Abbreviation from Latin *exempli gratia* meaning "for example." Replace with the English equivalent *for example* or *for instance.* Do not confuse with **i.e.**

elicit, illicit *Elicit* means "to draw forth." *Illicit* means "unlawful": It is **illicit** to **elicit** public funds for your private use.

emigrate from, immigrate to To *emigrate* is to go out of one's own country to settle in another. To *immigrate* is to come into a different country to settle. The adjective or noun forms are *emigrant* and *immigrant*: The Ulster Scots **emigrated from** Scotland to Ireland and then **immigrated to** the United States.

eminent, imminent *Eminent* means "distinguished"; *imminent* means "about to happen": Linda Hughes is an **eminent** scholar. The storm is **imminent.**

ensure   See **assure, ensure, insure.**

enthused   Informal usage, not accepted in formal writing. Use *enthusiastic.*

especially, specially   *Especially* means "outstandingly"; *specially* means "for a particular purpose, specifically": This is an **especially** nice party. I bought this tape **specially** for the occasion.

-ess   A female suffix now considered sexist, therefore unacceptable.

etc.   From the Latin *et cetera* meaning "and other things." In formal writing substitute *and so on* or *and so forth.* Since *etc.* means "and other things," *and etc.* is redundant.

everyone, every one   See **anyone, any one.**

except   See **accept, except.**

explicit, implicit   *Explicit* means "expressed directly or precisely." *Implicit* means "implied or expressed indirectly": The instructions were **explicit.** There was an **implicit** suggestion in her lecture.

farther, further   Generally, *farther* refers to geographic distance: six miles **farther.** *Further* is used as a synonym for *additional* in more abstract references: **further** delay, **further** proof.

fewer, less   *Fewer* refers to people or objects that can be counted; *less* refers to amounts that can be observed or to abstract nouns: **fewer** pencils, **less** milk, **less** support.

figure   Informal for *believe, think, conclude,* or *predict.*

folks   Informal for *parents.*

former, latter   *Former* refers to the first of two; *latter* to the second of two. If three or more items are mentioned, use *first* and *last.*

genus   Singular form for *genera.* Takes a singular verb.

go, goes   Inappropriate in written language for *say, says:* I say [NOT go], "Hello there!"

good, well   *Good* is an adjective frequently misused as an adverb; *well* is an adverb: He dances **well** [NOT good].

great   Overworked for more precise words such as *skillful, good, clever, enthusiastic,* or *very well.*

had ought   (meaning *ought to*) Omit the verb *had:* We **ought to** go home.

half a, a half, a half a   Use *half of a, half a,* or *a half.*

hanged, hung   *Hanged* refers specifically to "put to death by hanging": She was **hanged** at dawn. *Hung* is the usual past participle: He had **hung** the picture.

he   Used inappropriately as a generic term that possibly could refer to a woman. See **13c(2)**.

heighth   Unacceptable for *height.*

hisself   Use *himself.*

hopefully   Means "with hope." Used inappropriately for *I hope* or *it is hoped.*

i.e.   Abbreviation for the Latin *id est,* meaning "that is." Use *that is* instead. Do not confuse *i.e.* with **e.g.**

if, whether   Use *if* to mean *in the event that; whether* suggests alternatives. I can't go **if** you drive; **whether** I go depends on who is driving.

illusion   See **allusion, illusion.**

imminent   See **eminent, imminent.**

implicit   See **explicit, implicit.**

imply, infer   *Imply* means "suggest without actually stating," and *infer* means "draw a conclusion based on evidence": He **implied** that he was angry, but I **inferred** that he was satisfied.

ingenious, ingenuous   *Ingenious* means "creative or shrewd." *Ingenuous* means "innocent or unworldly": Terry's **ingenious** plan worked without complication. The criminal's **ingenuous** smile was misleading.

in regards to   Unacceptable for *in regard to.*

irregardless   Use *regardless.*

its, it's   *Its* is a possessive pronoun, as in "The dog buried **its** bone." *It's* is a contraction of *it is,* as in "**It's** a beautiful day."

kind of a, sort of a   Use *kind of* and *sort of*: This **kind of** [NOT kind of a] book. . . .

lay, lie   Use *lay (laid, laying)* in the sense of "put" or "place." Use *lie (lay, lain, lying)* in the sense of "rest" or "recline." *Lay* takes an object (to **lay** something), while *lie* does not. See also 13c(3).

> Lie   He had **laid** [NOT lain] the book on the table.
>   The man was **laying** [NOT lying] the carpet.
>
> Lay   He had **lain** [NOT laid] down to take a nap.
>   The woman was **lying** [NOT laying] on the bed.

learn   Unacceptable for *teach, instruct, inform*: He **taught** me [NOT learned me] bowling.

leave   Unacceptable for *let* in the sense of allowing: **Let** [NOT leave] him have the hammer.

less   See **fewer, less**.

like   Although widely used as a conjunction in spoken English, *as, as if,* and *as though* are preferred for written English.

lose, loose   *Lose* is a verb: did **lose**, will **lose**. *Loose* is chiefly an adjective: a **loose** belt.

lots   Informal for *many, much*.

mankind   Considered offensive because it excludes women. Use *humanity, human race*.

may be, maybe   *May be* is a verb phrase; *maybe* is an adverb: The rumor **may be** true. **Maybe** the rumor is true.

media, medium   *Media* is plural; *medium* is singular.

morale, moral   *Morale* (a noun) refers to a mood or spirit: **Morale** was high. *Moral* (an adjective) refers to correct conduct or ethical character: a **moral** decision. *Moral* (as a noun) refers to the lesson of a story: the **moral** of the story.

most   Use *almost* in expressions such as "almost everyone," "almost all." Use *most* only as a superlative: **most** writers.

myself   Use only when preceded by an antecedent in the same sentence: Chin and I [NOT myself] went swimming. BUT I made **myself** go swimming.

nauseous, nauseated   Frequently confused. *Nauseous* means "producing nausea"; *nauseated* means "enduring nausea": I felt **nauseated** when I smelled the **nauseous** spoiled meat.

nowhere near   Informal. Use *not nearly:* I had **not nearly** [NOT nowhere near] enough money.

nowheres   Unacceptable for *nowhere.*

number   As subjects, *a number* is generally plural and *the number* is singular. Make sure that the verb agrees with the subject: **A number** of possibilities **are** open. **The number** of possibilities **is** limited.

of   Often mistaken for the sound of the unstressed *have:* "They must **have** [OR would **have**, could **have**, might **have**, ought to **have**, may **have**—NOT must of] gone home.

off of   Use *off* in phrases such as "walked **off** [NOT off of] the field."

OK, O.K., okay   Informal usage.

on account of   Use the less wordy *because:* I went home **because** [NOT on account of] I was tired.

plus   Acceptable as a preposition. Weak when used instead of the coordinating conjunction *and.* I telephoned and [NOT plus] I sent flowers.

precede, proceed   To *precede* is to "go ahead of"; to *proceed* is to "go forward": His song will **precede** the fight scene. He will **proceed** with the song.

principal, principle   The adjective or noun *principal* means "chief" or "chief official." The noun may also mean "capital." The noun *principle* means "fundamental truth": The **principal** factor in the salary decision was his belief in the **principle** of sexual equality.

raise, rise   *Raise (raised, raising)* means "to lift or cause to move upward, to bring up or increase." *Rise (rose, risen, rising)* means "to get up, to move or extend upward, ascend." *Raise* (a transitive verb) takes an object; *rise* (an intransitive verb) does not: Retailers **raised** prices. Retail prices **rose** sharply. See **13c(3)**.

rarely ever Use either *rarely* alone or *hardly ever:* He **rarely** (or **hardly ever**) [NOT rarely ever] goes to the library.

real, really Use *real* as an adjective, *really* as an adverb: It is a **really** [NOT real] beautiful day.

reason why Redundant. Use *reason:* The **reason** I went home was that I was ill.

regard, regarding, regards Use *in regard to, with regard to,* or *regarding.*

sensuous, sensual *Sensuous* refers to gratification of the senses in response to art, music, nature, and so on; *sensual* refers to gratification of the physical senses.

sit, set Use *sit* in the sense of "be seated" and *set* in the sense of "to place something": Jonathon **sat** under the tree. Maria **set** the cookies on the table. See **13c(3)**.

so Overused as an intensifier; use a more precise modifier: She was **intensely** [NOT so] focused.

some Informal and vague when used as a substitute for such words as *remarkable, memorable:* She was a **remarkable** [NOT some] athlete.

someone, some one Distinguish between each one-word and two-word compound. See **anyone, any one; everyone, every one.**

sometime, sometimes, some time *Sometime* is an adverb meaning "at an unspecified time"; *sometimes* is an adverb meaning "at times"; *some time* is an adjective-noun pair meaning "a span of time": Let's go to the movie **sometime.** **Sometimes** we go to the movies. They agreed to allow **some time** to pass before going to the movies together again.

somewheres Unacceptable for *somewhere.*

sort, sort of See **kind of a, sort of a.**

specially See **especially, specially.**

stationary, stationery *Stationary* means "in a fixed position"; *stationery* means "writing paper and envelopes."

sure Informal when used as an adverb, as in "I **sure** like your new hat." Use *certainly* or *undoubtedly.*

take See **bring, take.**

thataway, thisaway Unacceptable for *that way* and *this way.*

that, which Use *that* with a restrictive clause: The cup **that** is on the table is full (distinguishes a specific cup that is full). Use *which* with a nonrestrictive clause: The cup, **which** is on the table, is full. ("which is on the table" gives nonessential information). Read the two example sentences aloud to notice the different intonation patterns. Some writers, however, prefer to use *which* for restrictive clauses if it does not cause confusion. See **17d.**

their, there, they're, there're *Their* is the possessive form of *they; there* is ordinarily an adverb or an expletive; *they're* is a contraction of *they are; there're* is a contraction of *there are:* **There** is no explanation for **their** behavior. **They're** making trouble **there** on the ball field. **There're** no tickets left.

theirself, theirselves Use *themselves.*

them Unacceptable when used as an adjective: **those** apples OR **these** apples [NOT them apples].

then Sometimes incorrectly used for *than.* Unlike *then, than* does not relate to time. He's better than [NOT then] he knows.

this here, that there, these here, them there Redundant; use *this, that, these, those.*

thusly Use *thus.*

to, too Distinguish the preposition *to* from the adverb *too:* When the weather is **too** hot to play ball, they go **to** the movies.

try and Informal for *try to:* I will **try to** [NOT try and] see him today.

unique Because it means "one of a kind," it is illogical to use *unique* with a comparative, as in *very unique.*

utilize Often pretentious; *use* is preferred.

wait on Unacceptable as a substitute for *wait for.*

ways Unacceptable for *way* when referring to distance: It's a long **way** [NOT ways] from home.

where Informal as a substitute for *that:* I saw on TV **that** [NOT where] she had been elected.

where . . . at, where . . . to   Omit the superfluous *at, to:* **Where** is the library [OMIT at]? **Where** are you moving [OMIT to]?

which   When referring to persons, use *who* or *that.* See **that, which.**

whose, who's   *Whose* indicates possession: **Whose** book is this? *Who's* is the contraction of *who is:* **Who's** going to the movie?

with regards to   See **regard, regarding, regards.**

you all   A regionalism for the plural of *you.* Not acceptable for formal writing.

your, you're   *Your* is the possessive of *you:* in **your** house. *You're* is a contraction of *you are:* **You're** gaining strength. See also **its, it's.**

Glossary of Terms

This glossary presents brief explanations of frequently used terms. Consult the index for references to further discussion of most of the terms and for a number of terms not listed.

absolute phrase A grammatically unconnected part of a sentence—generally a noun or pronoun followed by a participle (and sometimes modifiers): We will have a cookout, **weather permitting** [noun + present participle]; **The national anthem sung for the last time,** the old stadium was closed [noun + past participle with modifier]. Some absolute phrases have the meaning (but not the structure) of an adverb clause. See **1d(3), 9a,** and **12b(4).** See also **phrase** and **sentence modifier.**

acronym A word formed by combining the initial letters of a series of words: laser—light amplification by stimulated emission of radiation.

active voice The form of a transitive verb indicating that its subject performs the action the verb denotes: Emily *sliced* the ham. See **7** and **11d(1).** See also **passive voice, verb,** and **voice.**

adjective The part of speech modifying a noun or a pronoun. *Limiting adjectives* restrict the meaning of the words they modify: *that* pie, *its* leaves. *Descriptive adjectives* name a quality of a noun, including degrees of comparison: *red* shirt, *bigger* planes. *Proper adjectives* are derived from proper nouns: *Spanish* rice. See **23c.** *Interrogative adjectives* are used to ask questions: *Whose* book is it?

adjective clause A subordinate clause used as an adjective: people *who bite their fingernails.*

adjective phrase A phrase used as an adjective: The woman *carrying the large notebook* is my sister. See **1d(3).**

adverb The part of speech modifying a verb, an adjective, or another adverb: *rapidly* approached, *too* bitter, *very graciously* accepted. An adverb may also modify a verbal, a phrase or clause, or the rest of the sentence: *Usually,* an artist does her best work when she is focusing *entirely* on the task at hand.

adverb clause A subordinate clause used as an adverb: *Although he is usually quiet,* everyone listens to him *when he speaks, because he makes good suggestions.* See **1e(2), 17b(1),** and **12b(1).**

adverb phrase A phrase used as an adverb. See **1d(3)** and **9a(2).**

agreement The correspondence in number and person of a subject and verb (*the dog barks, dogs bark*) or in number and gender of a pronoun and its antecedent (the *team* boarded *its* bus, the *members* carrying *their* bags). See **6a** and **7a.**

allusion A brief, unexplained reference to a work or to a person, place, event, or thing that the writer expects the reader to be familiar with. See also **35a(4).**

analogy A rhetorical device using the features of something familiar (and often concrete) to explain something unfamiliar (and often abstract), or similarities between things that are not usually associated.

analysis A separation of a whole into its constituent parts.

antecedent A word or group of words that a pronoun refers to: *Pets* can be polite or rude, like *their* trainers. See **6b.**

antonym A word that means the opposite of another: *follow* is the antonym for *lead.*

APA American Psychological Association. See **34d–e.**

appeal The means of persuasion in argumentative writing; relies on reason, authority, and/or emotion.

appositive A noun or noun phrase placed next to or very near another noun or noun phrase to identify or supplement its meaning. See **17d(2), 9a(3), 12b(4),** and **12c(3).**

argument A kind of writing that uses various rhetorical strategies and appeals to convince the reader of the truth or falsity of a given proposition or thesis. See **appeal** and **thesis.**

article   *The, a,* or *an* used as adjectives before nouns. *The* is a definite article. *A* (used before consonant sounds) and *an* (used before vowel sounds) are indefinite articles. See **16a.**

audience   The person or persons for whom the writing is intended. See **28a.**

auxiliary   A form of *be, have,* or *will* that combines with a verb to indicate voice, tense, or mood: *was* going, *had* gone, *will* go. Modals such as *will, would,* and *may* are also considered auxiliaries. See **7** and **16b.**

bibliography   A list of books, articles, essays, or other material, usually on a particular subject.

brainstorming   A method of generating ideas about a subject; involves listing ideas as they occur in a session of intensive thinking about the subject. See **28b.**

browser   Software that finds and displays Web pages.

case   The form or position of a noun or pronoun that shows its use or relationship to other words in a sentence. The three cases in English are the *subjective,* which is usually the subject of a finite verb; the *possessive,* which indicates ownership; and the *objective,* which functions as the object of a verb or preposition. See **6** and **19a.**

cause and effect   A rhetorical strategy by which a writer seeks to explain why something happened or what the results of a particular event or condition were or will be. See **27d(4).**

CD-ROM   Acronym for Compact Disk—Read Only Memory. CD-ROMs store large amounts of information.

citation   Notation (usually parenthetical) in a paper that refers to a source. See **34a(1)** and **34d(1).**

chronological order   The arrangement of events in a time sequence (usually the order in which they occurred).

claim   A conclusion that a writer expects readers to accept. Should be supported by accurate and representative source material. See chapter **31.**

classification and division   A rhetorical strategy in which a writer sorts elements into categories (*classification*) or breaks a topic down into its constituent parts to show how they are related (*division*). See **27d(6)**.

clause A sequence of related words within a sentence. A clause has both a subject and a predicate and functions either as an independent unit (*independent clause*) or as a dependent unit (*subordinate clause,* used as an adverb, an adjective, or a noun). See **1e** and **9**. See also **sentence.**

cliché An expression that may once have been fresh and effective but that has become trite with overuse. See **14c**.

coherence The principle that all the parts of a piece of writing should stick together, one sentence leading to the next, each idea evolving from the previous one. See **5** and **27b**.

collective noun A noun singular in form that denotes a group: *flock, jury, band, public, committee.* See **7a(8)**.

colloquialism A word or phrase characteristic of informal speech. "He's *grumpy*" is a colloquial expression describing an irritable person. See chapter **13**.

comma splice, comma fault A punctuation error in which two independent clauses are joined by a comma with no coordinating conjunction. See chapter **3**.

common noun See **noun.**

comparative degree. See **degree.**

comparison and contrast A rhetorical strategy in which the writer examines similarities and/or differences between two ideas or objects. See **27d(5)**.

complement A word or words used to complete the sense of a verb. The term usually refers to a subject complement, an object complement, or the complement of a verb like *be.* See **1b**.

complex sentence A sentence containing one independent clause and at least one subordinate clause: *My neighbor noticed a stranger* [independent clause] *who looked suspicious* [subordinate clause]. See **1f**, **9**, and **12c(1)**. See also **clause.**

compound-complex sentence A sentence containing at least two main clauses and one or more subordinate clauses: *When the lights went out* [subordinate clause], *there was no flashlight* *at hand* [independent clause] *so we sat outside and gazed at the stars* [independent clause]. See **1f**. See also **clause.**

compound sentence A sentence containing at least two independent clauses and no subordinate clause: *The water supply was dwindling* [independent clause], so *rationing became mandatory* [independent clause]. See **1f, 17a,** and **18a**. See also **clause.**

concession Agreeing with a point made by your opponent in response to your own argument.

conclusion A sentence, paragraph, or group of paragraphs that brings a piece of writing to a satisfying close. See **28e(2)**.

conjugation A set or table of the inflected forms of a verb that indicates tense, person, number, voice, and mood. See chapter **7**.

conjunction A part of speech (such as *and* or *although*) used to connect words, phrases, clauses, or sentences. *Coordinating conjunctions* connect and relate words and word groups of equal grammatical rank. See **1c(7)** and **10**. See also **correlatives.**

Subordinating conjunctions (see list on page 14) mark a dependent clause and connect it with a main clause. See chapter **9**.

conjunctive adverb A word (*however, therefore, nevertheless*) that serves not only as an adverb but also as a connective. See **3b,** and **27b(3)**.

connotation The suggested or implied meaning of a word through the associations it evokes in the reader's mind. See **14a(3)**. See also **denotation.**

consonant A class of speech sounds represented in English by any letter other than *a, e, i, o,* or *u.*

contraction Condensing two words into one by adding an apostrophe to replace the omitted letter or letters: *aren't, don't.*

controlling idea The central idea of a paragraph or essay, often expressed in the paragraph's **topic sentence** or the essay's **thesis** statement. See **27a** and **28d**.

conventional Language that complies with the accepted rules of formal written English, generally termed *correct.*

coordinating conjunction One of seven connectives: *and, but, for, or, nor, so, yet.* See **1c(7), 17a, 9,** and **10**.

coordination The use of grammatically equivalent constructions to link ideas, usually (but not always) those of equal weight. See 17c(2), and 10.

correlatives One of five pairs of linked connectives: *both . . . and; either . . . or; neither . . . nor; not only . . . but also; whether . . . or.* Correlatives link equivalent constructions: *both* Jane *and* Fred; *not only* in Peru *but also* in Mexico. See 10c.

count, noncount nouns Count nouns are individual, countable entities and cannot be viewed as a mass (*word, finger, remark*). Noncount nouns are a mass or a continuum (*humor*). See chapter 1.

credibility The reliability of a person or evidence. See 31d.

cumulative sentence A sentence in which the subject and predicate come first, followed by modifiers. See 11b.

dangling modifier A word or phrase that does not clearly refer to another word or word group in the sentence. See 5b.

database A kind of electronic filing system. Computer databases are usually organized hierarchically so that computers can find information more quickly.

declension A set or table of inflected forms of nouns or pronouns. See the examples on page 31.

deduction A form of logical reasoning that begins with a generalization (*premise*), relates a specific fact to that generalization, and forms a *conclusion* that fits both. See 31f. COMPARE **induction**.

definition A brief explanation of the meaning of a word, as in a dictionary. Also, an extended piece of writing, employing a variety of rhetorical strategies, to explain what something is or means. See 27d(7).

degree The form of an adverb or adjective that indicates relative quality, quantity, or manner. The three degrees are as follows: *positive*, a quality of a single element; *comparative*, between two elements; and *superlative*, among three or more elements: *fast, faster, fastest.* See 4c.

demonstratives Four words that point out (*this, that, these, those*).

denotation The literal meaning of a word as commonly defined. See **14a(3)**. See also **connotation**.

dependent clause A subordinate clause. See **clause**.

description A rhetorical strategy using details perceivable by the senses to portray a scene, object, performance, and so on. See **27d(2)**.

determiner A word (such as *a, an, the, my, their*) that signals the approach of a noun: **the** newly mown *hay*.

diction The writer's choice of exact, idiomatic, and fresh words, as well as appropriate levels of usage. See chapters **13** and **14**.

direct address A name or descriptive term (set off by commas) designating the one or ones spoken to: Play it again, *Sam*.

direct object See **object**.

discussion list See **listserv**.

double negative The nonstandard combination of two negatives: We ca*n't* do *nothing* about the weather. See **4e**.

edited American English (EAE) The term adopted by the National Council of Teachers of English for the formal style expected in most college writing.

editing Reworking sentences for clarity, sense, and conformity to conventional rules of spelling, punctuation, mechanics, grammar, and sentence structure.

electronic mail See **e-mail**.

electronic sites Publicly available files on a computer that can be accessed through the Internet.

ellipsis Three or four spaced periods that indicate material omitted from a quotation. See **21i**.

elliptical construction The omission of words while retaining the meaning: Cats are cleaner than pigs [are].

e-mail Electronic mail; transfers messages over a communications network.

ethos Can be translated as "arguing honorably" and is employed when you tell others the truth and treat them with respect.

Effective arguments use not only ethos, but also **logos** (the logical use of language) and **pathos** (the use of language to stir the feelings of an audience). See page 222.

euphemism   An indirect or "nice" expression used instead of a more direct one: *Correctional facility* instead of *jail*. See chapter **14**.

example   Any fact, anecdote, reference, or the like used to illustrate an idea. See **27c**.

expletive   The expletive *there* shifts the order of subject and verb in a sentence: *There* were over four thousand runners in the marathon. The expletive *it* transforms the main clause into a subordinate clause: It is apparent that the plane is late.

expository writing   See **referential writing**.

expressive writing   Writing that emphasizes the writer's own feelings and reactions to a topic. See **28a**.

fallacy   A false argument or incorrect reasoning. See **31h**.

faulty predication   The use of a predicate that does not logically belong with a given subject: One superstition is a black cat. [The verb should be *involves*.]

figurative language   The use of words in an imaginative rather than a literal sense. See **14a(5)**.

file   A collection of computer-readable information. *Binary* files contain information readable only by computers unless the file is decoded. People can read *text* files.

focus   The narrowing of a subject to a manageable size; also the sharpening of the writer's view of the subject. See **28b** and **28c**.

fragment   A group of words that begins with a capital letter and ends with a period but forms only part of a sentence. See chapter **2**.

freewriting   A method of finding a writing topic by composing for a specified length of time without stopping to reflect, reread, or correct errors.

FTP   Abbreviation for File Transfer Protocol. People use FTP for transferring files on the Internet. See page 244.

function words   Words (such as prepositions, conjunctions, auxiliaries, and articles) that indicate the functions of other words in a sentence and the grammatical relationships.

fused sentence   Two or more sentences run together, with no punctuation or conjunctions to separate them. Also called a run-on sentence. Unacceptable in formal writing. See chapter 3.

gender   The grammatical distinction that labels nouns or pronouns as masculine, feminine, or neuter.

general/specific, generalization   *General* words are all-embracing, indefinite, sweeping in scope: *food*. *Specific* words are precise, explicit, limited in scope: *spaghetti carbonara*. The same is true of *general* and *specific* ideas. A *generalization* is vague and may be untrue.

gerund   A verbal (nonfinite verb) that ends in *-ing* and functions as a noun: *Riding* a bike is good exercise. [The gerund phrase—*riding* and its object, *bikes*—serves as the subject of the sentence.]

Gopher   A menu-based program for finding files on the Internet. See page 245.

grammar   The system of rules by which words are arranged into the structures meaningful in a language.

graphics   Images or pictures that can be displayed on a computer screen.

hardware   In computer terminology, the tangible components of the computer system such as the keyboard, the monitor, and the components inside the system box.

helping verb   A verb that combines with another verb to indicate voice, tense, or mood. See **auxiliary** and **modal.**

historical present   A tense used to describe events in literature or history that are permanently preserved in the present: The tragedy *is* that Iago *deceives* Othello. See 7b and 35a.

homophones   Words that have the same sound and sometimes the same spelling but differ in meaning (*their, there*, and *they're* or *capital* meaning funds and *capital* meaning government city). See 22b.

hyperbole An intentional overstatement made for rhetorical effect. COMPARE **understatement.**

idiom A fixed expression (within a language) whose meaning cannot be deduced from its elements: *put up a fight; to mean well.* See **14b.**

imperative mood See **mood.**

independent clause See **clause.**

indicative mood See **mood.**

indirect object See **object.**

indirect question A question phrased as a statement, usually a subordinate clause: We can ask *whether Milton's blindness was the result of glaucoma,* but we cannot be sure. See **8e.**

indirect quotation A report of the written or spoken words of another without using the exact words of the speaker or writer: The registrar said *that the bank returned my tuition check.*

induction A form of logical reasoning that begins with evidence and interprets it to form a conclusion. See **31e.** COMPARE **deduction.**

infinitive A verbal (nonfinite verb) used chiefly as a noun, less frequently as an adjective or adverb. The infinitive is usually made up of the word *to* plus the present form of a verb: Lashanda wanted *to continue* the debate.

infinitive phrase A phrase that employs the infinitive form of the verb: *to go to the store, to run the race.* See **phrase.**

inflection A change in the form of a word to show a specific meaning or grammatical function:

Verb	*talk, talks, talked*
Noun	*dog, dogs, dog's, dogs'*
Pronoun	*he, him, his; they, them, their, theirs*

informal Although often acceptable in spoken language, words or phrases that dictionaries label **informal, colloquial,** or **slang** are not generally appropriate in college writing. See chapter **13.**

intensifier　A modifier used for emphasis: *very* excited, *certainly* pleased. See **qualifier.**

intensive/reflexive pronoun　The *-self* pronouns (such as *myself, themselves*). The *intensive* is used for emphasis: The teenagers *themselves* had the best idea. The *reflexive* is used as an object of a verb, verbal, or preposition: He blames *himself.*

interjection　A word expressing a simple exclamation: *Hey! Oops!* See **21c.**

Internet　An international network of computers linked through telephone and fiber-optic lines.

interrogative　A word like *which, whose,* or *why* used to ask a question: *Which* is the more expensive?

intransitive verb　A verb (such as *appear* or *belong*) that does not take an object. See chapter **7.** See also **verb** and **transitive verb.**

invention　The process of using strategies to generate ideas for writing. See **27d** and **28b.**

inversion　A change in the usual word order of a sentence: Into the valley of death rode the five hundred. See **11f.**

irony　A deliberate inconsistency between what is stated and what is meant. Irony may be verbal or situational.

irregular verb　A verb that is not inflected in the usual way— that is, by the addition of *-d* or *-ed* to the present form to form the past tense and past participle.

jargon　Technical slang. It should be avoided in writing intended for a more general audience. See **13c(1).**

journal　A special-interest periodical. Also, a notebook in which a writer records personal thoughts and experiences.

journaling　Keeping a **journal.**

justification　Inserts spaces between words so that every line is the same length and makes the right or left margin, or both margins, straight.

linking verb　A verb that relates the subject complement to the subject. Words commonly used as linking verbs are *become, seen,* *appear, feel, look, taste, smell, sound,* and forms of the verb *be:* She *is* a writer. The bread *looks* burned. See **1a, 4b,** and **6g.**

listing   A way of gathering ideas in which a writer lists any ideas that he or she has.

listserv   A list of e-mail addresses to which messages can be automatically broadcast as if they were sent to a single user: a *discussion list* or a *mailing list.*

logic   The presentation of ideas that shows a clear, predictable, and structured relationship among those ideas. See chapters **8** and **31.**

log on   The process by which a user provides a username and a password in order to be recognized by a computer system and allowed to use its programs.

logos   See **ethos.**

loose sentence   See **cumulative sentence.**

main idea   The part of the paragraph or paper to which all the other ideas relate. See **topic sentence** and **thesis.**

mechanics   The form of words and letters, such as capitals, italics, abbreviations, acronyms, and numbers.

metaphor   An imaginative comparison between dissimilar things without using *like* or *as.* See **14a(5).**

misplaced modifier   A modifier placed in an awkward position, usually far away from what it modifies: I read that there was a big fire *in yesterday's newspaper.* Sometimes a misplaced modifier confuses the reader because it could qualify either of two words: To do one's best *sometimes* is not enough. *Sometimes* to do one's best is not enough. To do one's best is *sometimes* not enough. See **5a.**

mixed construction   A garbled sentence that is the result of an unintentional shift. See **8c(2).**

mixed metaphor   A metaphor that confuses two or more metaphors: Playing with fire will drown you. See **8c(1).**

MLA   Modern Language Association. See **34a–b.**

modal A helping verb (not conjugated). *can, could, may, might, shall, should, will, would, ought, must.*

modem A device that allows a computer to transmit data over telephone lines.

modifier A word or word group that describes, limits, or qualifies another. See chapters 4 and 5.

mood The way a speaker or writer regards an assertion—that is, as a declarative statement or a question (*indicative* mood); as a command or request (*imperative*); or as a supposition, hypothesis, or condition contrary to fact (*subjunctive*). See 1f and 7e.

narration A rhetorical strategy that recounts a sequence of events, usually in chronological order. See 27d(1).

network A group of two or more linked computer systems.

nominalization The practice of using nouns instead of active verbs: She *made a list* of the schedule changes. [COMPARE She *listed* the schedule changes.]

nonrestrictive Nonessential to the identification of the word or words referred to. My best friend, *Pauline,* understands me. See 17d.

nonstandard Speech forms that are common in informal writing but that should be avoided in formal writing. See chapter 13.

noun A part of speech that names a person, place, thing, idea, animal, quality, or action.

TYPES OF NOUNS

Common	a **woman**, the **street**, some **dogs**
Proper	**Ms. Wentworth**, in **Dallas**, the **White House**
Collective	a **team**, the **committee**, my **class**
Concrete	A **truck**, the **cup**, my **foot**, two **fish**
Abstract	**love**, **justice**, **fear**
Count	two **cents**, an **assignment**, many **revisions**
Noncount	much **concern**, more **consideration**, less **revenue**

noun clause A subordinate clause used as a noun. See 1e. See also **clause**.

number The inflectional form of a word that identifies it as singular (one) or plural (more than one): *river–rivers, this–those.*

object See **1b(2–3)** and **1c(6).**

A *direct object* is any noun or noun substitute that answers the question *what?* or *whom?* after a transitive active verb. A direct object frequently receives the action of the verb: Bill hit the *ball. What* did he hit?

An *object of a nonfinite verb* is any noun or its equivalent that follows and completes the meaning of a participle, a gerund, or an infinitive: Building a *house* takes time. She likes to grow *flowers.*

An *indirect object* is any noun or noun substitute that states *to whom* or *for whom* (or *to what* or *for what*) something is done. An indirect object ordinarily precedes a direct object: She gave *him* the keys. I gave the *floor* a good mopping.

An *object of a preposition* is any noun or noun substitute that a preposition relates to another word or word group: They play ball in the *park.* [*Park* is the object of the preposition *in.*]

object complement A word that helps complete the meaning of such verbs as *make, paint, elect, name.* An object complement refers to or modifies the direct object: They painted the cellar door *blue.* See **1b(3)** and **4b.** See also **complement.**

overgeneralization Lacking specificity.

paradox A seemingly contradictory statement that actually may be true. See **35a(8).**

paragraph Usually a group of related sentences unified by a single idea or purpose but occasionally as brief as a single sentence.

parallelism The use of corresponding grammatically equal elements in sentences and paragraphs. See chapter **10.**

paraphrase A sentence-by-sentence restatement of the ideas in a passage, using different words. See **33h(4).**

parenthetical element Nonessential words, phrases, clauses, or sentences set off by commas, dashes, or parentheses. See **17d, 21e(2),** and **21f.**

participle A verb form that may function as part of a verb phrase (was *thinking,* had *determined*) or as a modifier (a *deter-*

mined effort; the couple, *thinking* about their past). The *present participle* ends in *-ing*. The past participle of regular verbs ends in *-d* or *-ed;* for past participles of irregular verbs, see **7b**.

particle A word like *off, out,* or *up* combined with a verb to form a combination with the force of a single-word verb: The authorities refused to *put up* with him.

parts of speech The classes into which words may be grouped. See **1c**.

passive voice The form of the verb showing that its subject is not the agent performing the action of the verb but rather receives that action: The ham *was sliced* by Emily. See **7** and **11d(1)**. See also **active voice**.

pathos See **ethos**.

perfect tenses The tenses formed by the addition of a form of *have* and showing complex time relationships in completing the action of the verb (the present perfect—*have/has eaten;* the past perfect—*had eaten;* and the future perfect—*will/shall have eaten.*

periodic sentence A sentence in which the main idea comes last. See **11b**. COMPARE **cumulative sentence**.

person The form of pronouns and verbs indicating whether one is speaking (*I am*—first person), is spoken to (*you are*—second person), or spoken about (*he is*—third person). See **7a** and **8e**.

personal pronoun Any one of a group of pronouns—*I, you, he, she, it,* and their inflected forms—referring to the one (or ones) speaking, spoken to, or spoken about. See chapter **6**.

personification The attributing of human characteristics to nonhuman things (animals, objects, ideas): "That night wind was breathing across me through the spokes of the wheel." —WALLACE STEGNER.

persuasive writing A form of writing intended chiefly to change the reader's opinions or attitudes or to arouse the reader to action. See **28a**.

phrasal verb A unit consisting of a verb plus one or two uninflected words like *after, in, up, off,* or *out* and having the force of a single-word verb: We *ran out* on them.

phrase A sequence of grammatically related words without a subject and/or a predicate. See **1d** and **2a**.

plural More than one. COMPARE **singular**.

point of view The vantage point from which the subject is viewed. See **8e(6)**.

positive See **degree**.

possessive case See **case**.

predicate The part of the sentence comprising what is said about the subject. The *complete predicate* consists of the main verb and its auxiliaries (the *simple predicate*) and any complements and modifiers: We *chased the dog all around our grandmother's farm*.

predicate adjective The adjective used as a subject complement: The bread tastes *sweet*. See **1c(4)** and **4b**.

predicate noun A noun used as a subject complement: Bromides are *sedatives*. See **1c(2)** and **6g**.

prefix An added syllable or group of syllables (such as *in-, dis-, un-, pro-*) placed before a word to form a new word: *adequate–inadequate*. A prefix ordinarily changes the meaning.

preposition A part of speech that links and relates a noun or noun substitute to another word in the sentence: The dancers leapt *across* the stage. See page 9.

prepositional phrase A preposition with its object and any modifiers: *in the hall, between you and me, for the new van*.

prewriting The initial stage of the writing process, concerned primarily with planning.

primary source In research or bibliographies, the source that provides unedited, firsthand facts.

principal parts The forms of a verb that indicate the various tenses: the present (*give, jump*); the past (*gave, jumped*); and the past participle (*given, jumped*). See **7b**.

process analysis A rhetorical strategy either to instruct the reader how to perform a procedure or to explain how something occurs. See **27d(3)**.

progressive verb A verb phrase consisting of a present participle (ending in *-ing*) used with a form of *be* and denoting continuous action: *is attacking, will be eating.*

pronoun A part of speech that takes the position of a noun and functions as nouns do. See **1c(3)**, **6**, **7a**.

proofreading Checking the final draft of a paper to eliminate typographical, spelling, punctuation, and documentation errors. See **26d** and **29d**.

proper adjective See **adjective**.

proper noun See **noun**.

purpose A writer's reason for writing. See **28a**. See also **expressive writing**, **persuasive writing**, and **referential writing**.

qualifier Any modifier that describes or limits: *Sometimes* movies are *too* gory to watch.

quotation Repeated or copied words of another, real or fictional. See **20a** and **33g**.

redundant Needlessly repetitious, unnecessary.

referential writing Writing whose chief aim is to clarify, explain, or evaluate a subject in order to inform or instruct the reader. Also called expository or informative writing. See **28a**.

refutation A writer's introduction of reasons why others may believe differently followed by an explanation showing why these reasons are not convincing.

regular verb A verb that forms its past tense and past participle by adding *-d* or *-ed* to the present form: *love, loved.*

relative clause An adjective clause introduced by a relative pronoun: the programs *that provide services.*

relative pronoun A noun substitute (*who, whom, whose, that, which, what, whoever, whomever, whichever, whatever*) used to introduce subordinate clauses: He has an aunt **who** *is a principal.* **Whoever** *becomes treasurer* must be honest. See chapter **6**.

restrictive A word, phrase, or clause that limits the word referred to: Every student *who cheats* will be removed from the class. [Only those students *who cheat* will be removed.] See **17d**. See also **nonrestrictive**.

retrieval database A database system that allows users to search by keyword, author, or title and that may often provide the full text of a document.

revision Part of the writing process. Writers revise by rereading and rethinking a piece of writing to see where they need to add, delete, move, replace, reshape, and even completely recast ideas.

rhetoric The art of using language effectively.

rhetorical question A question posed for effect without expectation of a reply: Who can tell what will happen?

rhetorical situation The relationship between the writer, the audience, and the context that determines the appropriate approach for a particular situation.

run-on sentence See **fused sentence.**

search engine A program that searches documents for a specific word (keyword) and returns a list of all documents containing that word.

secondary source A source that analyzes or interprets **primary source** material.

sentence A grammatically independent unit of expression. A simple sentence contains a subject and a predicate. See chapter **1**.

sentence modifier An adverb or adverb substitute that modifies the rest of the sentence, not a specific word or word group in it: *Yes,* the plane arrived on time.

server A computer that manages resources; for example, a Web server, a network server, or a mail server.

sexist language Language that arbitrarily excludes one sex or the other or that arbitrarily assigns stereotypical roles to one or the other sex. See **6b** and **13c(2)**.

simile The comparison of two dissimilar things using *like* or *as.* See **14a(5)**.

simple tenses The tenses that refer to present, past, and future time.

singular One. See **number.** COMPARE **plural.**

slang Casual vocabulary of specific groups. See chapter **13**.

split infinitive   The often awkward separation of an infinitive by at least one adverb: *to* quietly *go*. See **infinitive**.

squinting modifier   An ambiguous modifier that can refer to either a preceding or a following word: Eating *often* makes her sick. See **5a(4)**.

standard American English   See **edited American English**.

stipulative definition   A definition that specifies how a certain term will be used within a certain context. See **14a(2)**.

style   An author's choice and arrangement of words, sentence structures, and ideas as well as less definable characteristics such as rhythm and euphony. See **8e(5)**.

subject   A noun or noun substitute about which something is asserted or asked in the predicate. The *complete subject* consists of the *simple subject* and the words associated with it: *The woman in the gray trench coat* asked for information. COMPARE **predicate**.

subject complement   A word or words that complete the meaning of a linking verb and that modify or refer to the subject: The old car looked *shabby*. See **1b, 4b, 6g**.

subjective case   See **case**.

subjunctive mood   See **mood**.

subordinate clause   See **clause**.

subordinating conjunction   See **conjunction**.

subordination   The use of dependent structures (phrases, subordinate clauses) that are lower in grammatical rank than independent ones (simple sentences, main clauses). See chapter **9**.

suffix   An added syllable or group of syllables placed after a word to form a new word: *light, lighted, lighter*.

summary   A concise restatement briefer than the original. See **33h(5)**.

superlative degree   See **degree**.

syllogism   A three-part form of deductive reasoning. See **31f**.

synonym   A word that has a meaning similar to that of another word.

syntax Sentence structure; the grammatical arrangement of words, phrases, and clauses.

tag question A question attached to the end of a related statement set off by a comma: She's coming, *isn't she?* See **3a**.

Telnet A program that connects a computer to a network server. The user then has access to programs and functions as if he or she were in the same physical location as the server. See page 245.

tense The form of the verb that denotes time. See chapter 7.

thesis The central point or main idea of an essay. See **28d**.

tone The writer's attitude toward the subject and the audience, usually conveyed through diction and sentence structure.

topic The specific, narrowed idea of a paper. See **subject**.

topic sentence A statement of the central thought of a paragraph.

transitions Words, phrases, sentences, or paragraphs that relate ideas and provide coherence by linking sentences, paragraphs, and larger units of writing. Transitions may be expressions or structural features a writer uses. See **32b**.

transitive verb A type of verb that takes an object: They *danced* the polka. See **verb** and **intransitive verb**.

understatement Intentional underemphasis for effect, usually ironic. See **hyperbole**.

Uniform Resource Locator See **URL**.

unity All the elements contributing to developing a single idea or thesis. See **27a** and **28d**.

URL Acronym for Uniform Resource Locator. A URL consists of several parts: the protocol to be used (e.g. (http://; ftp://; gopher://), the Internet address and domain name, and the path to the file.

Usenet A worldwide bulletin board system that is available on the Internet. It contains over 2,000 *newsgroups* on a wide variety of topics.

verb A part of speech denoting action, occurrence, or existence (state of being). See **1a** and 7. See also **inflection, mood, voice, transitive verb,** and **intransitive verb**.

verbal   A nonfinite verb used as a noun, an adjective, or an adverb. See **gerund, infinitive,** and **participle.** See also **1d.**

voice   The form of a transitive verb that indicates whether or not the subject performs the action denoted by the verb. A verb with a direct object is in the *active voice*. When the direct object is converted into a subject, the verb is in the *passive voice*. See 7 and **11d(1)**.

vowel   A speech sound represented in written English by *a, e, i, o, u,* and sometimes *y.*

World Wide Web (WWW)   A system of Internet servers that store documents formatted in a special computer language (HTML). These documents are called *Web pages* and a location containing several such pages is called a *Website*. Web pages can provide links to other sites as well as to graphics, audio, and video files. See page 241.

Copyright and Acknowledgments

Excerpt from *Reader's Guide to Periodical Literature*, 1990, p. 440. Copyright © 1990 by The H.W. Wilson Company. Material reproduced with permission of the publisher.

Excerpts from poems "I'm Nobody! Who Are You?" and "Because I Could Not Stop for Death" by Emily Dickinson. Reprinted by permission of the publishers and the Trustees of Amherst College from *The Poems of Emily Dickinson*, Thomas H. Johnson, ed., Cambridge, Mass.: The Belknap Press of Harvard University Press, Copyright © 1951, 1955, 1979, 1983 by the President and Fellows of Harvard College.

Excerpt from poem "You fit into me . . ." from *Power Politics* by Margaret Atwood, copyright © 1971, 1996. Reprinted with the permission of the House of Anansi Press, North York, Ontario.

Excerpt reprinted by permission from *Merriam-Webster's Collegiate ® Dictionary*, Tenth Edition © 1996. Merriam-Webster, Incorporated.

Excerpt from *The New York Times Index*. Copyright © by The New York Times Company. Reprinted by permission.

Specified three line excerpt from "To be of use" from *Circles on the Water* by Marge Piercy. Copyright © 1982 by Marge Piercy. Reprinted by permission of Alfred A. Knopf, Inc.

Specified eight line excerpt from "Musée des Beaux Arts" from *W. H. Auden: Collected Poems* by W. H. Auden, edited by Edward Mendelson. Copyright © 1940 and renewed 1968 by W. H. Auden. Reprinted by permission of Random House, Inc.

Excerpt from "Lullaby" by Leslie Marmon Silko. Copyright © 1981 by Leslie Marmon Silko. Reprinted by permission from

Storyteller by Leslie Marmon Silko, published by Seaver Books, New York.

Excerpt from "Walking Our Boundaries" from *The Black Unicorn* by Audre Lorde. Copyright © 1978 by Audre Lorde. Reprinted by permission of W.W. Norton & Company, Inc.

Excerpt sample page reprinted by permission from Yahoo!. Text and artwork copyright © 1996 by Yahoo!, Inc. All rights reserved. Yahoo! and the Yahoo logo are trademarks for Yahoo!, Inc.

Sample web pages from Netscape and Lynx, "Richard III: On Stage and Off," © 1996, 1997, The Richard III Society, Inc. Used with permission.

Index

Numbers and letters in color refer to rules; other numbers refer to pages.

ESL Index

Entries in this index identify topics basic to ESL usage. Numbers and letters in color refer to rules; other numbers refer to pages.

MLA Documentation Style

This index refers to items in the parenthetical citations, the works cited list, and the student papers in chapter 34. The italics indicate the page on which a given form is illustrated in a paper.

APA Documentation Style

This index refers to items in the parenthetical citations, the reference list, and the student paper in chapter 34. The italics indicate the page on which a given form is illustrated in a paper.